Catching DREAMS

Sports and Entertainment

Steven A. Riess, Series Editor

Catching DREAMS

Syracuse University Press

My Life in the Negro Baseball Leagues

Frazier "Slow" Robinson with Paul Bauer

Foreword by John "Buck" O'Neil

Introduction by Gerald Early

Library of Congress Cataloging-in-Publication Data

Robinson, Frazier, 1910–1997
    Catching dreams : my life in the Negro baseball leagues / Frazier "Slow" Robinson
with Paul Bauer : foreword by John "Buck" O'Neil : introduction by Gerald Early.
— 1st ed.
            p.   cm.   — (Sports and entertainment)
    Includes index.
    ISBN 0-8156-0563-3 (cloth : alk. paper) ISBN 0-8156-0658-3 (pbk. : alk. paper)
1. Robinson, Frazier, 1910–1997. 2. Baseball players—United States—Biography.
3. Afro-American baseball players—Biography. 4. Negro leagues—History.
I. Bauer, Paul, 1956–   . II. Title. III. Series.
    GV865.R596A3 1999
    796.357'   092—dc21   98-51650

Manufactured in the United States of America

Frontispiece: Frazier "Slow" Robinson as a member of the 1946
Baltimore Elite Giants. Courtesy of the author.

For Wynolia,
and for
Luther Robinson
and
Carolyn and James Robinson.
And in memory of
Benjamin Griggs
[FR]

For Francine,
and for my parents,
Nancy and C. Franklin Bauer
[PB]

Frazier Robinson played professional baseball in parts of four decades beginning in the 1920s. He caught Hall of Fame pitchers Satchel Paige and Leon Day and played with many other legendary Negro Leaguers. He retired to Kings Mountain, North Carolina, and lived there with his wife until his death in 1997.

Paul Bauer is a used and rare book dealer specializing in baseball. He lives in Kent, Ohio.

Contents

Illustrations

Foreword

John "Buck" O'Neil

Frazier "Slow" Robinson was one of the most delightful men I've ever been around. Father-like figure even to players older than he, yet, like a son to me. He'd come for advice, not only as how to pitch to a hitter or how to position his infield or outfield, but as to which player to hang out with or what places to be seen.

"Slow" was a religious person who enjoyed Negro spirituals and sang them very well. He organized a quartet on every team he played on. On the Kansas City Monarchs it was Satchel Paige, John Markham, I. V. Barnes and himself.

"Slow" had good, quick hands and a strong accurate arm as a catcher. A quick compact swing with average power as a hitter.

Joe Greene was our starting catcher, and I felt that "Slow" had too much to offer as second string. Therefore, I was very pleased when he went to the Elites.

At every reunion, I was most delighted to see "Slow" and Wynolia. God took a good man home when he took "Slow."

Acknowledgments

We thank Peter Golenbock who read the first draft of this book and made many useful suggestions. Thanks also to Mark Dawidziak, Harvey Pekar, Larry Lester, and JillEllyn Riley for their help and encouragement.

Introduction
Freedom and Fate, Baseball and Race

Gerald Early

> Materially, psychologically, and culturally, part of the nation's heritage is Negro American, and whatever it becomes will be shaped in part by the Negro's presence.
> —Ralph Ellison, "What America Would Be Like Without Blacks"[1]

> 'I thought it was "If a body catch a body,"' I said. 'Anyway, I keep picturing all these little kids playing some game in this big field of rye and all. Thousands of little kids, and nobody's around —nobody big, I mean— except me. And I'm standing on the edge of some crazy cliff. What I have to do, I have to catch everybody if they start to go over the cliff—I mean if they're running and they don't look where they're going I have to come out from somewhere and *catch* them. That's all I'd do all day. I'd just be the catcher in the rye and all.'
> —J. D. Salinger, *The Catcher in the Rye*[2]

What is remarkable about baseball is not simply the persistence of its popularity (it is the team sport with the longest history in the United States and whose records and statistics are most broadly known) but the persistence of its claim to significance as a reflection of our national values and as an architect of the national character. Baseball, it has been said from a certain cultural habit and with a certain cultural cogency, symbolizes our democratic values as a series of balances—a tautly dramatized individualism made possible within the context of teamwork; fair play guided by the principle of taking every possible advantage of your opponent in a game that does not require that the officials extract penalties; a rigidly structured, ordered game that requires improvisation and con-

---

Gerald Early is the Merle Kling Professor of Modern Letters and Director of African and Afro-American Studies at Washington University in St. Louis.

stant adaptation. It is a game that perfectly balances, in its way, both freedom and fate, in much the same way, some of the game's most passionate adherents say, that our nation itself does. But as a reflection of our national life, it must never be forgotten that for roughly sixty years black Americans were denied the opportunity to play professional baseball with white men, and the organized version of baseball that they played was considered inferior to white professional baseball. Indeed, for a good portion of that period, from the mid-1880s to the mid-1940s, blacks had their own separate leagues. It is perhaps a sign of our own confusion about this contradiction of the democratic ideal that segregated professional baseball represented for so many years in our nation—there was no freedom of athletic competition and one's skin color, not ability, was one's fate—that today we are not sure whether we should see Negro League baseball as an heroic achievement or a hideous, inhuman perversion. When we think of Negro League baseball, it should remind us that we know a great deal about baseball as a game, as a form of entertainment, as an astonishingly intricate and sometimes densely illusory set of records, but what do we know of baseball as an experience? What does baseball tell us about how blacks see the national character, democratic values, and their own travails as a persecuted minority that once was as enthralled with this game as anyone? That black men went through much adversity but, with great persistence and admirable energy and enterprise, played segregated baseball for a number of years is not simply a reflection that the game represented a kind of mainstream of Americanism in which they wanted to swim, although that motivation was clearly present. Negro baseball also showed blacks taking something that was peculiarly American and, at times, casting it in their own terms, refracting it through the prism of their own understanding of what it means to be American. This is, in part, why Negro League baseball was played in a different style from white baseball, half elegance, half degradation. Part of the experience of playing Negro League baseball meant playing clown baseball as "Zulus" with grass skirts or some such depraved nonsense. Part of the experience of playing Negro League baseball meant playing fiercely against white major leaguers in exhibition games. It was in this complex way that African Americans learned how their specialness both alienated them from and united them to other Americans.

"Geography is fate," wrote Ralph Ellison in his essay, "Going to the Territory,"[3] and, perhaps, this formulation might explain why Frazier Robinson, an Oklahoman like Ellison, became a professional baseball player in the Negro Leagues. Geography, to be sure, has a great deal to do with the game of baseball itself. Largely developed and codified in cities in the northeast and New England in the antebellum era with the New York version of the game winning out over the New England brand, baseball spread rapidly to the middle west and southwest, and professional and semiprofessional baseball was well established in those regions after the Civil War. Baseball, in its origins, was not a game of pastures and open fields as much as it was a game of small towns, cities, and the rising tide of industrialism, of labor wars, cartel-formation, and rowdy, drunken, gambling crowds. Baseball, symbolically, seems clearly to represent both the creation of the frontier and its conquest.

Black baseball has strong northeastern, urban roots as well, as Sol White's remarkable document *The History of Colored Base Ball* (1907) makes plain. Indeed, White describes 1906, for instance, as a year of "a base ball [*sic*] epidemic" when nine professional black teams within a one-hundred-mile radius on the east coast played against each other.[4] Yet it is now well known that Andrew "Rube" Foster formed the first successful Negro League (Sol White tells of the trials and tribulations of other such attempts before Foster) in Chicago, where Foster had formed, with the backing of a son-in-law of Charles Comiskey, the Chicago American Giants in 1911. Foster's inability to get support from eastern Negro teams led to his forming the Negro National League with teams in Chicago (two), Detroit, Indianapolis, St. Louis, and Kansas City, all owned by blacks except Kansas City, which became, arguably, the most storied of all Negro League teams. (Frazier Robinson, in his autobiography, says "As a teenager, my team was the Kansas City Monarchs.")

If geography is fate, in that a particular landscape provides the material and spiritual circumstances to make a group of people or individual do a certain thing inevitably, geography is also, in the American and especially the African American context, freedom as well. Blacks, for instance, came to the Oklahoma Territory, where Frazier Robinson grew up, to escape the harsh racism of the south. They came with a sense of the pioneer's or the immigrant's hope, a new sensation or sense of expectancy for most blacks, as they did not originally come to this country with such an air of aspiration. Indeed, they did not come here at all of their own volition. And it was the sheer independence that the new mobility of the post–Civil War African American represented that gave hope as much as any other kind of promise of a new order of things. But Oklahoma specifically offered a kind of promise. As Ellison wrote, "the state of Oklahoma had attracted many of the descendants of the freed slaves, who considered it a territory of hope and a place where they could create their own opportunities. It was a magnet for many individuals who found disappointment in the older area of the country, white as well as black, but for Negroes it had a traditional association with freedom which had entered their folklore."[5] But most found the middle west and southwestern territory of the country to be no haven, and certainly no hiding place.

Despite baseball's urban, eastern origins and despite black baseball's similar pattern of development, the middle west and the "frontier" literally and figuratively helped shape the game dramatically. But the freedom and fate of American geography also shaped the mentality of the men who played it. Once again, as Ellison said about Oklahoma in a 1973 interview, "In the atmosphere of the place there was a sense that you had to determine your own fate, and that you had a chance to it."[6] The very wildness of Oklahoma, as Ellison described it elsewhere, gave more than one African American a sense of the unique advantage he felt the white American had: the freedom to make his own fate. Perhaps this is what attracted some black men to baseball; it seems a game that ritualized that very possibility. In *Catching Dreams: My Life in the Negro Baseball Leagues,* Frazier Robinson writes about the Oklahoma of his childhood:

> Oklahoma was kind of a wild place when I was a boy. It hadn't been a state but for three years when I was born. The eastern part of the state had been Indian Territory and the law didn't go there. That made it a big

hangout for highway robbers and outlaws and that kind of carried over after it became a state. . . .

When I was growing up in Oklahoma, there were black folks, white folks, and Indians. The Indians were mostly Cherokee, Creek, and Osage, and they were very plentiful. . . . We didn't socialize with 'em although they would follow you around. They liked to associate with black people.

Not only did Oklahoma bring together in close proximity the three major groups of racial tragedy in America—Indians, blacks, and whites —but the state was also associated with outlawry, an intriguing sort of freedom for a black boy in those days.

Frazier Robinson was born on May 30, 1910 (four years before Ralph Ellison) in Birmingham, Alabama, but like many black families of the era, his migrated to Oklahoma while Robinson was still a young boy in hopes of a better life. Robinson's father was a very strict man, a minister, who never supported the idea of Frazier or his brother, Norman, playing baseball, not surprisingly because black Protestant religion is deeply opposed to anything as worldly and frivolous as sports, indeed, popular culture itself. "Looking back," writes Robinson, "I'm surprised he let us play at all. To tell the truth, in all the years I played baseball, neither of my parents ever saw me play so much as an inning." He writes elsewhere: "I don't think my father was proud of Norman and me playing baseball for a living. It was kind of against his teaching. He saw baseball as a worldly thing, and he wanted us to follow in his footsteps. We tried to follow his beliefs as best we could, but we just couldn't let go of that baseball."

From his youth, Robinson was attracted, not to athletics, but just to baseball. His younger brother, Norman, was a far more well-rounded athlete, learning to play several baseball positions as well as mastering other sports like track. Frazier wanted only to be a professional baseball catcher. In at least Robinson's case, we learn that baseball catchers are born and not merely made. Catching is probably the least glamorous position on a baseball team; and it is, without question, the most physically demanding. Foul tips and the back-swings from batters break fingers. The constant squatting ruins knee cartilage. And in the most dreadful heat the catcher must play the field weighed down with protective equipment. It is no wonder that this equipment is referred to as "the tools of ignorance." But catchers are often the captains of their teams, positioning the fielders, telling the pitchers what pitches to throw. The catcher is involved in every phase of the game and must have his mind on each pitch of each inning of the game. Catchers are often the most intelligent players on their teams. As Branch Rickey, the Brooklyn Dodger executive who signed Jackie Robinson and a former catcher himself, wrote: "You cannot win a pennant with a poor catcher. And how often the best catcher in baseball is in the World Series! . . . The catcher is in position to be the field general. He sees exactly where seven men are standing and he should be the master defensive tactician of the game."[7] Rickey also wrote that the catcher must be a great conversationalist and first-rate psychologist: "A clear indication of a catcher's exceptional intelligence is his social gift of engaging in enlightened conversation with batsmen while behind the plate. . . . If a catcher can place in the batter's mind the slightest suggestion that he must select one out of two or more prospective pitches in the next delivery, he has made a guess hitter out of the batsman."[8] While catchers may be very slow afoot, they must be nimble and quick to stop pitches thrown in the dirt and to catch foul pop-ups behind the plate. To be a catcher is not very glamorous life, but it is probably the most vital and the most obsessively strategic position in baseball.

What is most valuable about Frazier Robinson's memoirs is that the reader is given a close-up look at the trials and tribulations of playing this position and learns precisely how someone masters it. Moreover, because Robinson was a catcher he provides the reader with more insightful stories about how the game is played. He also provides us with some of the best stories about Josh Gibson, doubtless the most formidable catcher in Negro League history. He understood Gibson because they were both catchers.

Robinson joined the Negro Leagues during its second incarnation. After Foster fell ill in 1926, his league began to fall apart. By 1931, with the onset of the Depression, the Negro National League disbanded. But a new age, the era of the numbers bankers, the men in the black community with the money, expertise, and interest to start a sports franchise, was launched when Gus Greenlee took over the Pittsburgh Crawfords.[9] By 1933, Greenlee was instrumental in getting together enough black numbers men to start the Negro Leagues again. Robinson played the bulk of his career with the Kansas City Monarchs and the Baltimore Elite Giants.

Not surprisingly, Robinson encountered many incidents of racism in his professional life. One he describes took place in Hobbs, New Mexico, in 1936. Robinson had been playing in Abilene for the all-black Texas-Oklahoma-Louisiana (TOL) League. (Like many Negro Leaguers, Robinson led the barnstormer's peripatetic life and played in a number of settings, including several industrial teams.) But the TOL folded and Robinson in 1936 was playing for Odessa. The Odessa team played the local Hobbs nine: "it was so prejudiced that you just didn't feel up to your potential. This is what the umpire said over the public address system to begin the game. He said, 'Today's the day of the big ballgame. For the white boys, it's Ted Blankenship pitching and Beans Minor catching. And,' he said, 'for the niggers, it's a big nigger pitching and a little nigger catching.' I was catching and [Jack] Matchett was pitching. And we knew we were going up against the worst of it because this was the umpire saying this. I just looked around. It didn't make no difference to me because I'd heard that before."

The reader also learns from Robinson's narrative what a farce discrimination in professional baseball really was. He, like many black ball players, played against many white major leaguers, who were rehabilitating an injury, had been released and were trying to get back to the majors, or were simply trying to earn a little extra money to supplement their major league pay. And integration was common on the semiprofessional level. Robinson tells the curious story of former Cubs slugger Hack Wilson, against whom he played in 1935: "There were a lot of teams out there that were put together by business people, and in Texas and Oklahoma that meant oil companies. These oil men would sponsor these teams, get some advertising out of it, and get to tell their friends that not only did they know Hack Wilson or some other ex-big leaguer but also that he worked for them." This does not differ very much from what drives extremely wealthy and powerful men to own sports franchises today.

Here is a book that is full of riches for anyone interested in the intersection of African American culture and baseball: stories about Satchel Paige (whom Robinson caught for many years), ranging from his bad driving to his showmanship; accounts of Kansas City jazz (Robinson was a good dancer and a passionate lover of swing music) from Basie and McShann to Parker; tales of singing harmony with the fellows in Satchel Paige's Chrysler; detailed sketches of several Negro League personalities including Buck O'Neil, Double Duty Radcliffe, Cool Papa Bell, and Newt Joseph as well as some who made it to the majors like Larry Doby and Don Newcombe. How angry or upset were Negro League players about playing segregated baseball? Robinson's response to segregation in baseball (not every player's to be sure) and Jackie Robinson's signing with the Dodgers is remembered in this way:

> Looking back on Jim Crow and baseball's color line, I'd have to say that segregation was just something I'd gotten used to. I was brought up this way. I was used to it, and it didn't bother me. As long as I could get along, it didn't bother me. I knew this was just one of those things—the way it was. I knew it wasn't fair, but you had to accept it. There wasn't anything you could do about it. I'd played a number of times against all-white teams in Texas, Oklahoma, and Mexico. I played 'em and the fans seemed to enjoy it. It *could* work. I figured it was just a few people who didn't want to see integration happen. I didn't think everybody felt that way. When Jackie Robinson signed with Branch Rickey, I just said, 'So well and so good.'

Finally, in a book that is so affirming of a man's humanity, and the humanity of his race and, ironically, through his own stoic belief in himself to play this game, the triumphant humanity of his nation, we are given the gift of Robinson's language. For this book is told to us in his own voice, the wondrous plain lyrical bantering of an old-fashioned black vernacular. I do not mean to suggest any silliness here in praise of an exaggerated Dunbar-ian dialect or any overly self-conscious, so-called Ebonics. This black working-class speech is the English of everyman in its immediacy, its honesty, its humor, and its lack of pretension. His description of Jack Matchett during his days in Abilene with the TOL illustrates the point:

> Our best pitcher was a boy called Jack Matchett. Matchett was always a cutup. He was a guy who never did go to school. He didn't have no education. I learned him how to read and write his name. He was that type of person who figured that whatever he did, he would be right doing it on his own. You know how those people are. If you kind of talk to him or scold him about it, he'd get angry. You'd best serve him with kid gloves. He was that type but he was a good pitcher.

It is good to have Robinson's autobiography alongside of other ex-Negro Leaguers like Buck O'Neil, Wilmer Fields, Satchel Paige, Jackie Robinson, Roy Campanella, and Quincy Trouppe. For lovers of baseball, for students of African American and American culture, one can never get enough of these tales, even the ones that have been told over and over again. To learn that the catcher is something like the anchor of the team, and the symbolic guardian of home, who does, in effect, what any of us who have ever caught a baseball do: play catch with a pitcher. Throw back all the odd assortment of fastballs, junk pitches, and brush backs that life offers. To be a good catcher is no small thing. Frazier Robinson's autobiography, like the game of ball, is glorious.

Notes

1. "What America Would Be Like Without Blacks," in Ralph Ellison, *Going to the Territory* (New York: Vintage Books, 1987), 111.

2. J. D. Salinger, *The Catcher in the Rye* (Boston: Little, Brown, 1991), 173.

3. "Going to the Territory," in Ralph Ellison, *Going to the Territory*, 131.

4. Sol White, *Sol White's History of Colored Base Ball, With Other Documents on the Early Black Game, 1886–1936* (Lincoln: Univ. of Nebraska Press, 1995), 31.

5. "Going to the Territory," in Ralph Ellison, *Going to the Territory*, 132.

6. Maryemma Graham and Amritjit Singh, eds., *Conversations with Ralph Ellison* (Jackson: Univ. Press of Mississippi, 1995), 256.

7. Branch Rickey with Robert Riger, *The American Diamond: A Documentary of the Game of Baseball* (New York: Simon and Schuster, 1965), 160, 163.

8. Ibid., 157.

9. The most important black athlete of the 1930s, Joe Louis, was managed by two numbers men, Julian Black and John Roxborough. Caspar Holstein, of the Virgin Islands, and a well-known numbers man, supplied much of the prize money for the literary awards handed out by black publications like *The Crisis* and *Opportunity* during the Harlem Renaissance.

Catching DREAMS

1

Back Where It All Began

I couldn't say when I first picked up a baseball, but I must have been five or six. At that time we were living in Oklahoma City where we had moved before I was one. I was born in Birmingham, Alabama, on May 30, 1910, and was named Henry Frazier Robinson, Jr., the Frazier being my mother's idea.

When I was very young our family also included my grandmother, my mother's mother, who was part Creek Indian. Her name was Claudia Black and she saved my life. I was about a year and a half old when she saw me drowning in the bathtub and pulled me from the water. She passed away shortly after, but I still remember how she would always keep me on her lap. She was the only one of my grandparents that I ever saw. I always heard that she was a freed slave. I never learned very much about my grandfather, my mother's father, and can't say if he'd been a slave too. I'm quite sure my grandparents on my father's side had been slaves because my father was older than my mother by about seven or eight years and I heard him speak of his mother having been a slave. As far as I know my dad and his mother and father were from North Carolina.

My father, Henry Robinson, was a minister, and he and my mother, whose name was Corrine, made sure that my two sisters, four brothers, and I saw the inside of a church. They were very religious, and made us go to church all the time. They were very strict about that. My father was strict about everything, very strict. Because he was a minister, all the people gave him the utmost respect, and he demanded respect out of his children. I knew he would get you if you did something wrong. That's a known fact. And he kind of put a little fear in me to that extent. We were afraid to say anything bad in front of him. So instead of me going up to him and asking him direct for something, I'd go through my mother. I'd get her to do it. She would talk to him, and he'd give it to her or he'd tell her to have me come to him and he'd give it to me. He never would turn me down for anything. But I wouldn't go and ask him. I was pretty close to him, it's just that I didn't talk too much with him.

We just had to walk a tight rope and do as they said for as long as we were in their house. And if my father ever found out that we had been playing baseball on a Sunday, why there'd be trouble when he got home from his revival on Monday. That's the way we grew up, under those kind of rules. We couldn't do anything about it. We had to follow those rules, or you couldn't stay there.

My parents set a good example in our home. All I can say is that they lived a life before us that they wanted us to live. I never did know anything bad about my parents. My father, I never even heard him curse. Or my mother either. Sometimes my father would raise his voice enough to let us kids know that he meant business, but I never heard him ever say a mean thing to my mother. They got along real good, and I never heard them fight or argue.

My oldest brother's name was Edward G. Robinson, the same as the movie star. And the next one to him was Theophilus Robinson. After Theophilus there was Maybelle Robinson. And after Maybelle there was John Robinson, then it was Estelle Robinson, then me. Norman, who was born on April Fools' Day in 1913, was the baby. We all had to go to school, and we all graduated from high school. My father saw that we did. As a matter of fact, Edward, Maybelle, and Norman all went to Langston University, an all black school in Oklahoma.

We stayed in Oklahoma City for quite a while then we moved one last time, to Okmulgee, Oklahoma. Okmulgee is about thirty miles south of Tulsa and sits in a valley which is partly surrounded by tree-covered hills. It was an oil town, but there was also a lot of farming in things like cotton and pecans. Anyway, that's where I grew up and that's where my family remained until my mother died in 1956. We certainly weren't rich but

Catching Dreams

my parents took good care of us. We lived in an ordinary frame house on the outskirts of Okmulgee. It was what you'd call a bungalow. That's what it was. It had an outhouse and a pump out back. Near the pump we had tubs and washboards for the washing and a clothesline to hang it all out on. We didn't have electric either; we had oil lamps and lanterns. We finally got electric and city water and bathrooms put in when I was a teenager but my entire childhood, we'd use an outhouse, go fetch water in back, do our homework by the light of an oil lamp, cook over a wood-stove, and keep coal for the furnace. That's the way it was.

I was about fifteen when we got our first car. It was a Ford Model T, then later we got a Chevrolet. We never did have horses or any kind of livestock, so if my father had to go someplace and he couldn't walk it, he'd travel by train or get a cab. There were quite a few people that had cars in the neighborhood, and they would carry him where he needed to go too.

We had a garden for a while and grew some vegetables. It wasn't too big because vegetables were pretty cheap, and people would come around all the time with wagonloads to sell. Beside vegetables, my father rented some land from a nearby farmer and raised turkeys there. At Thanksgiving and Christmas he'd sell a lot of 'em. I helped when he was selling them. All he could raise, he could sell to people that he knew.

I didn't take care of the turkeys too much but me and Norman and John all took care of the dogs. We had a fox terrier called Spot and one called Jack that was a shepherd with a little greyhound or something in him.

Another favorite memory from my childhood was Christmas. It was always a treat because we were all together. We'd get together and do a lot of singing and then sit down to a table my mother had filled with turkey and dressing, cranberry sauce, greens, corn bread, sweet potato pies, and cakes. To this day, when I think of Christmas, I can almost smell my mother's cooking.

Because my father was pastor of the church, he'd run a lot of revivals and travel a lot. He'd do a whole lot of camp meetings. They'd put up a big tent that would seat maybe fifteen or sixteen hundred people, and then they would put straw down on the ground and benches in there for the people to sit on. And they'd put a pulpit up front. People would come from everywhere—all races of people. They'd come by car and horse and buggy. When I'd go, I'd usually go with my mother. I wouldn't go to all of them but went as often as I could. I enjoyed them. It kept me from going out and getting with the wrong people. Norman went more often because my father carried him around a lot. See, he was the baby and my father and mother kind of petted him. We'd sit out there in the crowd, and my father's words would roll all over us.

These revivals might run for ten days. There'd be quite a few preachers there, might be twenty ministers there. They'd have a choir. They'd do baptisms too. The camp meeting might be up in town, and then they'd have a nice spot along a river where they'd go in the afternoon for baptism. After a Sunday afternoon service, they'd stop to eat. The people from the church hosting the revival would prepare food in houses by the tents for the out-of-town people. They'd put together a full meal—fried chicken, fish, ham, beef, corn on the cob, pies—good home cookin'. All the people would sit down at picnic tables and eat. Then they'd go back to church that night.

Oklahoma was kind of a wild place when I was a boy. It hadn't been a state but for three years when I was born. The eastern part of the state had been Indian Territory, and the law didn't go there. That made it a big hangout for highway robbers and outlaws, and that kind of carried over after it became a state. When I was in my early twenties, a lot of the talk in Oklahoma was about Pretty Boy Floyd. He was a bankrobber from Akins, Oklahoma, and he had a reputation of takin' from the rich and givin' it to the poor. I don't know if that was true, but that's what everybody said. At least all the white farmers believed it because they'd put him up and hide him from the police. They had a heckuva time trying to catch old Pretty Boy. And when they'd catch him, they couldn't hold him. He was pretty slippery.

Another outlaw that was running around Oklahoma at that time was Clyde Barrow. Clyde was from Texas and it seemed like when he wasn't in Texas pulling off a robbery, he was in Oklahoma or Missouri sticking

Catching Dreams

somebody up. Later on, he teamed up with Bonnie Parker. I remember when they got a hold of these submachine guns and killed some policemen. The police couldn't seem to catch them either. When the police finally did catch them in Louisiana, there was a big shootout, and that was the end of Bonnie and Clyde.

The other big bankrobber in those days was Wilbur Underhill. They called him the "Tri-State Terror" because he robbed so many banks in Oklahoma, Arkansas, and Kansas. One of his biggest jobs was a bank right in Okmulgee. He got more than $10,000 on that one. Sometimes they'd catch him but they just couldn't keep him in jail. One time the police were carrying him to jail in McAlester, Oklahoma, and they had him manacled in the back of a car. They hadn't gone five blocks when, some kind of way, he got loose from those manacles, jumped out the door, and was on the run again. They finally did catch him and, just like Pretty Boy Floyd and Bonnie and Clyde, they didn't take Wilbur Underhill alive.

When I was growing up in Oklahoma, there were black folks, white folks, and Indians. The Indians were mostly Cherokee, Creek, and Osage, and they were very plentiful. In fact, Okmulgee was the capital of the Creek Indians right up to when Oklahoma became a state. They would come in on the weekends to buy whiskey. We didn't socialize with 'em, although they would follow you around. They liked to associate with black people. Mostly they liked to party and drink. And then they'd be uncontrollable. I only knew one of 'em to play baseball. He was a great ballplayer, about 6'3" and 250 pounds, and could play infield or outfield but he never got out of Okmulgee.

I never got in much trouble as a boy but one time when I was about sixteen. It was from having dogs to fight on a Sunday, and it got me the worst whupping from my father that I ever had. What happened was that there was this dog in the neighborhood that knew how to fight. He wasn't our pet dog; he belonged to somebody else. He was just mean and if a dog come close to him, he'd fight it and you'd have to separate them because he'd choke it to death. We kept our dog fenced in, but the people that had this dog let him get out. So he'd come around and we'd like to see him fight. This particular time it was my older brother John's idea to get the dogs to fighting. John was grown then and would have been about twenty-three or twenty-four years old. John was always kind of a problem child. So me and my brother let him fight and this mean dog killed a dog that belonged to a lady that lived a couple of doors from us. When my father come home, the lady came over. Her name was Robinson too but she was no relation. She had about seven children, some of 'em in college and some of 'em in high school. Mrs. Robinson told my father about her dog. We were sorry that it happened, but it did happen and we couldn't do anything about it. I was pretty good size and old enough to know better, but I wasn't too big for my father to take a switch to. He went and got him some switches that wouldn't break and cut 'em off on me. That's what he did. If he told you to do something, you'd do it. If you didn't, you'd get it. You didn't cross swords with my father. That's the way he was brought up and that's the way he brought his children up.

Other than that time with the dogs, I never was in too much trouble. Never did have no trouble with the police or nothing like that. The only other trouble I got into were little things I'd do around the house, maybe I'd get into fight or something like that. I never fought with Norman though. We was always close, real close. Norman didn't get in too much trouble either. I can't recall of anything bad he ever got into.

My favorite sport when I was growing up was baseball. I always loved that baseball. Norman felt the same way. Most fellows pick up the game from their fathers, but our dad wasn't interested in anything that didn't have to do with church. He didn't play baseball with us or take us hunting or fishing or anything like that. When he was home you'd catch him in there studying the Bible all the time. He wouldn't have anything to do with baseball. My dad was strictly a Baptist minister. He wouldn't be around no sports or nothing like that. Looking back I'm surprised he let us play at all. To tell the truth, in all the years I played baseball, neither of my parents ever saw me play so much as an inning. We picked up the game from other kids in the neighborhood and played nearly every moment that we weren't in school, sleeping, eating, or in church. When I was sixteen, the boys in our neighborhood on the east side challenged a team of boys on the west side to a game. We had a lot of fun, and it became a regular thing. We would play for ten or twelve cases of Coke or something like that. We *loved* to play baseball.

Sometimes the guys in Okmulgee would play the guys in Clearview, which is about twenty miles away. The Clearview team had Willie and George Jefferson. Willie and George were brothers that made it all the way to the Cleveland Buckeyes. Both of 'em could pitch. Clearview had a bunch of guys down there that could play, *good* players. Cause we used to play 'em a lot of games on Sundays. We just made sure my father didn't find out.

As a teenager, my team was the Kansas City Monarchs. I especially liked a hustling catcher from Okmulgee named T. J. Young. He played for the Monarchs for a long time. I also admired the third baseman, Newt Joseph, who was scrappy and smart, but I kind of patterned myself after Frank Duncan. He was a terrific catcher with a great arm. Runners thought twice before trying to steal second on Frank Duncan. He was an average hitter but always seemed to hit a line drive to the gap with the game on the line. He always found time to talk to me on the side and ask how I was doing. That means a lot to a boy.

At the time I was catching for our high school team in Okmulgee. I was always a catcher, but I did play outfield sometimes. If we played a doubleheader, I'd catch one game and play outfield the next one. I never did like the outfield like I did catching. I just felt comfortable catching and didn't ever concentrate on another position or another sport. Norman, on the other hand, played everything—baseball, basketball, and football and after he come out of high school, he was fortunate enough to go to Langston University for a year and lettered in all three sports. His best track event was the 100-yard dash. Whatever sport Norman participated in, he would condition himself, keep himself in shape, and play it. He was just a good athlete, that's what he was.

In school I liked math and history, so that's what I studied hardest. I especially liked American history and read a lot about Abe Lincoln and the Civil War. But my sole ambition through high school was to get out and play baseball. That was all. I was determined to be a baseball player. I don't know why because I didn't know how long the Negro Leagues would be paying salaries. But I knew that, should I keep playing, I had a chance to go up there and find out. From Newt Joseph, I knew that. Joseph lived in Muskogee during the off-season, and we used to take the Monarch cab line to see him. He was the one that kept on encouraging us to keep playing.

In addition to catching for our high school team, when school let out in the spring I played for a local Okmulgee team. I was about seventeen then, and this team was run by a Catholic priest named Father Bradley. He wanted me to go to Catholic school in Okmulgee but that never worked out. Just the same I played baseball for him. One day a team from Tulsa, Oklahoma, the Tulsa Blackballers, came to town and the owner, a Mr. Louis, wanted me to go with them. Father Bradley begged me not to go with them. He wanted me to go to his Catholic school, get an education, and play baseball for him. I guess he had just taken a liking to me, and he figured if I could stay with his team, he'd have an extraordinary team. He also thought that I was too young to turn pro.

It got to the point where Father Bradley and Mr. Louis like to come to blows because the priest didn't want Louis around. That was a shock to me. What I mean is, I didn't want to see them fighting over me, so I knew I had to make a decision. I figured that since my goal in life was to be a professional ballplayer and Tulsa looked like the first rung on the ladder, I'd better take my chance. So I went with Mr. Louis and became a Blackballer. He had a good sandlot team consisting of a bunch of guys older than me. I ended up playing two years for the Blackballers.

The hardest part about my time with the Blackballers was being away from home and facing strange racial situations. In Okmulgee, I knew where I could and couldn't go. The high school was segregated, but the movie theater wasn't. That sort of thing. It never made sense to me why I could sit next to the white kids in a movie theater but not in a classroom, but that's the way it was. On the road with Tulsa in 1927 and 1928, I never knew what to expect. Texas and Louisiana were the worst. The reason I say that is that when we did go down south, we almost always had a little trouble. Guys you'd never seen before would come up to you and demand certain things. I remember one time I was walking to the ballpark in Denison, Texas, when this guy walked up to me and said that I had come to his farm and asked him if I could pick his cotton. I didn't know him. I had never seen him before in my life and told him so. He got angry when I said he must be mistaken and threatened to hit me. He had some overalls wrapped up that he had just bought, and I didn't know what he was hiding in there. Fortunately, the other team's starting pitcher had been watching, and when he walked up and said something, the farmer moved on.

When we were kids I always looked up to my oldest brother, Edward. He was like a second father to me. He became a minister like our father, finally quit his job as a mail carrier, and moved from Oklahoma to Akron, Ohio, where he got a job in the boiler room with the Goodyear Tire and Rubber Company. My parents were often traveling between Oklahoma and Ohio, going to revivals or just visiting Edward. I hadn't had much luck finding work in Oklahoma, so when I was 19, I went to Akron with my father, got a job with Goodyear, and moved in with Edward. According to my father, I was in Akron to work and help my brother. But I also played baseball for Goodyear's company team, the Wingfoot Tigers. That was my first time away from home, but it wasn't too bad because I was with Edward.

It was during my time in Akron that I had my first real experience with the death of a loved one. My brother Theophilus had been working as a mail clerk in Chicago when he got appendicitis in 1929. He died from poor judgment. The lady where he was rooming wouldn't give the OK for them to operate on him, and they let his appendix burst. He had his whole life ahead of him.

I continued to work and play ball for Goodyear, and the Wingfoots beat most everybody they played. One of our pitchers had played in the Negro Leagues for several years. That was Lewis Hampton. "Hamp," they called him. He started with the Columbus Buckeyes back in 1921 and played with the Indianapolis ABCs, Atlantic City Bacharach Giants, and Detroit Stars before fooling around with the Goodyear team where I met him. As much as Hamp wanted to talk baseball, I was willing to listen.

Our Goodyear team was pretty well known in northeastern Ohio and western Pennsylvania, so in 1930 when a young fellow from Pittsburgh named Bullock decided he wanted to put a Negro League team in Pittsburgh, he went shopping for players in Akron. He signed me and four other guys off the Wingfoots. Bullock stocked his new team with eighteen ballplayers and we played a few exhibition games around Pittsburgh while we waited to get into the league.

Homestead, Pennsylvania, is a small steel mill town just across the Monongahela River from Pittsburgh. Back around 1910 a group of steelworkers put together a team called the Homestead Grays. One of their outfielders, Cum Posey, eventually took over the club and by 1930 had made a great team out of them. They had a stocky second baseman named George Scales who was good at turning curveballs into line drives. Vic Harris was a good contact hitter who played outfield. The Grays' best player though was a pitcher named Joe Williams. Smokey Joe they called him. His fastball was legendary. So while I waited for Mr. Bullock's team to get their league bookings, I went to as many of the Grays' games as I could and even got to see the great Smokey Joe pitch a couple of games. He was an old man then. He would have been around 45, but he could still throw smoke. His catcher with the Grays was a veteran named Bucky Ewing.

I always heard that later that season old Smokey Joe was pitching in a night game against the Kansas City Monarchs. The Monarchs were the first to carry lights around with them, and they had them set up this night. They were hooked up to generators and sometimes these generators would kind of sputter and this would cause the lights to fade in and out. That could make it tough for the pitcher to see the signal and the catcher to see the ball. They said that's what happened to Buck Ewing. He got crossed up on one of Smokey Joe's fastballs and messed up his hand. That was it for Buck Ewing. The Grays knew about a local boy named

The Grays' best pitcher
was a fellow named Joe
Williams. Smokey Joe
they called him. His
fastball was legendary.
Courtesy of NoirTech
Research Inc.

Josh Gibson who caught for a sandlot team called the Pittsburgh Craw-fords. They put a Grays uniform on him and were gonna use him until Ewing got better. Within a couple days though, Josh had four or five home runs. After hitting the ball out of the ballpark like that, you knew the Grays weren't gonna let him get away. Ewing never did get back in there. I heard he retired to upstate New York, but he didn't play any more in our league. Anyway, that's how Josh got his start with the Grays.

That wasn't the end of the Crawfords though. A numbers operator in Pittsburgh named Gus Greenlee took over the Crawfords and made a reg-ular team out of them. He got a tough veteran infielder from New Orleans named Bobby Williams to manage his team. Bobby Williams knew quite a few good ballplayers, and Gus kept getting them. They had good pitch-ing led by Harry Kincannon who threw a big curveball. Roy Williams was another pitcher they had and his brother, Harry, was the Crawfords util-ity man. They also had Vic Harris's brothers, Bill and Neal. Bill played third and Neal played left. That's the way the Crawfords formed. But most important of all, later on Gus signed the best pitcher in baseball, Satchel Paige, and then he went out and got the best hitter in the game by getting Josh back from the Grays. When Satchel and Josh were with the Crawfords, they were one of the greatest teams of all time.

Gus Greenlee was able to get all these players for his team because the players knew that Gus was a man that believed in treating his players right. He did everything for his players. If something happened to a player's family, Gus was right there. If a player needed money, Gus'd give it to him. Other owners weren't like that. Other owners thought that Gus Greenlee treated a ballplayer too good, and they would get even with him years later.

The Grays of the 1930s had a good team too. They still had Vic Harris in left. Bill Evans was in right. They had Jelly Jackson playing shortstop. He was a little guy who could catch everything. Another little guy named Lick Carlisle played second. The Grays always had a lot of power over at first with Jap Washington, Oscar Charleston, and, beginning in 1934, Buck Leonard. Raymond Brown was the Grays top pitcher for a long time. He

Catching Dreams

was a right-hander with an outstanding curve. Edsall Walker was their top left-hander and had a great sinker. That's when the Grays dominated.

Cum Posey did not appreciate Gus Greenlee's going after his players, so he would go after Gus's players. Since they were always stealing each others players, a lot of these fellows like Josh, Jap Washington, Harry Kincannon, and the Williams brothers played for both teams. All of this made for a pretty tough rivalry.

Anyway, in 1930 when it came time to vote Bullock's team into the league, Cum Posey voted us out. And Bullock was married to Cum Posey's niece! So after two months in Pittsburgh, Bullock had to turn us all loose. He paid all of our fares home but instead of staying in Akron, I returned to Oklahoma.

I played a little ball in Oklahoma, and then I went to Texas and hooked up with the Abilene Eagles of the Texas-Oklahoma-Louisiana League or TOL. The TOL was an all-black league. They had the Eagles, the San Angelo Sheepherders, the Tulsa Oilers, the San Antonio Black Indians, and the Waco Cardinals as well as teams in Odessa, Dallas, Fort Worth, and Louisiana.

Some of my teammates on the Abilene Eagles were the brothers Tom and Rich Gee, both catchers, both veterans of the mid-1920s New York Lincoln Giants. We also had a good outfielder by the name of Ollie Waldon and an outstanding first baseman by the name of Bonnie Serrell. Bonnie was just a kid when I first met him, but you could see the natural ability he had. He come out of Dallas, Texas, and he could play. Our best pitcher was a boy called Jack Matchett. Matchett was always a cutup. He was a guy who never did go to school. He didn't have no education. I learned him how to read and write his name. He was that type of person who figured that whatever he did, he would be right doing it on his own. You know how those people are. If you kind of talk to him or scold him about it, he'd get angry. You'd best serve him with kid gloves. He was that type but he was a good pitcher.

There were some good ballplayers in the TOL. For example, the San Angelo Sheepherders were managed by the former player-manager of the

Birmingham Black Barons, Reuben Jones. And one of the Sheepherders pitchers was Schoolboy George Walker who went on to a good career with the Grays and Monarchs.

The TOL teams traveled in cars, not in buses. Like when we'd go to Waco to play the Waco Cardinals, we'd travel in cars on hot, dusty roads. We were always on the lookout for where we were gonna sleep. At that time we'd sleep in people's homes, and then we'd play maybe a couple of games in that town and leave.

While I enjoyed playing in the TOL, I wanted to move up and jumped at a chance to try out with the Kansas City Monarchs in 1932. They trained in Arkansas City, Kansas, and although they knew I was a youngster, they wanted to see what I could do. At that time their ace was Wilber "Bullet" Rogan, and I wish I could say that I got the chance to catch him back then. Since I didn't catch him or hit against him, I can't say for sure but some guys said he was faster than Satchel. He was an outstanding pitcher and about one of the best hitters you'd want to see to be a pitcher. Yes, sir, Bullet was a good hitter and a great pitcher. I'd watched him pitch with the Monarchs since I was a little boy. The Monarchs manager was Andy Cooper and a pretty good pitcher himself.

Here's what happened on my tryout. Some of the Monarchs threw the ball everywhere, bad as they could throw it, and I had to catch everything. I feel sure that this wasn't Andy Cooper's idea. They were doing this on their own. Newt Allen, their second baseman, was the worst. He was the main guy that didn't want to see a youngster make it. Sometimes they'd fire the ball at you when you weren't looking for it. One time they did that, and I got my hand in that glove too fast and jammed my finger. The next day Cooper wanted me to catch against the Wichita Watermen. They were a semipro team that played every year in the National Baseball Congress Tournament there in Wichita, Kansas. They had a lot of major leaguers on that team. One that I remember was Freddie Brickell who played outfield for the Pirates in the twenties. Andy Cooper wanted me to catch a big left-handed pitcher named Army Cooper, who was no relation to Andy. I started to catch him but my finger was hurting me pretty bad, so I had to ask Andy Cooper to take me out.

I went back to Abilene of the TOL and knew that if I played hard, my time would come. That short stint against the Wichita Watermen wasn't the first time I got to play against major league players. The TOL teams played a lot of teams with ex-major leaguers. As a matter of fact, when we'd go to Wichita, Kansas, for the National Tournament, there weren't many of those teams that didn't have major league ballplayers on it. Most years the Wichita Waterman were loaded with major league ballplayers. These were guys that had been up and come back because they had leg cramps or something like that and couldn't play the regular, full season in the majors. Besides the Wichita Watermen, we'd play the Enid Eason Oilers, the Duncan Halliburton Cementers, and a team out of Arkansas City whose name I forget. There were several of them and most of these teams were nothing but major league ballplayers, and you had to play to beat them. I remember hitting against Wilcy Moore, and he'd won 19 games for the '27 Yankees and even won a couple of World Series games. You'd have these veteran players that were just a notch below sticking in the majors. Those boys could play. Didn't look like they'd lost too much or nothin'.

One of the most famous major leaguers that I played against was Hack Wilson. That was in Texas in 1935 when I played a couple games for the San Angelo Sheepherders. My regular team out of Abilene was waiting on their booking, and to keep in shape, I played with San Angelo. Hack Wilson had finished his career with the Philadelphia Phillies the year before and then hired on with a Texas team called the Borger Huber Oilers. The Borger Huber Oilers weren't a regular TOL team. There were a lot of teams out there that were put together by business people, and in Texas and Oklahoma that meant oil companies. These oil men would sponsor these teams, get some advertising out of it, and get to tell their friends that not only did they know Hack Wilson or some other ex-big leaguer but also that he worked for them. In 1930, Hack Wilson had 56 home runs and 190 RBIs with the Chicago Cubs, and five years later he was with an oil company team in Texas and glad of it. Hack was happy to get the work, happy to get paid to keep playing. He knew the work wouldn't be hard. Hack and these other ballplayers had to go somewhere, so why not play for these big oil companies? That's all the oil companies did. Pick 'em up and play a little baseball.

Hack Wilson was a little, short guy, and he was kind of stocky. But he could hit that ball if you threw it in the wrong place. Yes, sir, he could hit. He was playing right field. I think Hack's team beat us 5–3, and I think he got a home run and a triple that night. If Hack was drinking you sure couldn't tell by talking to him or watching him play. Of course, I wouldn't ask him about his drinking noways. He acted kind of regular the two nights I seen him. He was nice.

We had a good team at Abilene, and every year we got to play in the Wichita Baseball Tournament. The TOL was a pretty good league, but it had trouble drawing and never did get up off the ground. I know we never got paid that much. During the week when the people were working on their farms, ranches, and oil fields, they were tired after being out in that sun all day, and they'd go home. This was the heart of the dust bowl in the middle of the Great Depression, and life was pretty rough for most folks. Even on weekends when people would come out to the ballgame—and on a Sunday or a holiday you couldn't hardly get in the park—they would divide the gate up on a percentage among the players, but the man that booked the games would get his off the top. A lot of times, if it wasn't a TOL game, people would pass the hat around. That would be about the size of it. We didn't make no money, but after all you might realize a couple dollars out of it. Of course, you wasn't looking for much. You never did stop playing though. Despite the depression, some kind of way they played a little baseball.

I played with the Abilene Eagles until the TOL finally folded, and then Jack Matchett and I caught on with a team out of Odessa in 1936.

Being on the road could put you in bad situations now and then. People would yell some pretty awful things at you. This—being threatened—didn't stop you. A lot of times maybe it'd be one guy in a bunch. Maybe he'd be betting or something like that, and you'd get those kind of threats. When I was playing for Odessa, we played a local team in Hobbs, New Mexico, which in 1936 was an oil booming town. A fellow named Johnny Carter had rounded up the best players he could find from Abilene and other teams that had been part of the TOL League to play for Hobbs. He even picked up Beans Minor who later had a long career as the catcher for the House of David. We practiced about a week together, and then we played the Hobbs team. A whole lot of money was being exchanged on that game, and it was so prejudiced that you just didn't feel up to your potential. This is what the umpire said over the public address system to begin the game. He said, "Today's the day of the big ballgame. For the white boys, it's Ted Blankenship pitching and Beans Minor catching. And," he said, "for the niggers, it's a big nigger pitching and a little nigger catching." I was catching and Matchett was pitching. And we knew we were going up against the worst of it because this was the umpire saying this. I just looked around. It didn't make no difference to me because I'd heard that before.

The umpire's comments didn't upset Matchett either, but you can imagine the sort of strike zone he had to pitch to. The umpires weren't giving you any breaks at all—they was takin' em. And Hobbs didn't need any help, they had a helluva club. But to make matters worse, we're playing and come to find out that a white man had bet all his life's earnings on us. They run seven runs on Matchett in the first inning, so we brought a boy in named John Childress and he stopped it right there. The fellow that did all the betting on us and his wife come into our dugout and sat with us. I guess they wanted to keep an eye on their investment. It was twilight when we began the top half of the seventh inning, and we were down by plenty. This poor guy and his wife were pretty sad. It looked like they were going to lose everything. And then the roof caved in—for Hobbs. We scored a bunch of runs to tie it and kept right on going. The next thing I know the happiest guy in the park is begging us to *stop* scoring. Since the park at Hobbs didn't have lights and and it was getting dark, he was worried that the umpires would call the game on account of darkness, wipe out our big inning, and give a six inning victory to Hobbs. So we just stopped making runs and then finished the seventh inning and started the eighth inning, and they had to call the rest of the game. The guy that won all that money celebrated with us until about five o'clock in the morning, spending money like a congressman in an election year.

Something that both Abilene and Odessa did was to have a little parade when they'd get into town. See, people didn't read newspapers too much, and they had to have some way to let the people know they were fixin' to play a ballgame. So what they would do was put a guy with a bull horn and five or six ballplayers in uniform on the back of a haywagon or open truck and drive them around town. And if they could find a few local musicians, especially trombones, tubas, and drums, they'd carry them too. And they could almost always count on boys and dogs running alongside. Now how many people can hear a bull horn, a small brass band, howling boys, and barking dogs and not stop what they're doing to see what the fuss is all about? And the longer they drove, the longer the line of boys and barking dogs would get. That got the word out.

It was while I was with Odessa that we played the Zulu Cannibal Giants. They came to Odessa on a holiday and stayed about three days because they were drawing so good. They had a show like the Clowns had later on. In fact, the Clowns got the idea from the Zulus. The Zulu Cannibal Giants had these grass skirts that they would wear and they'd put war paint on their faces. Some of 'em were good ballplayers but they looked ridiculous. This guy from Kentucky named Charlie Henry ran the team. They'd have a booking in a certain town and he'd leave there with two or three ballplayers and let the rest of them go. As he'd go on his way, he'd pick up the rest of the ballplayers he needed to play. He'd get players any way he could to make a date. He'd keep them as long as they had bookings and then they'd break up. He'd just make sure to get those grass skirts back before they drifted off. The whole thing was kind of insulting. You might think they'd have been reluctant to slide with those grass skirts on but they always had pants and pads on underneath. When they came to play us in Odessa though, they had a pretty rough time. We ran the skirts right off 'em.

I was on the road most of the time but kept a room in Lubbock, Texas, at Jack Matchett's father's house. I had just gotten back from a road trip when Mr. Matchett handed me a telegram. It was from my sister Maybelle saying that my father had died. He was 86 and had had pains in his head for a long time. The telegram had been there for several days while I had been out of town. The day I got it was the day they was burying him. It wouldn't have did me any good to leave then because Lubbock was a long ways from Okmulgee. No way could I get there in time. Regardless of where I was, I kept in touch with my parents, so this really got to me. I called my mother and explained to her why I couldn't make it back for the funeral. In fact, I didn't know when I could make it back to Okmulgee. It wasn't the team, I couldn't put it on the team, it was my condition. I didn't have the money. And after talking to my mother and my brothers and sisters, I wasn't in shape to go home anyways. I cried because they told me that he kept asking for me. I figured that he wanted to tell me something, but I was down in Texas playing ball. I felt very bad but I tried not to feel that guilty about not being there because I wasn't making any money and it was the middle of the depression time. I finally did get back six or seven months later.

I don't think my father was proud of Norman and me playing baseball for a living. It was kind of against his teaching. He saw baseball as a worldy thing, and he wanted us to follow in his footsteps. We tried to follow his beliefs as best we could, but we just couldn't let go of that baseball. It would have been nice to have his blessing, but we understood. He had always been a big part of my life, and it was pretty rough to go on without him.

My father had suffered with that head pain for a long time. I never did know what it was because he didn't believe in going to a doctor. He never did go to no doctor. Us kids and my mother never did have no doctors either. The only remedy we'd get was that my father believed in prayer. We never did have no medicine around. No home remedies or anything like that. If we got sick, it was prayer and that's all. He'd pray for you and he believed that the Lord answered prayers and that's what happened. I never saw a doctor until I was twenty-three but then, until recently, I didn't ever get sick but one time. That was many years ago when I ate a watermelon that was hot because it hadn't been put on ice. I got a fever and that's the only time. Other than that I never was sick.

Another thing I'll never forget about my time in Texas was in 1936 when I first saw Satchel Paige pitch. I'd always heard about him but never seen him. The Satchel Paige's All-Stars were playing thirty to forty miles away from us, so a bunch of us piled into a car and drove to the game. They had just won the Denver Post Tournament and, in addition to Satchel, they had Felton Snow at third, Leroy Morney at short, and Cool Papa Bell in center. Their other pitchers were Bob "Schoolboy" Griffith and Harry Kincannon and their catchers were Josh Gibson and Pepper Bassett. They called Bassett "Rocking Chair" Bassett because he would catch Satchel while sitting in a rocking chair. Fans loved that. Oscar Charleston was in right field and, as it turned out, this was the only time I got to see him play. I think he went two for four that night but he was nearly forty and on his way out. They say he was the greatest outfielder of all time. He might also have been the toughest. That's what they were telling us. Satchel's All-Stars played semipros and teams of ex-major leaguers. Four of those guys, Satchel, Josh, Cool, and Oscar, are now in Cooperstown. The boys from Odessa were mighty impressed that day.

2

Satchel Paige's All-Stars

My brother Norman, who had been playing ball in east Texas with a team out of Mineola called the Black Spiders, and I were back home in Oklahoma in the winter of 1938 when the Kansas City Monarchs called. They wanted Norman. My brother was an outstanding defensive center fielder with excellent speed and he was an excellent switch hitter, so I wasn't surprised he got the call. I was happy for him and knew someday I'd get my chance too. So Norman caught a train to New Orleans to join the Monarchs in the spring of 1939, and I headed back to Odessa. When the Monarchs needed another catcher, Norman reminded them of me, and they sent for me too.

When I arrived at training camp in New Orleans, I met with my old friend Newt Joseph who was now the player-manager of the Kansas City Monarchs' second team, the Satchel Paige's All-Stars. The Monarchs were one of the best teams in the Negro Leagues and the All-Stars, led by Satchel Paige, was their barnstorming B-team. Later that night Newt introduced me to the fellows. I guess I didn't have sense enough to be nervous. I knew that people had always praised my catching. And I wasn't afraid to catch anybody. I'd caught guys that threw harder than Satchel, although they didn't have his control. Satchel had the best control of anybody. And at that time Satchel wasn't throwing that hard anyway because he'd hurt his arm pitching in Mexico. That's the reason he wasn't with the Monarchs. The All-Stars was a way for him to get his arm back into shape and for the Monarchs to develop new ballplayers and, with Satchel's name on all the advertising posters, sell some tickets.

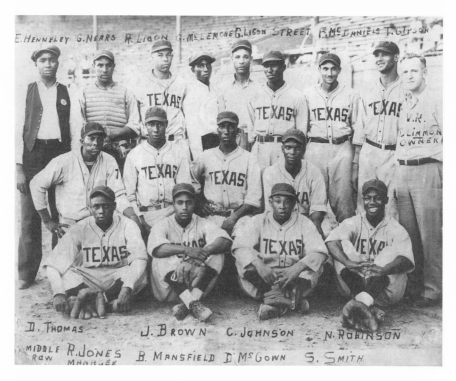

The Mineola Black Spiders, 1938. Norman is sitting in the lower right and looks like a man who enjoys his work. While Norman was playing in east Texas, I was playing with the Abilene Eagles and a team out of Odessa. Courtesy of the author.

I made the Satchel Paige's All-Stars team in spring training and signed a contract with J. L. and Lee Wilkinson, the brothers that owned the Monarchs. Finally, after seven years of professional ball down in Texas, I was going to earn a real, guaranteed salary playing baseball. I also knew that catching Satchel Paige would be a great experience and that if I played the way I knew I could play, I'd make it to the big club.

In addition to Newt Joseph and Satchel, the All-Stars had pitchers Dick Bradley, Ivory Barnes, Ted Alexander, John Donaldson, John Markham, and Monte Elmore. At third base was Herb Souell and at shortstop was

Satchel Paige's All-Stars, 1939. *(Standing left to right)* Ivory Barnes, Paul Hardy, John Donaldson, George Giles, Jack Matchett, Leandy Young, Ted Alexander, Fred McDaniels. *(Kneeling left to right)* Byron "Mex" Johnson, Jesse Douglas, Herb Souell (who sometimes played under the name of Herb Cyrus), Norman Robinson, John Markham, and Newt Joseph. I had broken my thumb and gone on home. Satchel was on the team but most likely was off moonlighting when this photo was taken. Courtesy of the author.

Mex Johnson who was really out of Arkansas. Second base was Jesse Douglas, first base was George Giles, and I was catching along with a veteran by the name of Paul Hardy. Our regular outfielders were Gal Young, my brother Norman, and Fred McDaniels. That was most of the team.

The Israelite House of David was a religious group out of Benton Harbor, Michigan. Their religion was based on the Book of Revelations. If you're old enough, you'd remember them for two things. One, they wore their hair long—really long—and let it hang down past the middle of their backs. They also liked shaggy beards. And two, they supported themselves by fielding a barnstorming baseball team. They'd been together so long that they had put together a good team. You can pretty well imagine what a sight these long-haired white boys were for small town crowds in the 1930s and 1940s. They were our first booking when we broke spring training in 1939, and we barnstormed west with them.

The House of David was a good drawing card but more so when matched with a team that had Satchel's name out in front. We almost always played to good crowds. They had Doc Talley pitching, Long John Tucker at first, George "Andy" Anderson at second, Eddie Lick at short, and Beans Minor, who was one of the few to wear his hair short, catching. These were the mainstays and the team was built around them. They

House of David baseball players Doc Talley, George "Andy" Anderson, and Long John Tucker. Courtesy of the State Archives of Michigan.

Catching Dreams

were friendly but kept to themselves and stayed at different hotels than us. They had a little "pepper" show that they put on that always went over big with the crowd. Talley, Anderson, and Tucker would play a shell game with the baseball. It was sort of a group juggling act where the ball would disappear from the hands of one player and reappear with another. The crowds could never figure out which one was hiding the ball. People liked to see their show, and we drew pretty well. Despite their show and crowd-pleasing, they played good, scrappy baseball. They knew that losing games wasn't gonna help their bookings any and beat most of the teams they faced—except us. They were good but we were better. Occasionally, the House of David had other bookings, and we'd go our separate ways for a few days only to meet up later in the week.

I had kind of a rough start on account of I broke my thumb early in the season. Before going back to Texas to wait for my hand to heal, J. L. Wilkinson took me aside and asked me to keep my eyes open for good ballplayers. He said to send 'em up to Kansas City and if they needed travelin' money, to just let him know and he'd send a check down to me. So the first thing I did was to look up some of my old teammates from Abilene. When I caught up with Bonnie Serrell, Bonnie wanted to know if I would talk to Wilkinson about him. Bonnie didn't need to ask since I had him in mind all along. I told him I would, and after I talked to J. L. Wilkinson, the All-Stars sent for Bonnie, Jack Matchett, and Ollie Waldon. Eventually Jack and Bonnie wound up going on to the Monarchs.

I'm especially proud to say that I got Bonnie Serrell his first job. Bonnie was a fun guy. He was a young, lively fella and a good, good ballplayer. Bonnie went up there as a first baseman. He had a snap throw. All he'd do is snap his wrist and throw anywhere. Give Newt Joseph credit for moving him to second. Newt Joseph took one look at Serrell's snap throws and said, "We've got the best second baseman in the league playing first." Bonnie was good at whatever he did, and he got to the point—you know how people do when they get good and confident—where he'd wanna drink and clown with the guys. But on the field, he was all business. That's all he ever wanted to do was play ball. Bonnie Serrell was something special.

I'm especially proud to say that I got Bonnie Serrell his first job. Bonnie was a fun guy. He was a good, good ballplayer. That's all he ever wanted to do was play ball. He was something special. Courtesy of NoirTech Research Inc.

Catching Dreams

After six weeks I rejoined the team for a series of games against the House of David and took over for Paul Hardy who had been doing the catching while I waited for my hand to get better. I got off to a great start by breaking up four games in a row with big hits in the late innings. It felt good to be back, and I was happy to prove to everybody that I could play. Later on Joseph decided we had too many catchers and got rid of Paul. Paul ended up barnstorming with the Clowns and then managed and caught for the Harlem Globetrotters baseball team before becoming the equipment manager of the Globetrotters basketball team. With Paul gone, I did the bulk of the catching.

All of our bookings were made before the season started by the Monarchs' booking agent. The Monarchs' office handled the finances and scheduled the games. All we had to do was play. Most of our barnstorming games were at night. The ballparks weren't the best but the groundskeepers did the best they could so we had to play on it. As you can imagine, the infielders had the worst of it. Some of the places we played in weren't even regulation parks.

Sometimes we had to play two and three games a day, but the stops weren't so far apart when we played three games a day. When we did play three games a day, I caught all three. Sometimes, but not often, if we were leading in the third game, Newt Joseph would relieve me in the seventh or eighth inning. He'd put me in left field to keep my bat in the lineup. When we'd play three games like that, it would be on the Fourth of July or some other holiday. That's the only place people knew to go was to the ballpark. You'd be booked in the morning at ten o'clock, and that park would be full. Then you'd go over to the next town a little later in the afternoon and play that game. Then you might have to travel about twenty miles to the next town that evening. This was all up in Iowa and Nebraska and the midwest. And I caught lots of doubleheaders. Later in my career when I'd be catching a doubleheader and feeling a little tired, I'd think back, "Well, at least there ain't no third game." Catching could really wear you down, but I loved being behind the plate because you had the whole game right in front of you.

I'll tell you about Satchel Paige. When I first started catching him with the Satchel Paige's All-Stars in 1939, it was worse than just working a sore arm back into shape. He was washed up. His arm hurt real bad, and everybody knew it. Even though he was trying to get back in shape, nobody really believed that his arm would ever get right again. I was in my late twenties and on my way up, and Satchel was in his early thirties and sinking fast.

He had been just a dominant pitcher. In his prime, his fastball came in like a rifle shot, and since he was tall with long arms, it seemed like he was right on top of the batter. He made sixty feet, six inches feel like twenty feet. But Satchel had hurt his arm in winter ball while pitching in Mexico City and at spring training in New Orleans you could tell something was really wrong. All he could throw was off-speed junk. The Monarchs were very worried and had our trainer, Jew Baby, stay with Satchel day in and day out. I don't know why they called him Jew Baby. His real name was James Floyd. Anyway, Satchel saw more of Jew Baby than his own wife. They were always rubbing his arm down with hot towels, lotions, and epsom salts to try and work this cold out of his arm. I knew it could be done because I'd had sore arms before and after you take hot towels, you do a lot of jogging, get your legs in shape, and then your arm comes around—if you're lucky.

We certainly weren't the first team to take an injured or old star, name the team after him, and hit the road. That's what they did with Grover Cleveland Alexander. His team would barnstorm all over the place, or he'd hook up with the House of David and play with them for a while. When we played against Grover Cleveland Alexander in Oklahoma and Texas, he would pitch two or three innings but he didn't have nothin'. He was just a drawing card like Satchel. A lot of times when Satchel was standing there talking to him, I'd come over and talk with him. He was a nice guy. If he had a drinking problem, I couldn't tell. A whole lot of them guys drank, and you couldn't tell whether they were drinking or not. Grover Cleveland Alexander was nice to the black ballplayers. It would have been fun to catch him in his prime.

About five weeks after spring training we had gotten as far from New Orleans as Oklahoma City. We were getting ready for a Sunday afternoon

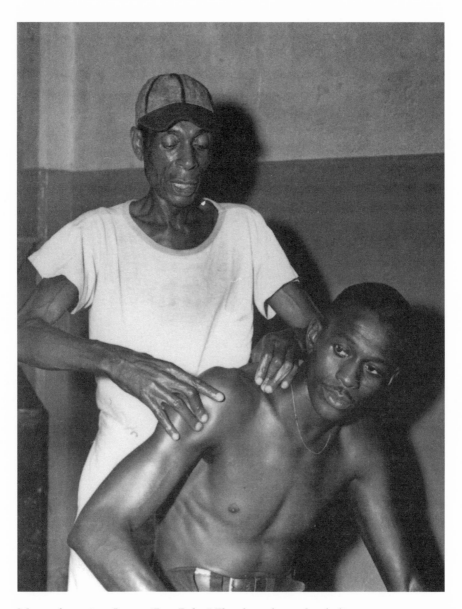

Monarchs trainer James "Jew Baby" Floyd works on Satchel's arm.
Courtesy of UPI/Bettmann.

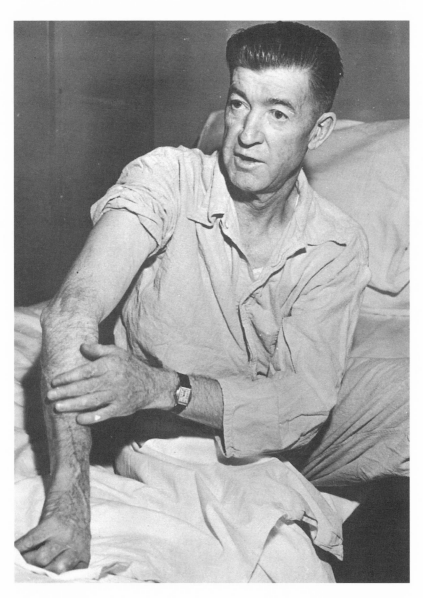

Grover Cleveland Alexander and his famous right arm. It was against his barnstorming House of David team that Satchel's arm returned to full speed. Courtesy of the author.

game against the Grover Cleveland Alexander House of David team, which fielded several ex-major leaguers. It was a nice warm Sunday— in the low eighties. Satchel came up to me and said, "You better be ready because I'm ready today." And I told him, "I can catch what you been throwing in a work glove." I warmed him up and it was like catching marshmallows. He was throwing underhand and lobbing the ball to me as usual. When the leadoff hitter came to bat, I called him for a fastball and that's what he threw. Satchel threw that baseball so hard that he knocked the mitt off my hand. I walked out to the mound, handed the ball back to him, and said, "I'll be ready from now on." I shouldn't have been surprised because he threw that pitch overhand, and he hadn't done that in a long time. We beat them that day, Satchel beat them pretty bad. And his arm never did get sore no more. Years later he told me his secret for not having a sore arm after Jew Baby got it back in shape. His secret was to urinate on his hand and rub it on his arm and shoulder.

With his arm right again, Satchel was about as fast as anyone I ever caught, but it was his control that carried him as far as he went. He had superb control. The way he'd warm up was to tear the top off a book of matches, put it down, and throw the ball over that. That was his target. He'd pitch over that. That made the plate look like a mattress when he was out there. He could throw the ball over any part of the plate.

When I first started catching Satchel, he told me, "I don't need a signal. Just catch what I throw."

I couldn't go for that. It's the catcher's responsibility to call the game. For the first few batters of that first game, no matter what I called, Satchel threw the fastball. I went out to the mound.

"Look," I told him, "You missed the signal."

"Just catch. You don't need no signal."

"Well, I don't know about that," I said. "If you throw a fastball and I've called you for a curve, you'll cross me up. There's a possibility I could hurt my hand."

"I'm not gonna cross you up because I can get *everybody* out with my fastball." That's what he told me. He said, "You look for a fastball all the time. Just give me a target and catch it."

The truth was that he didn't have any kind of a curveball. He just threw the ball hard. One day we finally got together on signals, and he decided to go with what the catcher asked for. There wasn't a whole lot to choose from. I'd call him for a fastball, change-up, or his hesitation pitch.

Satchel was smart out there by outthinking the hitter. He could change his pitch, if he saw a batter shift some kind of way. If you were a good low ball hitter, he would pitch to your weakness so much that when he threw the ball in your power, you'd miss it. He knew how to get you out because when he wasn't pitching, he was studying how to break your stride. He'd figure out what he wanted to do with a particular batter, and then he'd set them up. He was very good at changing speeds. He might start a batter out with a fastball or two and then, just when the batter figured he knew what to expect, Satchel would take something off the fastball. The batter would readjust again and then Satchel would throw you another one that looked like it wasn't ever gonna get up there. That's what he called his trouble ball—that real slow one. He'd take everything off the ball, but he'd make a strike out of that pitch. A whole lot of pitchers could throw a change-up, but not too many could throw it over the plate for a strike. Satchel threw his for a strike. That's where his control came in. Satchel believed in breaking your stride, and he knew that you couldn't get but so much wood on the ball. That was his main objective, to break your stride. If you go so far, you haven't got nothing left to swing with but your arms. No power. You've given it up. Same thing in golf. If you lose that twist in your body, you ain't got nothing left to hit with. You got to get your weight into it. Satchel was smart enough to outsmart the hitter, and he had excellent control. This made him as great as he was.

Satchel's most famous pitch, after his fastball, was probably his hesitation pitch. He always had that hesitation pitch when his arm was healthy. The hesitation pitch was like his trouble ball in that it ruined the hitter's timing. He would go through his wind-up and stop. Then he would just put his left foot down and throw from right there and still have a whole lot on it. He could throw the ball like a catcher, from the waist up. Most of the time when Satchel stopped or paused momentarily, a hitter would shift his weight. Broke their stride. By the time they'd get the bat back up, Satchel'd done thrown the ball past 'em.

Catching Dreams

Despite all of Satchel's stops and starts on the mound, I never saw our umpires call Satchel for a balk. Not once. Even in the late forties when he played for Lou Boudreau and the Indians in the majors, they didn't bother him much with balk calls. It wasn't until he came back with the Browns in the early fifties that the umpires started to call him regularly for balks.

Now if it's a fastball pitcher like Satchel, you just hold that bat up there, keep your eye on the ball, and punch at it. That's the only way you're going to hit him. If Satchel caught you slugging at him, you never would hit him. Never would.

That's what I called him for—fastball and change-up, in and out, high and low. That's all. And he had enough on the ball that you wouldn't get the big part of the bat on the ball. The first year I caught him, that's the way we worked. He'd experiment with other pitches though. He wasn't ashamed to ask another guy how to throw a different pitch, and then he would practice it. Pretty soon he would develop that pitch.

And after he had gotten good with a pitch, he would name it. Satchel had all kinds of names for his pitches. He called one his bee ball, another his jump ball, there was Long Tom, and so on. Those are just some of the pitches that he threw. I couldn't tell the difference between most of them except that one might be his fastball and the other would have something taken off it. He had a way of naming pitches because it made a good story. People loved it. If he called one of his pitches a bee ball, that was fine with me, but it still looked like his fastball to me. Sometimes he'd call that bee ball his hummer. It was still his fastball, but he'd throw it a slightly different way. That was all. I never actually called him for the bee ball or the drop ball or any of those crazy pitches. It was strictly fastball, or, if you wanted a change-up, you'd kind of wave your mitt. I'd let him know the location by the way I'd hold my mitt. I would straddle the plate and make him hit my knees—that's right on the corner. That's where he'd pitch. But as far as separate signals for Long Tom and the rest, that was just Satchel talking. He loved to tell stories. To this day, I still don't know which one Long Tom was.

The only weakness that Satchel had was that he didn't have such a good move to first base. But since Satchel could throw hard from the stretch, you didn't get that far off first off him either. If a guy was fixin' to run, and you called Satchel for an off-speed pitch, he'd still get it up there fast enough to where you could throw the runner out.

Satchel never really did have too good a curve as long as I caught him, which was 1942. He could throw what you'd call a little slider. Satchel had what he called a curveball but I would call it a slider. It broke just enough to throw the hitter off a little but not enough to be a real curve. But he could throw it for strikes and he could throw it hard. And he would throw it not in the middle of the plate but over the corner. Later on he went to school and was smart enough to keep on trying until he developed a good curveball.

You won't be surprised to hear that the best fastball I ever caught was Satchel's, but Dick Bradley could throw just about as hard. It's kind of scary to think that Kanas City had *two* guys that could throw that hard. Dick was out of Louisiana, and he's still living there. His ball was a little heavier than Satchel's. Satchel threw a light ball, and it was easier to catch. Satchel's fastball also had a little hop on it.

If you include the guys that I saw but never got to catch, I would say this: Bullet Rogan, Smokey Joe Williams, and Satchel were about the fastest. This boy Rogan was as fast as anybody for five or six innings. He just didn't have the stamina, but for five or six innings he was faster than anybody. He wasn't no big man. He was about my size, I guess. I don't know where he got his power from, but he could throw.

It was great to play on the same team with Norman but people expected me to do something about his rough style of play. Norman played baseball like Ty Cobb. Where I would try to keep from hurting you, Norman would hurt you. He went into the bases rough. He'd even come in hard on me. He was that type of ballplayer. You just couldn't take it away from him. He played the game like that. They said that when Ty Cobb saw somebody waiting to tag him out, that rather than hit the base, he'd get his spikes up in your chest and try to shake that ball loose from you. Pete Rose was another one would do the same thing. Remember the way he ran over that boy Fosse in the All-Star game and like to put him out of baseball? This is the type of player Norman was. You had several ballplayers in the league like that. He would hurt his own brother. Norman would. He had the reputation in the league where you'd get out of the way or you were going to be cut. That's the way he played the game.

Well, Norman hurt a bunch of those people at the House of David. When I came back after my thumb was hurt, I found out that he had cut their shortstop, Eddie Lick. He was a white boy—like all the House of Davids—and a good shortstop. Norman cut him so bad, they had to send him home for the rest of the season. They came to me when I rejoined the team because I knew the House of David catcher, Beans Minor. I knew him from when I was kid. I'd grown up watching Beans play with Wilson Moore, Jimmy Walker, and Stormy Davis on the Okmulgee Drillers of the Western Association. We knew each other very well, so Beans came to me and said, "I know you boys. I knew you when you started playing. I knew you when you was kids. Your brother is going into the bases too rough." And he said, "I'm sure you can tell him because you're a couple years older than he is. Tell him that people are complaining about him." So I talked with my brother about it, and my brother talked to our manager, Newt Joseph. This rough style was also Joseph's way of playing. Joseph liked the way he was going into bases. This was his way of playing too. Finally, Joseph said, "The hell with what they say. You go to get safe. Don't you be trying to keep from spiking somebody. You'll hurt yourself." Newt Joseph understood that this is what made Norman a good ballplayer and didn't try to change him. He figured the House of David would just have to get used to it.

Newt Joseph was pretty tough himself. One time he was pitching batting practice to Gal Young, and Gal hit a line drive right back at Joseph that hit him in the groin. Hit that line drive and broke his cup, he hit it so hard. His privates swole up so that he went back to the clubhouse and laid down. Me and Satchel went in there trying to cheer him up. Satchel was kidding him. Told him, "Next time you pitch batting practice, don't you let nobody know what's coming." I don't think Newt thought this was as funny as we did, so he told Satchel and me to get the hell out of there. He laid up there for a while, and it wasn't long before he was back out on the field. He was the manager and there was a game to play.

The truth is I'd had my own problems with the House of David. We even got into a big fight during one game in Reno, Nevada. What happened was, they had bet a whole lot of money with some gamblers on the game. This was wrong and we didn't know anything about it. We didn't know what people were betting, who they were betting against, or who stood to lose what. So we were in Reno that night and along about the seventh or eighth inning, with us leading about 5-3, George Anderson got on. Anderson was standing on second base, and Booker McDaniels was pitching when somebody singled to the outfield. That Anderson tried to score from second base on a line drive single! The outfielder threw the ball in, and I covered him way up the line and tagged him several feet from homeplate.

When I tagged him out, he jumped and started hollering and going on. I'm not sure why but the umpire was slow making the call, so I said to him, "Well this is all he'd do. He's a troublemaker. He's hollerin'. You know he's out." And then Anderson run up to me and pushed me, and I pushed him back. And it started. People were coming out of the stands, hollering, fussing, fighting. They told us to just go to the dugout and take cover. So that's what we did. They finally got it straightened out, and we went on and won the game. You could get hurt like that with people betting all that money. Because one player can start something. They know this man's out because he's out from here to next Saturday. 'Cause I done tagged him. I got the ball and he was about half way home from third base, and I got him way up the line. He was touching my hand with the ball, he's out. I can't say betting was the cause of this incident, but it sure did make it worse by getting the fans involved. I didn't know it at the time, but this brawl would come back to haunt me later.

The Negro Leagues didn't fool with betting. To tell the truth, I never know'd a player, not on our team, to bet on no ballgame. That was one thing that was definite. Would have got him home fast for betting. But later, when I was playing in Baltimore, I had people come up to me and say, "What do think about the game?" I'd say, "I think we're gonna play hard; we're gonna try to win." That's all. Because there's guys that want you to give them the assurance that you're gonna win. We weren't allowed to pass out no information like that. Although at times we knew we were going to win because we had a pitcher that was gonna win. People come up and ask you some terrible things about a ballgame.

That wasn't the last of my little problems with the House of David. Later in the season I had some words with a couple of their guys—again it was their second baseman Andy Anderson and Long John Tucker, the first baseman. It happened during a game with Satchel pitching. They had been crying on every pitch for several innings, when Tucker came up to bat again. Satchel fired a fastball strike over the plate, and Tucker thought it was inside and started complaining again. Tucker was a big crybaby anyhow, and I was tired of listening to him. I said, "He's gonna throw another one in the same place." Tucker turned and drew his bat back like he was going to hit my head into center field and cussed me. Tucker was another one, I guess, that didn't like you talking to him. It was OK for him to talk but not you. Whole lot of guys didn't like you talking to them when they were at bat, but they couldn't stop it. That's part of the game. So I walked out to the mound to cool off. Satchel had seen what he did and said, "Don't say nothing." I walked back to the plate and crouched. Satchel broke two of his ribs on the next pitch. That was the first time I'd seen Satchel get angry in a ballgame, and the only time I ever saw or heard of him throwing at anybody.

Satchel Paige, beside being the greatest pitcher in our game, was also our greatest attraction. When we were going to play in a town, they would put big placards up all over town, and if Satchel was billed to pitch on the placard, he would pitch even if it wasn't but three innings. I don't care if it was everyday, he would have to pitch. That's the way they did it because people would come from all over to see Satchel pitch.

Satchel would pitch here today and pitch for somebody else tomorrow if he didn't have to pitch for us. That's the way he made his extra money. Since the idea was to get Satchel to make as many appearances as possible, J. L. Wilkinson, the Monarchs' owner, bought a little two-seater Piper Cub and Dick Wilkinson, J. L.'s son, would fly him around to his games and appearances. They covered a lot of ground that way. Everything was fine until the plane came down in a farmer's corn field in Nebraska. While

Satchel and Dick were looking at the wreckage, trying to figure out what to do, the farmer walked up and said that somebody was gonna pay for that corn. They'd messed up a lot of rows of his corn. So Satchel told him he'd just give him what was left of the plane and they walked away. That was the last time he fooled with a small plane.

Satchel loved to play to the crowds, and the crowds always turned out to see him. There was always the feeling that with Satchel on the mound, you might see something you'd never seen before. Something once-in-a-lifetime. One time in Spokane, Washington, when I was catching for the All-Stars, he called in all three outfielders and moved them to the infield. Then he set the third baseman down on third base and the first baseman down on first base. Then he struck out the side. He would do things like that just to excite the fans. He knew that when these fans talked to their friends over in the next town where we'd be scheduled to play, they'd say, "Do you know what that Satchel Paige did?" And when they heard, they'd buy tickets and tell their friends. He knew that you had to get people talking about you the morning after in order to have another good turnout that night. Satchel was really made for barnstorming.

He'd only try things that he knew he could pull off. For example, once before a night game in Ogden, Utah, against the House of David, a reporter asked Satchel if he would try something. The reporter would get the crowd quiet, and he wanted Satchel to throw a fastball so hard that the crowd could hear it hiss. Satchel had to tell him that he couldn't do it and didn't know of anybody that could. Not with a clean baseball. Maybe if the cover was torn but then everybody would know it was a stunt. You couldn't hear Satchel's fastball; you were lucky to just see it.

After his arm got better, Satchel wasn't the only great pitcher I caught in 1939 with the All-Stars. John Donaldson goes way back with the Monarchs to when they first got together. They said that he had been a great pitcher in his prime, and he'd won as many games as anybody. A lot of people think he should be in the Hall of Fame, but he was older than Vaseline when I caught him with the All-Stars. He would have been in his late forties, and he didn't have too much left, but he knew all the tricks.

He was a left-hander whose best pitch was a big curveball. And he had one of the best pick-off moves I've ever seen. One of his favorite tricks was to walk a good hitter just to pick him off first base. He could pick you off first base just as easy as 1-2-3. He had that good of a move to first base. Nowadays, umpires would call him for a balk. What he did was to drop his right leg like he was going home, and when the runner moved, he'd whip the ball to first. That's a balk these days, but I never once saw him get called for it. He especially liked pulling this on the House of David boys. He was slick enough to keep you in a ballgame. He'd throw you that old junk, and you couldn't hit it but too far. He couldn't throw that hard no more, but he had good enough control to spot pitch you and make you hit the ball like he wanted you to hit it. He'd break your stride and keep you off balance. He could trick you. I guess the booker let him stay with the team because of his past reputation. I don't know whatever became of him after he left the club.

I'd caught John Markham back in my days in the Texas-Oklahoma-Louisiana League. The best knuckleball I saw was thrown by John Markham. He threw his knuckleball pretty hard. You had to knock it down a lot of times—especially if runners were on base. You had to block it. It was pretty hard to catch, and I didn't like to use that big mitt they had. I'd use my regular mitt all the time. You never could tell which way his knuckleball was going. It might break outside this time and inside the next time. They were pretty hard to handle, but I found I could catch them with a little practice. Of course, Markham's knuckleballs were pretty hard for batters to handle too.

John Markham, my brother Norman, and I rode with Satchel. Satchel had this big old Air-Flow Chrysler and that's how we traveled out west. The rest of the guys drove Mercurys. This way you could carry your own uniform. I had my catching equipment to carry and my uniform. I kept my catching equipment rolled up nice and neat, so I could just grab it from the back of the car, put my uniform on, and be ready to go. It was certainly easier traveling by car than by bus except for one problem.

Satchel was a terrible driver. I couldn't stand his driving because I'd be scared he'd get us killed at any second. He'd look like he wasn't keeping his eye on the road, and he sure wasn't going by the signs and rules that he had to go by. Satchel was liable to run into anything at anytime. He would take chances where you or I wouldn't. If three cars made it through an intersection on a yellow light, he'd just go on through it too. He was like that. "If they made it, I'm going to make it." And he'd go on through it too, green or not. Somebody else coming through could hit us. Running through red lights can hurt you quicker than anything else. I told him the only excuse a person would have to drive like that would be if he was following somebody because he didn't know where he was going and was afraid the other cars would get out of sight. You couldn't talk to him about his driving though; he'd just keep on going. I was fortunate that nothing ever did happen. As a matter of fact, we never even got pulled over by the police when I was riding with him. And as long as I knew him, he wasn't in any serious accidents. I don't think he ever was a good driver. I really don't. He was just terrible, and it kept John, Norman, and me on the edge of our seats the entire season.

We spent a lot of time in Satchel's Chrysler, and about the only thing we could do to keep from worrying about getting killed by Satchel's driving was sing. We'd blend our voices pretty good. Sometimes we'd sing spirituals. Sometimes we'd sing those little old love songs. We'd just sing whatever songs were popular at the time, like "Blue Skies." Now the Grays team just before the war had a little singing group. Josh was in it, along with Buck Leonard, Sam Bankhead, Jerry Benjamin, and Vic Harris. And this was their theme song: "Blue skies smiling at me, nothing but blue skies do I see."

Me, Satchel, Norman, and John Markham finally had us a little group too. Sometimes Satchel played the ukulele. Satchel went in for a variety of music. His mother was a good church lady, and his brothers and sisters were church people too. So naturally Satchel liked spirituals and gospel. He also liked little things he picked up out on the streets, popular tunes and a cappella and that sort of thing. He liked all of it, and he had a good voice. He was just fun to sing with. So we sang "Blue Skies" and a song called "Sweet Sue". "Sweet Sue" goes: "All the stars above, know the one I love, Sweet Sue, it's you." That's the way it went. Our favorite was "I Know That You and I Will Never Meet Again" which was made famous by Andy Kirk and His Clouds of Joy. Not many people remember Andy Kirk's big band today, but they were very popular at the time and even replaced the Cab Calloway band at the Cotton Club in Harlem. He had that girl playing piano with him, Mary Lou Williams. She was terrific and that band could really swing. Satchel and I both loved Kirk's band, and I don't understand why they're so unknown today. Later on when I was with the Monarchs, our little singing group used to get together and try to outsing the Grays. It was a lot of fun and just something to break that spell of traveling and playing all the time.

Out on the west coast the All-Stars played the House of David team from Walla Walla to Reno and beat 'em most of the time. In fact, in Spokane, Washington, I caught Satchel in a no-hitter against those boys. After the game we went out to a club for a little celebration. Norman, Satchel, Fred McDaniels, and I were all at a table, and we all had girls with us. One thing about Norman, when it came to spending money, he was Satchel's opposite. Norman was one of the real cheap ones. Norman saved almost 50 cents a day out of his eatin' money, and we wasn't getting but a dollar a day. He was that tight. Norman was the sort of guy that would take big steps just to save on shoe leather. Tight, *tight!* But he would still look for his big brother to spend a little something on him. So when the time come for Norman to buy a round, he leaned over and asked me to pay for it. I'd already paid for my round, but I just went on and paid for his too. I knew him. I knew he was tight, but I was his big brother and I just figured, "Well, I'll just forget about it." And I would because me and him was real close. We didn't have a lot of money when we were growing up, and I think that was in the back of Norman's mind. I remembered our childhood a little differently. Nobody went hungry, we had good clothes, and we had a roof over our heads so I never worried too much about money. Somehow we always got by.

Anyway, Satchel thought Norman was hilarious. Norman would do something to save a nickel, and Satchel would just look at him and bust up laughing. He'd tell him, "Why don't you spend some of that money?" Satchel would say something to kind of get under his skin, just playing. We had a lot of fun with each other.

Norman finally loosened up after he got up there with the big clubs a while. After that he was just like everybody else; he bought a brand new car when he needed one and all that stuff.

I liked playing out on the west coast and thought most of the people treated us very well. One time in Washington, for instance, we played a game where people were having a big barbecue. They were very nice and fixed us up real well after the game. We also played a lot of minor league teams starting in Washington state and working our way down to San Jose. We were scheduled to play two night games against this AAA team in San Jose which had won just about everything that season. They told us, if we didn't beat them the first night, don't bother to come back to play the second night. So we beat them the first night 6–5, and the second night Jack Matchett used fastballs, curveballs, screwballs, and change-ups to shut them out until the seventh inning. That was as far as he was supposed to pitch. Satchel was supposed to finish up because he was billed to appear. Remember, Satchel Paige on the mound meant fans in the seats and money in the cash drawer. The crowd had waited all night to see him step out of that dugout and walk to the mound, and they were getting restless. They had to wait a little longer because Satchel wasn't going anywhere.

Satchel had managed to pile up fifty-two traffic citations in California for running red lights and speeding and was afraid he'd be arrested on the mound. That crowd might still be waiting if it hadn't been for Lee Wilkinson convincing Satchel that he would get him out of trouble if the authorities were at the game and tried to haul him in. Satchel finally put on his uniform and went out there cold. He wasn't warmed up and one of the guys hit the ball over the fence on Satchel with two men on. That tied the score. Then Satchel got kind of warm and we went fourteen innings. We finally beat them when Gal Young—who was an outstanding bad ball hitter—hit the ball over the fence.

After our booking with the House of David ran out, we'd barnstorm with different teams. One of the teams that we played was the Brooklyn Royal Giants. We barnstormed about twenty games with them. They had Jimmie Crutchfield in the outfield. He didn't play every game, just about

Catching Dreams

ten of them. He wasn't no big man; he was kind of a small guy. He played a long time for the Crawfords when they were great in the thirties. He was a hustlin' little ballplayer.

When we finished on the west coast, we barnstormed back across the country and by late in the season had made our way to Chicago to play the American Giants. Satchel was pitching for us, and they had a boy called Davis who had been pitching for Chicago's Palmer House Hotel semipro team. He wasn't with the Giants very long. That's all he knew to do was cut the ball. That's the only way he could get you out. If he didn't cut it, it was going over that fence.

Satchel told him, "Now, y'all are scratching. If you keep cutting the ball, I'm going to have to throw that same ball, and I don't know where it's going. If I hit a batter, somebody's gonna get hurt. So you keep cutting it, but I'm gonna keep throwing it too," Satchel told him. "I've got to pitch the same ball, and you guys better look out because I don't know where it's going."

So Satchel threw a cut baseball, and it moved like Davis's ball but it wasn't Satchel's fault. He didn't cheat. Satchel's speed without Satchel's control was scary. Nobody even thought about digging in on Satchel that game.

None of this bothered Davis. He cut two dozen balls over the course of that game. Finally, our owner, J. L. Wilkinson, said, "Let him keep on cutting them. We're gonna make him pay for them balls." We beat him 2-1 but they made this guy pay for two dozen balls.

There were several pitchers that fooled with the ball in our league. They wouldn't do it all the time but save it for when they were in a jam. Dave Barnhill, the New York Cubans pitcher, was one. I hit against him and at first, when he had that great fastball, he didn't mess with the ball but later on in his career he started cutting it. Double Duty Radcliffe was another that was known for cutting the ball.

The Clowns had two that cut the ball. One was called Peanuts and the other was called Salem. Peanuts real name was Edward Davis and Salem was just Salem. They all cut the ball. It wasn't hard to tell when they started cutting it. When the ball acted funny, you'd look at it and you'd see it'd been cut. You'd tell the umpire about it because when Peanuts and Salem didn't cut it, the ball would be bouncing up against the outfield fences. It was just like the time when Roy Campanella was batting against Birmingham's Jimmy Newberry, and Newberry was cutting the ball. Campanella complained, "When y'all don't cut it, it goes up against the fences."

They said that old Smokey Joe Williams scratched the ball too. That would have been *really* unfair. A guy like that didn't have to scratch the ball, he threw hard enough to get everybody out as it was.

Chet Brewer, who pitched for the Monarchs, the Cleveland Buckeyes, and a bunch of other teams, was another one that would cut the ball. It's hard to score against somebody that cuts the ball. They said Joe Williams and Chet Brewer once hooked up in a game that went eighteen innings at nothin' to nothin'. Nobody at bat got anything off either one of them. They were both pitching that emery ball. Now if you see somebody pitch eighteen innings and nobody's getting hits, you know something's wrong.

I notice in the major leagues now, from time to time the umpire looks at the ball likes something's wrong. The umpires rub those balls up but every once in a while something is wrong with one and they throw it out. On certain pitchers like Gaylord Perry they'd keep on throwing it out. Gaylord'd always mess with the ball or have them thinking he was doing it, but he was slick enough to get away with it. At least he was tagged as throwing a spitball. Don Sutton was the same way. If they throw out too many balls on a certain pitcher and they think he's doctoring it, they'll put him out of the game.

That didn't happen with us. About all the umpires would do was throw the ball out and keep an eye on the pitcher. A lot of these guys would scratch it with their wedding ring. The pitcher didn't always cut it, though. Now Oscar Charleston and another old-timer by the name of Chippy Britt could scratch or cut the ball with their hands. That's how strong they were. They'd do that right there in the coach's box and then they'd get the ball to their pitcher. Or the pitcher might throw it to the third baseman, and he'd cut it for him. You had to watch them too because they'd have a Coca-Cola bottle cap right under their belt, and they'd scratch the ball anywhere it was rough, so it wouldn't be too obvious. They'd wait until the ball hit the concrete and if it wasn't thrown out, they had their rough spot. The pitcher would know to look for the cut when he'd get the ball—especially if he was in trouble with a couple men on base in a close ballgame.

As far as batters go, I saw people putting a lot of tar on their bats but that was about it. Guys would have their individual bat, and they'd usually take care of it themself. I didn't see them doctor no bats.

I'd also heard that Rube Foster, the father of the Negro Leagues, used to wet down the infield and use cold baseballs when the other team came to bat, but I never saw that when I played. No, the big thing that I saw was cut and wet baseballs.

From Chicago the All-Stars moved on to Toledo to play the Crawfords who had moved from Pittsburgh to Toledo at the start of the '39 season. Oscar Charleston was managing them. It didn't happen often, but Satchel lost his temper in this ballgame. I believe Jerry Benjamin was leading off and I called Satch for a fastball and that's what he threw. I didn't move the glove. I just left it there. And the pitch was just above his knees, right on the corner of the plate. And the umpire called, "Ball one!" I threw the ball back and called Satch for another fastball. And he threw the ball right to my glove. The umpire called, "Ball two!" Now these are *perfect* strikes he's throwing.

I turned around and asked the umpire, "Where is your strike zone at?" I didn't let the grandstand see me say that.

"You better get back there and catch," he said, "or you'll go out of this game."

So I got back in and Satchel threw another strike, right over the plate—*right down the heart!*

"Ball three!"

I turned around again and said, "Man, lookyhere. Are you blind or something?"

That did it. He put me out of the game right then. Threw me out. That's when Satchel really got angry. And then Newt Joseph, our manager, come out. Newt mainly played third but could catch enough to back me up if he had to. He was high-tempered anyhow and said to the umpire, "Look. I'm gonna catch this game. And if you put me out, you won't put me out like you put Robinson out. You'll go out before I do." Newt was only about 5'6", but I guess he got his point across because the strikezone reappeared, and he caught the rest of the game without a problem. As mad as Satchel was, he didn't let it bother his pitching one bit. He didn't try to throw any harder than usual. He pitched his game and beat 'em 4-2. I don't know where they got this umpire from because I never did see him anymore.

As a rule, Satchel didn't fuss much with umpires. Sometimes he kind of got angry with them because they wouldn't give him the corners. Just like they do in the majors. If they don't give the pitchers the corners, they get kind of upset. Sometimes the umpire might throw them out of the game. Pitchers get upset and Satchel was a pitcher.

In September of that 1939 season I saw the most amazing thing I've ever seen a ballplayer do in a game. That player was, of course, Satchel. We were back in Chicago on a hot Sunday afternoon to play the American Giants again. People knew Satchel would be pitching and they had an S.R.O. crowd at the park that day. It wasn't a big league park. It wasn't the White Sox park, but it was a huge crowd, maybe 40,000, and they were standing everywhere in foul ground. They were crowded as close to the diamond as they could get. And they were all fired up. We were leading them 2-1 and along about the eighth inning their catcher, a big guy by the name of Pep Young, led off. Satchel told him, "You can't hit nothing. What're you doing coming up?" And Satchel just lobbed the ball up there to the guy. Pep hit it over my brother Norman's head in center field. He hit it up against the wall for a triple, and there was nobody out. Satchel walked over to third and told Young, "You sit there. You ain't goin' no farther."

Pep Young was a guy who never said much, and he didn't say anything then but I know what he and everybody else in that park was thinking: Satchel's tired. He's on the ropes now!

The next man up was Joe Sparks, the Giants shortstop. He went down swinging. Then Satchel faced their first baseman—we called him Little

Sox. He and his brother, who sometimes played shortstop for Chicago, were from Fort Smith, Arkansas. The brother, who was the bigger of the two, was Big Sox, but he didn't play too long. Little Sox was a pretty fair hitter, but Satchel struck him out swinging too. To tell you the truth, I doubt if those guys ever saw the ball. And then, with the crowd screaming and carrying on, Alex Radcliffe came up. Alex played third and always hit for a high average. He was known for being a clutch hitter. Satchel got a strike on him, then got him to foul one off. I called Satchel for a curve, but he didn't want to throw one. I went out to the mound and talked him into it. He threw the curveball and Radcliffe swung and missed but the ball hit the plate. My first thought was that if it gets by me and goes back into the crowd, not only would Young score, but Radcliffe could get into scoring position. I managed to block the ball, pick it up, and tag Radcliffe for the third strikeout. Satchel struck out the side with Pep Young watching from third!

Satchel was noted for doing things like that. That's the way he liked to work the crowd. I wouldn't underestimate nobody like that to where you just lob the ball up there because he could have hit it over the fence. Newt Joseph was very hard-nosed as a player, but as a manager he understood it was best to let Satchel be Satchel. He knew Satchel wouldn't hurt the team, and I never knew his fooling around to cost us a game. Satchel picked his spots by checking the line-up and knowing who was coming up. If Satchel decided that he was gonna get you out, you was gonna get out. Especially if he was warmed up, he was *sure* he was gonna get you out. That kind of confidence makes a good pitcher a great pitcher.

To tell the truth, the only game I caught Satchel where you could say that he lost the game for us was also late in that season with the All-Stars. Our bookings had run out so they brought us in to face the Monarchs. This was the Kansas City B team playing the A team. Satchel really wasn't pitching that good that day. He didn't put any effort into it. He was tired and they beat us 7-5. Hilton Smith beat us. We got a kick out of playing them that close. Hilton won about as many games as anybody and had a good curveball. Since this was the end of the season, you couldn't blame Satchel for being tired. He'd pitched a lot of innings, most of them two or three inning appearances, but sometimes he'd go eight or nine innings if he didn't have to pitch no more that week. Most of the losses Satchel was tagged with were those two or three inning jobs, not the serious games.

I figure if Satchel had been in the major leagues, there's no telling how many games he could have won because they'd have pitched him every fourth day and he would have been rested. In our game he would pitch here today or tonight and tomorrow pitch somewhere else. I think this kind of schedule puts a strain on your arm.

There are a lot of stories out there about Satchel being a ladies' man and before he got his family he had a lot of girls in different towns. But after he got his family and started having children, he settled down. I credit J. L. Wilkinson, the man who owned the Monarchs, for getting in his corner. He was the one that convinced Satchel that he had to settle down. To have something in life, he told Satchel, he had to make a change from what he was doing. Satchel was the type of guy that was easily led, but once he got with the Monarchs he made a complete turnaround.

Before Satchel got with Kansas City he would get money from anybody, jump a contract, and go anywhere. That's what he did to Gus Greenlee when he was with the Crawfords in the thirties. Didn't nobody do Gus Greenlee as bad as Satchel did. When he was with the Crawford's, Satchel did a lot of things to Gus Greenlee that he shouldn't have done. Satchel used to get money from Gus—big money—and as soon as Gus turned around, Satchel would've jumped and gone to the Dominican Republic or anywhere the money was. That's the way he did Gus. Gus deserved a lot better. Just up and leave for Latin America after taking that man's money. I remember one time, Gus was talking about putting him in jail to be sure that he'd be around to pitch. Even the threat of jail didn't phase Satchel—didn't bother him one bit. Satchel was Satchel and he knew that he could do what he wanted. He knew he could pitch, and he knew that meant he could do things like jump a contract and get away with it. He knew that if he was gonna pitch, he was gonna charge some-body top dollar for it. It was disloyal but Satchel didn't see it that way. To him it was just business. He was wasting this money on different women. He was just running through his money. Before he got with Kansas City he did a whole lot of things that he couldn't get away with later. He stopped all this when he got with Kansas City and J. L. Wilkinson.

Part of the problem was that I don't think Gus Greenlee ever had Satchel under the right kind of contract. As soon as Satchel went with Kansas City, J. L. Wilkinson put him under the right kind of contract and his jumping stopped. And Wilkinson made sure that Satchel understood that he meant business, that a contract was a contract. He told Satchel, "If you think about jumping, I'll put you out of baseball. You won't play any-more in the United States." This got to Satchel; that this man could put him out for good. Wilkinson made Satchel see that it was in Satchel's best interest not to jump.

I know this impressed Satchel because of something that happened with the lady that owned the Newark Eagles, Effa Manley. Mrs. Manley was married to Abe Manley. He was from Virginia and was one of the best gamblers around. He played cards and they said that's how he got the Newark Eagles. But he didn't have time to fool with no ballclub so he turned it over to her and she ran the club. That was a smart move on his part because the lady was as shrewd as they come. And on top of that, Effa Manley was a very attractive looking lady. I was told that she went out with some of the ballplayers. I don't know whether Abe didn't know or didn't care.

At any rate, the Satchel Paige's All-Stars had played a Sunday game in New York, and we were playing the Eagles in Newark the following Monday when Mrs. Manley talked to Satchel and me about playing for her. She mentioned that if she could get me and Satchel that she knew she'd win the championship. She knew about Satchel. She knew about every move he made.

Satchel asked me what I thought and I told him, "No sir. I ain't goin' nowhere."

"Nooo, uh-uh. I ain't gonna leave Kansas City," Satchel decided.

Satchel couldn't leave. He was under contract. The money that they were going to give Satchel tempted him, but he remembered Wilkinson's threat to run him out of baseball if he ever broke a Monarchs contract. So he couldn't go nowhere noways. Now she could have been trying to make a deal with Wilkinson. She couldn't afford to just try to take somebody's ballplayer. They didn't do that.

The other thing about J. L. Wilkinson was that I think he understood what made Satchel tick. He knew that as long as Satchel lived out of his suitcase, there was still the risk that Satchel could vanish at any time. So in the mid-1940s he got Satchel this house in Kansas City and that's the first time Satchel had any home to go back to. Before that, Satchel had never thought about settling down or anything like that. This house finally settled him down. Before that house, Satchel had been wasting everything he got. He liked to party, liked to buy a lot of expensive clothes, liked to spend money. But after Wilkinson got a hold of him, Wilkinson let him know the value of making money while you were able to make it. Especially playing baseball. To do something with it. And so he just got that home for Satchel, but Satchel had to pay for it, I'm quite sure. Otherwise, Satchel never would have gotten it. Wilkinson made Satchel see that what he had been doing was wrong—that if he wanted to make something out of himself, he'd have to change his way of living. So Satchel stuck with it, and he never did jump anymore. And when the Cleveland Indians wanted him in 1948, they went through Wilkinson to get him.

3

The Kansas City Monarchs

After the 1939 season ended, a first baseman and nightclub owner out of Phoenix named Johnny Carter decided to put together a winter-ball team. He sent and got the guys that he wanted on his team. I was one of them. I stayed in Phoenix that winter, and he gave me money all the time—enough to keep me going. I'd broke a thumb in '39, and I needed that practice because I was going back to the Paige's All-Stars in '40. Carter's team would play just twice a week, sometimes three times a week, but it was enough to stay in shape and put a little something in my pocket.

That spring I went to New Orleans to train with the All-Stars and Monarchs. Norman didn't go with me. The reason he didn't want to stay with Kansas City was that he didn't like the All-Stars manager, Newt Joseph. I liked Joseph a lot but Newt would cuss all the time—especially if you made a bad play. Norman took this personally. I tried to explain to him that this was just Newt's way of living, but he wouldn't hear it. So Norman went to Baltimore to play.

The big promoter down there in New Orleans was a fellow that owned the New Orleans Black Pelicans and the Little Page Hotel on Dryades Avenue. His name was Allen Page and when we broke spring training, he booked us in a night exhibition game against the Grays. Late in the game we were leading them 5-3 with Hilton Smith on the mound when Jerry Benjamin dragged the ball and got on. Then Buck Leonard singled and Benjamin stopped at second. As Josh came up he was swinging four or five bats to loosen up. He came to the plate and said, "Hey Robinson, we got y'all again."

"Wha'chu mean?"

"This is it."

I know a warning when I hear one, and I do *not* want Josh Gibson busting up this game. If we pitch around Josh, we've got the bases loaded and Boojum Wilson coming up behind him. No bargain because Wilson was one you didn't want up there late in a close game. He would give himself up to get a hit. Let a pitcher hit him or anything. And Wilson hit line drives all over the place but at least you'd keep the ball in the ballpark. I called time and went over to the dugout to talk it over with the Monarchs manager, Lefty Cooper. "Skip, there's some room for him out there on the bases. Can we pitch around him?"

Lefty paused a second, scratched his head, thought about all the times he'd watched Josh Gibson trotting home wearing that big grin of his with a bunch of baserunners waiting at the plate to slap him on the back, and then said the words I wanted to hear. "Go ahead and pitch around him."

I walked to the mound. "Hilton, Skip said put him on. You pitch to him bad and put him on."

Hilton wouldn't go for it. "I can get him out."

Uh-oh. That sounded like trouble to me. I couldn't agree with him, but I admired his spirit. "Well if you're going to pitch to him, knock him down on the first pitch."

Josh came to the plate, and Hilton threw it right at my target, right up by his head. Josh backed out and said, "That don't mean nothing. Y'all trying to hit me but that's all right."

Then Hilton threw him a fastball on the outside corner, and Josh fouled it off. On the next pitch I made Hilton knock him down again. Then he came back and Josh fouled off the next pitch. Now the count is 2-2. So far, so good. This is our pitch, only Hilton fooled around with a curveball and went to 3 and 2. Now he's in a count I didn't want him to get in. I called him to throw another fastball on the outside corner, and he shook me off. He wanted to throw him what he called his dropball—a ball that would get there and drop. So that's what he did. Last time I seen it, it was going over that center field flagpole with height to spare. Josh did just like he said. He got us. He beat us 6-5. When Josh crossed the plate, he shook his head, grinned at me, and said, "I told you I'd get you." Usually after a home run he'd have a little something to say. Nothing mean, he'd jive to you and we'd jive at him. You might be mad that he got you, but you couldn't be mad at him.

The Satchel Paige's All-Stars and the Monarchs split up until a little past midseason when our bookings with the House of David ran out. The Wilkinsons brought me, Satchel, and a pitcher named Washington up to the Kansas City Monarchs big team, and we finished the season with them. The rest of the fellows from the All-Stars had to go home.

My salary with Kansas City was $325 a month. Kansas City never did pay big salaries like the Homestead Grays or the Pittsburgh Crawfords. They paid more. And the Newark Eagles paid more. Kansas City never did pay. The salaries just weren't that big, but the Monarchs' Muehlebach Field was an improvement over most of the little fields and parks the All-Stars visited. At Muehlebach Field the fans were close to the action and, at least when we played, blacks fans didn't have to go to separate sections. It was definitely a pitcher's park. You had to hit it a long way to get it out of there.

Buck O'Neil, our first baseman, understood this. He wouldn't try to pull the ball. Instead he'd hit these shots to right field that would find the gap between the outfielders. He was an outstanding first baseman. Buck played a long time. He didn't go no place else but the Monarchs.

When I was at Kansas City they had Jesse Williams at shortstop and, beginning in 1942, Bonnie Serrell at second base. They were the best double play combination that I saw in our game. Both of them had steady hands, quick feet, and could make that snap throw to Buck over at first.

Here's how good they were: One night somebody was on first and Cool Papa Bell was at the bat. Cool was the fastest man I ever laid eyes on. That man could play tag with jackrabbits and never get caught. I walked to the mound to talk it over with our pitcher. Jesse came in from short, and Buck O'Neil walked over from first.

Jesse turned to Buck. "Buck, you ever see Cool hit into a double play?"
"Can't say I ever have."

No quicker than he said that than Cool hit the ball right to Jesse who flipped it to Bonnie. It looked like the ball never went into Bonnie's glove. He had such great hands and feet, and you should have seen him pivot!

He got rid of the ball so quickly because he could throw by just snapping his wrist. The ball smacked into Buck's glove just ahead of Cool. Doubled him up. Yes, sir, they doubled Cool Papa Bell up! We'd never heard of anybody doing that, but they got him. It was just bang-bang. You can imagine how how many normal guys they doubled up. They were the keystone, Serrell and Williams. These boys were just like Phil Rizzuto and Snuffy Stirnweiss when they were with the Yankees. They were that good. In the mid-1940s, Bonnie jumped and went down to Mexico to play. A whole lot of them guys did that. Some of them liked it down there, and some of them didn't. You didn't jump a contract with J. L. Wilkinson and get away with it, and Bonnie found out that he was blackballed from playing in the States for a while. When he was allowed back in 1949, he returned to the Monarchs.

Over at third we had Herb Souell. He started losing his hair in about 1941, and they started calling him Baldy. It didn't bother him at all. He was a good little third baseman. He didn't have any size, but he could hit the ball just fine. I don't care what it was, you had to knock him down to get that ball past him. He may not hit it far, but he'd put the ball in play.

In the outfield the Monarchs had a fellow named Willard Brown that some people believe was as great a player as Josh Gibson himself. I think this. I wouldn't consider him as great a ballplayer as Josh because Josh was just a good all-around ballplayer, but Willard Brown was a great hitter. He could hit those home runs. I think he hit fifty-six one year. But see the only thing about Brown was that he never did get serious about baseball. He acted like he didn't care about playing because he'd stand out there like he wasn't in the ballgame. In the outfield it would look like he wasn't going to get to the ball. He never did drop anything, and he got to all the balls he should have, but Willard couldn't throw that good. It just seemed like he never tried to put that much on it. You'd watch him and you'd think he wasn't hustling, but I guess this was his way of playing. He didn't make too many mistakes, but it just looked like if he would have put a little more effort into it, he could have been classed as a great outfielder.

Catching Dreams

What Willard could do was hit. He was a big right-handed power hitter with very good speed. There were some guys you absolutely did not want to see carrying a bat toward home plate late in a tight ballgame. One of 'em was Willard Brown. He was a little like Reggie Jackson in that he was at his best in big games. He could even hit the emery ball that they used. He wouldn't mind. Now if you worked at it, you could get Brown out. You could get him out with a good curveball or something like that, although he could hit a curveball out of the park too. He was just the type of hitter that they wanted to class with Josh but he wasn't as consistent as Josh. If you were good, you'd get Willard out. If you were good *and* lucky, you *might* get Josh out. I guess Josh's reputation made you fear him more. Willard was a good hitter, but folks seemed to think he could have played the outfield better, and he could have let the fans know that he was hustling at all times.

One thing about Willard though—nothin' bothered him. The Chicago American Giants had a pitcher named Davis that cut the ball. This was a different guy than the one we faced in 1939. This one was an old-timer by the name of Roosevelt Davis and, just like the other Davis, he wouldn't throw nothing but a cut ball. When I was with the Monarchs, he faced us and all the guys were complaining about him cutting the ball. Everybody except Willard Brown that is. Willard said, "Let him throw it because I can hit it anyway." Didn't matter to Willard, if somebody was throwin', he was swingin'. This Davis cut two dozen balls too, and just like before, J. L. Wilkinson made him pay for all of them. He'd just rough it up. He wasn't gonna pitch unless he cut it.

Willard Brown wasn't the only outfielder we had with dynamite in his bat because Turkey Stearnes was over in center. Turkey must have been close to forty, but he could still make a pitcher pay for a mistake. He hit four home runs in one game out on the west coast. I didn't see it but everybody knew he did it because a lot of people told me about it. This would have been around '34 or '35, something like that. I don't know what team this was against, but I do remember that two of those home runs came against Larry French. And if you don't know who Larry

French was, I can tell you that Larry French spent the thirties pitching for the Pirates and Cubs. In his prime, Turkey was a major league ballplayer. Should have been, anyway. He was known as a long ball hitter. Stearnes wasn't doing much when I seen him with the Monarchs, he was kind of ageless, but he still liked the game, liked to be around it. Wilkinson gave him a chance because he'd been around a long time.

All of our other outfielders could throw the ball. Ted Strong, who played several seasons with the Monarchs, had a powerful arm. Having Ted in right field helped make up for having Willard Brown in center. Our other outfielder in Kansas City, Bill Simms, would get plenty on the ball. Sometimes Newt Allen played in the outfield, and he could throw the ball too.

Andy Cooper managed the Monarchs until he died in the spring of 1941 and Frank Duncan, my favorite player when I was growing up, was made manager. His son, Frank Jr., was also getting started with the Monarchs, and he and I got on real well. Several years later our first baseman, John O'Neil, took over from Duncan as the Monarchs manager. It didn't surprise me a bit that Buck ended up managing. As a player, when the rest of us would be singing and cutting up, Buck might watch but he'd never join in. He just had a certain way that he carried himself—a manager's way. He was always friendly, but he kept to himself.

Our pitching staff in Kansas City was, of course, led by Satchel but the other guys weren't too shabby. We had Hilton Smith who threw an excellent curveball and a very good fastball to go with it. I couldn't say who had the best curve ever because they say an old timer named Trent had the best one of all. Ted Trent. He started back in the twenties with the St. Louis Stars and finished with the Chicago American Giants in the late thirties. He was a tall right-hander who came right over the top. They said he had *several* different curveballs. Anyway, Hilton Smith had the best curveball that I ever saw and a good pick off move too. Hilton was the ace right-hander for a long time until Satchel came along. He was with Kansas City his entire career.

The Monarchs also had Allen Bryant, Lefty, who threw a knuckleball and all kinds of slow and breaking balls. Connie Johnson and Jack Matchett were both right-handers with a variety of pitches and good control. Booker McDaniels was also a right-hander. He lived on his fastball. He didn't quite have the control that the other fellows had, but he really liked pitching in the clutch. McDaniels went to the Los Angeles Angels of the Pacific Coast League and then pitched in the Cubs farm system. He never did get to the majors. Connie Johnson also pitched in the minors, but he eventually made it to the majors with the White Sox and Orioles. These guys were the heart of Kansas City's pitching staff.

While most of my teammates on the 1940 Monarchs welcomed me to the ballclub, it could be pretty rough on a new guy. Newt Allen, the second baseman who'd messed up my tryout eight years before, was the one that did all the dirty work. He was kind of snobbish to begin with, and then he'd pull a whole lot of jokes or tricks on you that would make you feel not welcome, make you want to go home. A young ballplayer come up there—he would make life hell for them. He liked to break in the youngsters. I guess he'd call it initiation or something like that.

He did little things like sneak into your room while you'd be sleeping and put soap in your eyes and slip out. Then he'd be laughing about it the next day and say, "You put the soap in your eyes so you'd be sharp and see good." Things like that he did. I mean he never did do anything too bad, something that would hurt you. I remember when I was catching and I'd throw the ball to second base, and he'd take his glove off and shake his hand like I'd thrown the ball too hard. He'd do anything to try to upset you, but that didn't bother me because if somebody's going to second base, I'm gonna throw it to second base whether he can catch it or not. And if you did something wrong, you could count on Allen to rub it in and put you in the doghouse. This is what went on in Kansas City.

He was a little showman too. Newt Allen would go to center field and shag a few balls, and then he'd throw home like he was throwing out people. And the next one he'd throw it over the grandstand. He could do that. He should've been with the Clowns. He was stylish and the people would be hollering and clapping while he put on his show.

Newt Allen had been a great ballplayer in his day, but he was almost forty and near the end of the line as a player. Except that he figured he would play ball the rest of his life. He didn't think he would ever grow old. There were a few old-timers like Newt Allen that didn't like a youngster to come around. They thought the youngster was gonna take their jobs, I guess. They should have known that eventually they were gonna have to give way to a young ballplayer. It seemed like Newt Allen was always around and he was always up to some little nasty work. Because he'd been with the Monarchs for so long and was a friend of Wilkinson's, he could do little things to you and get away with it. I didn't go for those things when I was a rookie, and I didn't go for those things when I was a veteran. He and I didn't get along noways and I didn't try, but it was tough to avoid him. We didn't have too much to say to each other. We had to get along to play on the same team but so far as associating with him, no. Willard Brown was all right. Buck O'Neil was great. Ted Strong our right fielder. Those guys were all right to be with after the game but Newt Allen . . . I couldn't stand him. That's one of the reasons I eventually wanted to leave Kansas City, on account of him.

For all the guys like Newt Allen that tried to grind you down there were more guys that tried to pick you up. Guys like George Giles, Newt Joseph, Frank Duncan, and Buck O'Neil. These guys would kind of encourage you. And although I wasn't around him as much, Josh was another one. Most people don't know he encouraged a whole lot of young ballplayers. He'd go out of his way to help young ballplayers. Josh might be walking down the street and see kids playing and he'd go and play with them. That was the type of guy he was. Josh played baseball just like you would do anything else. You've got to love the game to play it and Josh loved the game and loved life. He was just a good guy, one of the best. If you were on the other team, Josh would do everything he could to beat you, even hurt you, if you didn't get out of the way. Once the game was over, he'd be the first one to stop by your locker and encourage you. I'll tell you, young players—and just about everybody else— loved that man. Now Newt Allen wouldn't do anything like that. He didn't try to help you. I guess that was his way of living.

As we entered that 1940 season, I picked up the nickname that stuck with me as long as I played. Actually, I didn't so much pick it up as have it given to me by Satchel. Most of the guys called me Hank, but Satchel started calling me "Slow" because I talk slowly, and then Josh and the other ballplayers picked up on it. For the record, I ran well enough to score from second on a single, I just talk slow.

I wasn't going to get to start, that spot went to Joe Greene. He was a good catcher, had a good arm. And he was a good hitter, hit the ball out of the ballpark a bunch. But he was kind of ageless. He wasn't no young man, but he could still get the job done. And when Joe caught Connie Johnson, they had a Stone Mountain battery. Both of 'em come out of Stone Mountain, Georgia.

I found out that they had talked about bringing me in to do the Monarchs' catching the year before. The manager wanted to bring me up then but the owner, J. L. Wilkinson, said, "I'm not ready for Robinson to come in yet." That's when they got Greene from the Grays. Wilkinson was thinking of that fight in Reno with the House of David early in the '39 season. That game left some bad blood for a while and that was one of the reasons that Wilkinson wouldn't let me come to the main team as a starter. He thought that I was the cause of something like that. If they thought you was gonna be a little troublemaker, they wouldn't bring you in. They thought I'd caused that.

Traveling with the Monarchs was different than traveling with the Satchel Paige's All-Stars. Where the All-Stars toured mostly in the northwest and west coast, the Monarchs traveled from Kansas City to Chicago, Memphis, Birmingham, St. Louis, and other parts of the midwest and south. Also, with the exception of Satchel who still traveled in his own car, the Monarchs traveled by bus instead of the Chryslers and Mercurys the All-Stars used.

Being stuck inside of a bus brought the team together for long periods of time, so we'd sing. It didn't sound as good as the year before when Norman and Satchel were with us, but it was something to pass the time.

Not everybody sang though. Some of the guys on the bus played a kind of Rummy called Rum and Trump. The guys I knew weren't betting.

They might play for nickles and dimes, but just as a way to keep score. They would play cards sometimes, but they didn't play too much and when we were playing two and three games a day, they didn't play at all. A lot of the time, most of the guys would be back there trying to get a little rest. If you could get the back seat, you might even be able to lay down and get some sleep. Later on, Newark and Baltimore finally got modern buses with reclining seats, so you could get a nap but not back then. There were times we didn't even have time to change our uniforms. We just had time enough to change our sweatshirts and get to the next town. But for the most part it was a lot of fun traveling with the Monarchs. We'd be laughing and singing, going to the next town. Quite a few of them guys were fun to be around, and that made the time pass.

When I was riding with the Monarchs just before the war, meals were very cheap. You could get fried fish, rice, chicken, even steak for about fifty cents. Breakfast would be bacon and eggs or pancakes and run you about 35 cents. It was a good thing food was cheap because you weren't getting much meal money. There wasn't much problem getting something good to eat in the big cities. Like when we were at home in Kansas City, we stayed at the Streets Hotel. That's right in the city, and there was a big cafe there. But say in Des Moines you didn't have as much to choose from; there was one nice cafe and we stuck with that.

Sometimes we wouldn't have time to get to a hotel, clean up, and go to a cafe that could serve a whole lot of players. So we'd stop in a grocery store and buy cold cuts or something like that, eat fast, and go on and play that game. There was no such thing as fast food. The worst was when you played an afternoon game and you had maybe eighty miles to go to get to a night game that would start around seven o'clock. You'd drive over there and all you could do was pull off your shoes and pull off that sweatshirt that was wet. And if your outer shirt was damp, you'd change that too, go ahead and warm up, and you'd be ready to play again. This happened quite often. After a day on the road like that, if you were like me, you'd go on and have your dinner, go back to the hotel, relax a little while, maybe look at the paper, then go on upstairs and go to sleep. That's what I did.

Catching Dreams

Not every small town would have a little hotel with enough rooms to take care of us so often we'd stay at people's houses. The business manager took care of all that before we'd get to town. Sometimes it might be rough finding enough rooms, but people were very nice and you could usually find someone to let you stay in their home. That's the way we got by. Most of the time, I'd say 95 percent of the time, we'd come up with somewhere we could stay. If we couldn't find anything, we'd travel to the next town, find something, and try to get a few hours sleep before the next game.

Sometimes we'd have a little problem finding a meal or a place to sleep because of race. Having a hard time finding a place to eat or sleep may not seem like such a big deal until you've played a couple of ballgames, been stuck for a couple of hours in a hot bus, and are tired and hungry. Race was always something you were aware of, and it seemed like just when you'd pushed it to the back of your mind, you'd see or hear something to remind you that you were black in a white world.

There were a few ballplayers who could "pass" and go back and forth between black and white. One was a boy called Floyd Cranston that pitched for the Kansas City Monarchs in about '37, '38, and '39. I think he went out of baseball along about '40. He didn't stay up there but about four years, a good pitcher though. Right-hander. I don't know what ever happened to him. They called him Pretty Boy Floyd Cranston. His daddy was a Jew. He run a big Jewish clothing store down there in Texas. And Pretty Boy Floyd could pass.

Another guy that could pass was Harry Kincannon, that's the one that pitched for the Grays and Crawfords. He could pass for white. But these boys like Cranston and Kincannon wouldn't pass if their teammates were around. Most likely they wouldn't do it during the regular season at all. They'd do it in the offseason, if they did it at all. We wasn't around when they would do it because we would frown on guys passing if they did it to show that they were better than the rest of us. So they wouldn't do it around their teammates, not to your face they wouldn't. They might do something like, "Watch I can go in that cafe and you can't go in there." And then they'd go on in, get something to eat, and come on out. But it would be in fun, not to rub it in that the rest of us were a shade too dark. They wouldn't do that. Sometimes having a guy that could pass on the club would come in handy on the road because they could go into a place to get cold cuts and sandwiches when the rest of the guys wouldn't be allowed in.

It seems like most of our problems came when we were traveling. When we were crossing the Mississippi on a ferry, they wouldn't let us come upstairs. We had to stay down there with the cars. They wouldn't let us go up on the top deck with the people.

Another time we were traveling through Florida and the highway patrol saw us going in the opposite direction, and they turned around and pulled over all our cars. They took us over to a field to find out about us. I mean, for no reason. We couldn't understand that.

There were several bad experiences like these, but it could have been worse and we mostly got along OK. We were playing baseball, and we believed if we just went on and played baseball and took care of our business, we wouldn't have any trouble. Even so I'd heard about guys threatening your pitcher if you were playing their team. Back when I first went to Texas, I heard that one left-handed pitcher did get killed. I forget his name now. Some guy shot him down. Happened right on the field they said. He'd struck out about ten of their players. Now whether this happened or not, I can't say but that's what I'd heard.

There was a feeling on the Monarchs that this team was special. You were expected to act right and dress right. Here's what we did. If we were going to some special event, then we would dress. Most of us wore sport coats and open shirts. As long as they were clean and pressed. You also had to be in bed at a certain time. They had a curfew and whenever you've got a curfew, you've got somebody trying to beat it. I guess that's human nature. And sometimes if you broke curfew, you got caught. The guy that got caught the most was Bonnie Serrell. He got caught a lot of times. Bonnie drank all the time, but they knew that when they signed him. They knew that because I told them about Serrell and Matchett drinking when I sent them up there from Texas. When Bonnie first went up to Kansas City, he wasn't drinking that much, but after he'd been around for a while, he began to drink a lot more and go on. When we played together, he was drinking nothing but beer but later on I heard he got a taste for whiskey too. If Bonnie missed curfew, they might talk to him but they never got too mad. After a fellow got himself established, they knew he would stay in condition. That's what they'd look for—to be ready to play. And Bonnie Serrell was always ready to play. To watch that man play, you couldn't tell whether he'd had a glass of milk and gone to bed at nine or run a brewery dry at three in the morning. It's just a fact: Bonnie Serrell could drink a ton and *still* outplay everybody. Man, that guy was something to look at. Bonnie was a guy you'd enjoy seeing play. After he'd make one of those impossible plays, you'd look around the dugout, look at the fans, and everybody'd be smiling, shaking their heads. Beer or no beer, this man could *play*.

You could have a good time, but you couldn't overdo it and hurt your game. If I drank so much as a can of beer, I couldn't play. That's why I never drank that much. What Satchel and I liked to do was get a couple of girls and go dancing. I have to admit that, for being a tall man, Satchel was one of the best dancers I ever saw. He learned all the dances. When he went to Latin America, he could speak that language fluently, and he wasn't the kind of guy to hang around the hotel in the evening. He'd go to the different clubs, and he learned all the dances to that Latin music. He could mambo with the best of 'em. He was good at it, but when he came back to the States, he couldn't find anybody else that knew the steps. He was an excellent dancer. Josh was just the opposite. You wouldn't see Josh fool around much like that. Josh wouldn't go to a dance. He was kind of shy that way. The only thing Josh would do was to try to get you to go with him and drink a lot of beer. I never did seem him drink nothing but beer. Him and Sam Bankhead, the Grays shortstop. I went out with them a couple times and that's what they were drinking. They didn't mess with that whiskey. So I never did see Josh dance, although he liked to sing.

I didn't mind the traveling that much but I did look forward to getting back to Kansas City for one reason in particular. Jazz music. When people talk about black music, they think about New Orleans or New

Count Basie, the piano player at the Blue Room of the Streets Hotel in Kansas City. We saw a lot of Count when we lived upstairs of the Blue Room. Courtesy of the author.

Catching Dreams

York or Chicago or maybe Memphis, but there was a lot going on in Kansas City in the late thirties and early forties. Kansas City's where I saw a lot of Count Basie back in '39. He played piano at the hotel where we lived—in the Blue Room of the Streets Hotel in Kansas City. He was already pretty well known around Kansas City. Usually I'd head down to the Blue Room by myself. Kansas City was a place that I had a whole lot of friends, but I just never did find anybody on the ballclub that liked jazz like I did. Oh, Ted Strong or Willard Brown might go with me from time to time but more for something to do than anything else. Sometimes John O'Neil would go hear 'em for a little while, but you'd look up and see where John'd be gone. You'd never see Buck at a nightclub for very long. He'd go home to his wife and not stay out too late. I think he was always determined—had his mind made up—to become a manager, and managers don't hang out at nightclubs till all hours. This was way before Billy Martin.

Anyway, when I'd first seen Count in the early thirties, he was known as a singer; he wasn't playing much piano. A guy by the name of Bennie Moten had a stompin' swing band that was based out of Kansas City and played all over the Midwest for several years. Moten seemed to get the best musicians around. At one time or another he had Ben Webster on tenor sax, Jimmy Rushing who sang and shouted bluesy vocals, Hot Lips Page on trumpet, Walter Page on bass, and Count Basie on piano. They'd play these ballrooms and things would really heat up. Everybody'd be out there dancing and Moten's boys'd like to blow the roof off the place. Having a tonsil infection isn't a big deal these days, but back then they'd want to operate on you. That's what happened to Bennie Moten. He went in to have his tonsils operated on and died. That's when Count Basie took over his band, and Count kind of patterned himself after Bennie Moten.

Count Basie's band was probably the best known act out of Kansas City, but they weren't the only ones. Because he was born in Muskogee, Oklahoma, I'd heard Jay McShann's name for a long time. He was a piano player who put together a solid band that had this young alto sax player who would blow these incredible solos. His name was Charlie but everybody called him Yardbird. This would have been around '40. We'd go to

His name was Charlie but everybody called him Yardbird. Parker was always trying to figure out how to improve a note on that horn, always practicing, always trying to work it out, always blowing his horn. Courtesy of the author.

Catching Dreams

the Stagecoach House on 18th and Vine in Kansas City. This was before Bird moved to New York and teamed up with Dizzy Gillespie and started playing that bebop. I never got the chance to meet Charlie Parker, but a whole lot of guys that I know talked to him. Parker was always trying to figure out how to improve a note on that horn, always practicing, always trying to work it out, always blowing his horn. Dizzy Gillespie was the same way. I never would have thought that Parker would change music like he did. But this man changed music, and Gillespie tried to follow in his footsteps. Not being a musician I couldn't say exactly what they did differently, but they would play a song in so many beats. Where it might take you thirty-two beats to play it, they'd play it in sixteen. Where you'd put one note, they might put four. Those guys knew how to use those reeds and those horns. That's their claim to fame. They completely changed jazz. Then along came John Coltrane, and he changed it again. All we knew back in Kansas City was that Charlie "Yardbird" could play.

Actually there were a lot of great, great sax players passing through Kansas City in those days. Lester Young was another one. He played with Bennie Moten too, and then with Count for a long time until he refused to play on the 13th of the month because he was superstitious. That's when he left Count Basie and started playing with Billie Holiday. She's the one that started calling him Prez.

I already called Ben Webster from Moten's band, but he's best known as one of Duke's boys. Webster's sax had sort of a breathy, deep, soulful sound.

Coleman Hawkins also started out in Kansas City back in the twenties. He played with Fletcher Henderson's band for a while and then moved to Europe. He stayed there until around '39 when he came back to the States and made Johnny Green's "Body and Soul" his theme song. Coleman didn't play as many notes as some of the other saxophone players, but he played "Body and Soul" like nobody else could.

There were so many great ones in those days that I can't hardly call them all. Cab Calloway had a great tenor man named Chu Berry, and I saw him several times. And Duke had so many great ones in his band. Besides Webster on sax, Duke had Ray Nance, Cat Anderson, and Cootie Williams on trumpet. His bass players were two of the greatest ever: Jimmy Blanton and a boy from my hometown of Okmulgee named Oscar Pettiford. His brother Harry went to school with my brother Norman. They were a family of musicians and they started out playing together. Father played drums, mother played piano, Oscar played bass, Ira played trumpet, and Alfonso played trombone. The girl, Leontine, played the alto sax and went on to play with Bennie Moten. Harry played with Moten too. He stayed with him for a long time, and then I think he went with Count for a while. Alfonso went on to the McShann band. The Pettifords used to play on these big Mississippi riverboats and at dances in Okmulgee, which is where I saw them. I knew every one of them and went to school with some of them. Anyway, these are some of the musicians that made me look forward to ending a road trip and getting back to Kansas City.

I loved catching except for one thing. Foul tips. The problem was just keeping your fingers out of the way. That's the reason I got two bad fingers. On my right hand I can't straighten my thumb or my ring finger. Well after he'd retired, I remember seeing Biz Mackey, who'd begun catching in the teens, and his fingers were the same way.

My other big headache catching was guys trying to steal on you. There were three in particular that you had to watch or they'd steal you blind. Sam Jethroe of the Cleveland Buckeyes. Speed Merchant of the Clowns. And, especially, Cool Papa Bell. Those guys would steal on the pitcher. They'd know when he couldn't come to first base, and they'd take that jump. And you couldn't shoot 'em out.

Sam Jethroe wasn't as fast as Cool, but he was fast enough. He could run. Steal bases. He'd steal home on you if you weren't careful. He could fly on the bases. If he came up and hit a double, you could count on him stretching it into a triple. Cool was the best at doing that. After Cool left first base on a long hit, he was a blur. He'd put it in high gear and never hit a base on the outside. He'd always hit it on the inside. That way he wouldn't take that big turn. And when he'd slide and hit the ground, he'd stand straight up—ready to keep going if the ball got loose. Jethroe could run and steal bases just fine, but when he hit the ball between outfielders, he wasn't as fast as Cool. Nobody was that fast, but Jethroe and Merchant were fast enough. Cool Papa was just extremely fast. That's the way Cool played that long because he didn't do all that much hitting. He'd bunt the ball, lay it down and get on base like that.

Cool Papa Bell had a technique . . . Aww, he could just run, that's all. He would telegraph when he was gonna leave. He'd get about six feet away from the base and stare at the ball. And there wasn't no use throwing over there because he'd get back. But the minute he'd put his feet on the grass and hitch his pants up, I knew he was going. That's the way he telegraphed it, and you still couldn't shoot him out. Couldn't shoot him out with a rifle. And he done telegraphed it! He telegraphed it! Didn't too many people pay much attention to him, but I always did. I'd know when he was fixin' to go but . . . see, the man was so fast, it didn't matter. The only time I threw him out, he kind of stumbled. Even with Satchel pitching, as fast as Satchel could be, Cool'd still beat you. He could just run that fast. I'm convinced that catcher's hell is papered with pictures of Cool Papa Bell.

Actually, there was one other guy who should have been in that group with Cool, Sam, and Speed Merchant. He was with the Grays in the early 1940s. This boy was called Speed Whatley, and he could run too. Just like Cool. His real name was David, and he was faster than Jethroe and Merchant and nearly as fast as Cool. He played outfield and he could have been as great as Cool but he drank so much, he drank his way out of baseball. Who knows how great he could have been if he had taken better care of himself?

I think the most exciting thing that I saw these guys do was hit inside-the-park home runs. Sam Jethroe hit quite a few of them. Speed Merchant did it several times. So did my brother Norman. Several guys I knew hit inside-the-park home runs, and they usually ended up in close plays at the plate. If I was behind the plate, all I could do was watch, get in position to block the plate, and hope the ball got to me in time. The fans, of course, loved it.

I'd rate myself as a good defensive catcher. People gave me credit for handling the pitchers well and having a good strong arm. And if I had to compare myself to another player, I think I'd most remind you of Elston Howard behind the plate. I didn't have any problem throwing out the average guy, but when those good guys like Merchant, Bell, and Jethroe stole, I didn't feel bad because they'd steal on the pitcher. And with Cool, it was terrible because you just knew that this man was gonna score somehow. When Cool was taking his lead off first, the straight steal wasn't the only thing you had to worry about. After he'd get to first base, he was just terrible to handle because he was either gonna steal second or, if the batter laid down the bunt, he was going to third. Cool's steal-and-bunt play worked like this: Cool would break for second, the batter would bunt to third, and if the third baseman goes to first, Cool would often go on to third. Now this steal and bunt play goes back to Rube Foster, but Cool worked it better than anyone. In the 1950s I saw the Cleveland Indians run this first-to-third-on-a-bunt play quite often. Al Smith would go all the way to third when Bobby Avila bunted. They used to execute that play pretty well, but I think they got it from watching Cool Papa Bell.

One time Cool pulled that steal-and-bunt play, and I *still* don't believe what happened. By the time the batter bunted the ball and I went and threw the ball to first base, Cool was at third base. Now how could he get there that fast? Even Cool couldn't be *that* fast, could he? So I asked the umpire, "Were you watching where he was going? He might have cut across behind the pitcher." And the umpire looked at me and kind of smiled.

He didn't do it too often, but if you didn't pay attention to him, Cool would steal home. Cool might try it or my brother might try it too. Sometime they were successful at it, so you had to keep the pitcher aware of this. If you're up there on the mound and you don't look at Cool or Norman over there on third, they might break for home before you see it. By the time you see them, you might be in your windup, break your concentration, and throw the ball high or wide while they slide on home. You had some guys try that but not very often. Stealing home was another favorite of the fans.

Several players loved to showboat to get the crowd going. Once Sam Jones, who pitched for the Grays and Cleveland Buckeyes, was in the ninth inning of a no-hitter and walked the bases full by pretending to be wild. Then he struck out the side. Larry Doby said Jones was flow-showing. I hadn't heard that expression before but it seemed to fit. Another one was Speed Merchant of the Clowns who would holler about stealing to the pitcher and catcher—and then take off. Josh and Cool Papa never showboated. They were too good and sweet-natured. Oscar Charleston was too evil, too mean to showboat.

And, of course, there was Satchel. I already talked about some of the things that he did with the All-Stars. He'd showboat just to keep people interested and to jive the other team a little. He didn't do it to be mean, just to have fun. Like the time before a game when he told Sam Jethroe, "You ain't gonna get a loud foul off me today." And he didn't either. Or Satchel would walk over to a team before the game and knock over their bats. "Are these what you're going to use to hit me? You better get something else," he'd say, and everybody would laugh.

Satchel stopped calling in the outfield later in his career. He'd still have fun with the ballplayers, but he just didn't go in for showboating no more. It didn't matter. People always thought of him as an entertainer, and he was treated like a celebrity. This was at a time when black people, even the ones that didn't care about sports, cheered for Satchel and Joe Louis. The Italians had Joe DiMaggio, we had Satchel and Joe Louis.

Satchel was very popular with celebrities—people like Joe and Marva Louis. He'd talk to Joe and Joe'd say, "Well, I'll be at the game." And they'd come to the game whenever they could. A lot of movie stars liked Satchel. James Edwards, a black actor who was in the movie *Home of the Brave* was just one of many that would come out to see Satchel pitch. An-

Satchel Paige in his Monarchs days. Courtesy of the author.

Catching Dreams

other was Herb Jeffries. Most people remember that Duke Ellington had a female vocalist in his band. Ivie Anderson. Not too many remember that Ellington had a male vocalist with a terrific baritone. That was Herb Jeffries. He also sang with Earl Hines's band for a spell. Black folks who were kids in the late 1930s and early 1940s would remember Jeffries best as a singing cowboy in several westerns—kind of a black Gene Autry. He had a pencil-thin moustache, a fancy cowboy outfit, and a horse named "Stardusk." Anyway, all those big-time people would come to Satchel's games. They knew Satchel. They knew Josh. They all turned out. Satchel was very popular with them. Satchel was popular with entertainers going back to his days in Pittsburgh. That's where he met Lena Horne. And he knew this fighter that Gus Greenlee, the Pittsburgh Crawfords owner, managed. John Henry Lewis. That's the boy that fought Joe Louis in early 1939, and Joe Louis liked to beat him to death in the first round. Satchel knew all of them.

And of course the sportswriters at the Negro papers absolutley loved Satchel. They might criticize him for jumping a contract or being late for a game or something like that, but they knew they could count on Satchel for a good story. They would come into the locker room after a game and talk to the players. Sometimes they'd go so far as to come to the hotel where you lived. My favorites were Sam Lacy of *The Baltimore Afro-American*, Wendell Smith of *The Pittsburgh Courier*, and Bill Yancey out of Philadelphia. You read quite often today where a particular player won't talk to reporters but that was very rare in my time. We understood that these writers were just like us—fellows trying to make a living. A guy like Sam Lacy would write what he sees. If he was writing about a particular ballplayer, he would get every detail about that ballplayer. If one of those guys did write something critical about Satchel, it didn't bother him. Satchel might talk with them about it. If they wrote something about him that wasn't right, he'd explain it to them. And if it still wasn't right, you wouldn't quote him no more because he never would talk to you again. Now Lacy had Paige down just about right. It wasn't always pretty but it was honest and Satchel had no problem with that. I last saw Sam at the All-Star Game in Baltimore in 1993 when we were there. He made several speeches and came down to the hotel where we were. He's an old man now. To me, he was one of your top men up there in the east. Sam and Yancey and Wendell Smith.

There's a recent biography of Satchel that says that Satchel wasn't very popular with his teammates. That's wrong. I feel this way. The only thing Satchel would do differently from the other guys was that he had his own room. Satchel didn't ever have a roommate. But when he was with the guys, he was just as regular as anybody else, I thought. All the guys that were on the team when I was there liked him. After the ballgame Satchel kind of stayed off by himself. He carried a woman with him most all the time and he'd go off with her, but sometimes he would call me or my brother or John Markham or some of the other guys to come up to his room and talk. Sometimes we'd go up to his room and sing and carry on.

Satchel was one that comes along once in a lifetime. He was that type of guy. He would participate in a whole lot of off-field things that another player wouldn't do. Like Satchel would pitch a night game and then he might get a girl and stay with her. That's why Satchel never wanted a roommate. We were told when we were playing baseball not to run around chasing girls and stuff. You couldn't keep yourself in shape if you did. Staying in shape didn't affect Satchel, so he figured the rule shouldn't apply to him. Satchel believed he was special, and he *was* special. And Satchel would take drinks occasionally until his stomach got bad. He used to drink Old Taylor. He carried it in his suit roll. He wouldn't be drinking when he was pitching but after he was finished pitching, if it was cool, he'd take him a drink. He didn't do it to extremes, but he would take a drink or two. After he got a bad stomach, he started drinking milk. They said it was good for ulcers. Satchel had ulcers a long time. And when it came to not wanting a roommate, they say Ruth didn't have a roommate either. He didn't want nobody to be around. He didn't want nobody to know how much he was having to drink or if he was with a girl. He just played and didn't let nobody dictate to him and tell him what to do. Satchel was the same way. He could be stubborn that way.

Satchel was just Satchel. Satchel knew if he made $500 one night, he'd make $1000 the next night. It would come in as fast as he could spend it.

You couldn't keep up with Satchel. He always had money. Satchel was making all that money because Wilkinson gave him whatever money he needed and Satchel didn't have to worry about paying it back. Wilkinson had gotten Satchel to save some of his money, but Satchel still spent plenty. When we played together, he'd want me to hang around with him. I said, "Man, I can't hang out with you. I can't be spending the money like you because I don't get it like you." He'd look at me and laugh. That didn't bother me; I wouldn't go nowhere. And I couldn't do it, wasn't gonna try to do it, because I knew I had to pay that money back. I wasn't gonna follow him.

Satchel was never the type to flash a big bankroll. If he had a wad of cash on him, you'd never know anything about it. He was careful that way. If he was gonna have a party or something like that, he would go ahead and have the guy bring him the tab, but he never made a big show of having cash. I don't know where he kept all his cash. He could have kept it hidden in his suitcase because he'd have the best luggage you could get. I just know he always supported his habits.

Nobody made the kind of money Satchel made, but there were still guys who could run through money like Satchel. You had Ted Strong, you had one of Newark's pitchers, Terris McDuffie, you had a bunch of guys wouldn't save their money. They'd just go on. They figured they'd have some fun. Ted Strong also played basketball with the Globetrotters. He was a very good athlete. There wasn't no telling how good he would have been if he'd have just played baseball and stayed away from that bottle. That's where all his money went. Once, before the war, Strong was at the All-Star Game, and they was looking for him to put him in the lineup. When they went to his hotel he was laying up there in bed—dead drunk. They had to put him in a bathtub to try to sober him up. He'd just stay in them nightclubs and drink. He had a good voice. He liked to sing. He just messed up like that. He spent a lot of his money.

The other problem with running with Satchel was you couldn't keep to any kind of schedule. He liked to got me left behind one time when I went with him. I didn't want no reputation of being late or holding the club up or nothin'. If they say they're leaving the hotel at ten o'clock, you better be there and have your things. No, they wouldn't wait. Newt Joseph wouldn't wait. They'd leave you behind. Satchel got left behind a whole lot of times, but he never got in trouble because of it. All he'd do was call Wilkinson and say, "They left me." Then he'd catch a plane the next day. Satchel was Satchel. There wasn't no other Satchel just like there wasn't no other Babe Ruth.

4

From Kansas City to
Baltimore and Back Again

After the 1940 season with the Monarchs, I went to Baltimore to spend
the winter with Norman. Norman had spent the season as a utility player
for the Baltimore Elite Giants and a starter for a team that was just south-
east of Baltimore called the Sparrows Point Giants. The Sparrows Point
Giants were owned by a medical doctor, Dr. Joseph Thomas, who wanted
to get them into the Negro National League, which is where the Elites
played. There was a big Bethlehem Steel plant in Sparrows Point and a
huge shipyard. I think Dr. Thomas saw how the Homestead Grays filled
their park with steelworkers, despite having had the Pittsburgh Crawfords nearby, and figured the same thing could happen in Sparrows Point.

Norman introduced me to Dr. Thomas and we talked a little baseball.
He was a colored guy who just about owned Turner Station, which was
a little town near Sparrows Point. He had his own baseball park, his own
recreation park, and all kinds of other businesses there. He was about the
popularest doctor in that city. He'd taken care of all the people. I guess
that's the way he made his money. And he knew the people that ran the
steel mill and the shipyard. All we had to do was go over there and say
Doctor Thomas sent us, and we'd get a physical and go to work.

Sometimes you'd go to work with the bricklayers, sometimes at the steel
mill. They had quite a few things you could do. Norman was working
as a shipping clerk at the shipyard, and I got a job there too, working the
third shift. We would work about seven-and-a-half hours a day. I went

from signaling cranes to welding. I didn't know a thing about welding when I started, but they trained you right there in the yard. I liked welding until it went to messin' with my eyes. We were doing production welding, making those big ships for overseas. You'd be welding a big inner bottom and sometimes when you'd raise that mask up, another guy'd strike an arc on his torch, and that light'd hit you right in the eyes. That's what they called getting a flash. Pretty soon your eyes are all messed up. It was like you had a whole lot of gravel in your eyes. You'd have to rub white potato juice into your eyes to get it out. It did help some, but I knew this couldn't be good for a ballplayer.

After work, when I'd thawed out, Norman and I would get all dressed up and take our girls to the Edmondson Avenue Club or some other nightclub. We caught Billie Holiday several times. Baltimore was Lady Day's hometown. Louis Armstrong and his band also came through town. I even went to a dance in Baltimore, and it was the only dance I ever knew Nat King Cole and his Trio to play. He had Oscar Peterson with him. Oscar was just a teenager—maybe fifteen or sixteen—but he had come to the right guy to learn piano. Today people think of Nat as a singer, but it was his piano playing that got people into the clubs. I can listen to Oscar today and hear things that Nat used to do more than fifty years ago. Nat was playing "Straighten Up and Fly Right" then. I'd never miss a good trio and Nat and Oscar were the best. After the show I got to talk with Nat for a long time. The crowd had been so loud and had done so much clowning around that he swore he'd never play another dance again. Those years before the war were great ones for jazz fans.

When spring rolled around, I went with Norman to the Sparrows Point Giants camp. I hadn't planned to leave the Monarchs but after hanging around with Norman and the Giants, one thing led to another, and I ended up starting the season as the catcher for the Sparrows Point Giants. If it wasn't for wanting to be close to my brother, I wouldn't have left Satchel and the Monarchs, although I didn't miss Newt Allen one bit. So I played for the Giants—without getting my release from Kansas City. I figured I'd play with Norman's team for a while and then hook back up with the Monarchs. If I had to do it over again, I'd do things differently and get my release. I know now that J. L. Wilkinson would have understood and released me but when you're young . . .

Dr. Thomas put together a team that included my brother and me, Showboat Thomas at first, Sonny Williams in right field, Murray Watkins at short, Charlie Humble at third, and Rocky Ellis and Laymon Yokeley pitching. That Laymon Yokeley was a great pitcher. He's the one the major league boys never did beat. He was a right-hander. I think he was from Winston-Salem. He had been around, so I knew about him but it was great to finally get to catch him.

It was a good team and everything was fine until the Monarchs came to play. Then I wouldn't suit up because I hadn't gotten my release from Kansas City. There's no way I was gonna play against them. They weren't gonna let me. I'd usually watch from the stands with my girlfriend.

There's one game in particular that stands out from the 1941 season. I was catching for the Sparrows Point Giants, and we had a booking in Louisville for a doubleheader with the Chicago American Giants. Chicago had Cool Papa Bell playing for them. That Sunday started out hot and got hotter with every inning. We beat Chicago in the first game 3-2 and had Joe Fillmore pitching for us in the second game. He pitched for the Philadelphia Stars for a long time. That second game was tied up early and stayed tied. And it was so hot. In the twelfth inning we were still tied 2-2. In a tie game, the last thing you need is Cool Papa Bell on base. The only way he was gonna get on off of Fillmore that day would've have been to lay that ball down because Fillmore was a good pitcher. Some kind of way Fillmore kept Cool off base during that time we were all tied up and Cool hadn't hurt us any. Fillmore just wouldn't let him get on base. If Cool got comfortable up there, he'd knock him down. When I came up in the bottom of the twelfth, we had a man on second. Cool Papa, who was playing center field, looked like he wasn't too far behind second base. He was very shallow. I hit that ball dead to center field, and do you know he made what looked like an easy catch of it! And it was right up against the fence, and he had been standing right behind second base! When he heard the crack of the bat, he showed you his number, and he went back and made an easy catch out of it. I hit it, I saw it, and I still can't believe it. I said, "How can this man be that fast?" We had to go fifteen innings before we beat them 3-2. If he wasn't beating you stealing, he was beating you with his glove. Cool Papa Bell. That man was something to watch.

The other thing I remember about that game in Louisville was Chippy Britt, Chicago's third base coach, kept on picking at Joe Fillmore. Fillmore was fighting the heat and scuffling anyway he could to keep them from beating him. And Britt just kept on picking at him. The heat was bad enough, Fillmore didn't like Britt's talk making things rougher for him. Finally I told Fillmore, "Don't say anything to him. Just don't pay attention. Let's go on and try to win." Because Britt was saying things to get you to start something. He wanted to fight. Britt was a 50-year-old man then, but he had been the same way his whole career. He was just plain mean. He, Oscar Charleston, and Boojum Wilson. What I mean is, they wasn't rough about starting no fights, but they wouldn't turn none down neither. They had the reputation of not backing up from nothing. Britt would get to talking to you and sneak up on you and knock you down. He was that kind of guy.

Part way through that '41 season with the Sparrows Point Giants, I started catching for the Baltimore Elite Giants too. When I first got to Baltimore, George Scales, who had played second with the Grays when they dominated in the thirties, was playing a little outfield, but he was about at the age where he was thinking of hanging them up. After he retired as a player, he managed with Baltimore. As a player, he was a natural curveball hitter. You'd better not throw him a curveball. He said he could hit a curveball as far as he could a fastball—and he could, too!

As my manager with the Elites, George Scales was easy to play for, but he believed in you playing hard because he was always a good hustling ballplayer. He just believed in you giving 100 percent.

I went back with the Elites and Sparrows Point Giants in 1942. Felton Snow, the Elites third baseman, took over managing the team, and George Scales became the first base coach. As a first base coach, George Scales was one of the best signal catchers that there was in the league. Yes, sir! If you wanted to know what was coming, Scales was your man. Some batters didn't want to know. As a rule I didn't like guys to catch signals for me because you could get crossed up and even hurt. With some pitchers it *did* help. I always wanted him to steal the Grays signals because their left-handers always gave me trouble. Here's what he'd do: when he'd get the signal, if he'd show you the number on his back, it's a curveball. He'd leave the coaching box and walk toward right field. That's a curveball coming. If he didn't do anything but kick the ground, it's a fastball. I'll tell you another guy caught signals like that. Bob Turley. He pitched for the Yankees. He was one of the best signal catchers in the major leagues. And George Scales was the best that I saw in our league.

I remember one guy called Bill Anderson who was pitching for the Philadelphia Stars. He pitched the first part of a doubleheader against the Elites in 1942, and I went four for four against him. I hit him like I owned him. Later in the clubhouse he came up to me and said, "What are you doing? There's something you're doing because you hit me better than Josh has hit me."

"I'm not doing anything," I said. "What do you mean about something I'm doing?"

"There's *something* going wrong. Somebody's telegraphing my pitches."

It was George Scales catching his signals the whole time.

George eventually became the Elites road secretary, and that's where he stayed until Baltimore folded. Then he got a job scouting for one of the major league teams. The last time I saw him was a few years ago in California when Monte Irvin spoke to all of us about donating our things to the Hall of Fame. George and his son were there and a year later he passed.

Stealing signs was just one of the games within the game. Occasionally you would catch guys trying to rattle guys on the other team but not too much. That just didn't go on too much in our league. If you were in a slump and going bad, you might hear Minnie Minoso or somebody make remarks to you, but it wasn't too bad. Instead we had a lot of talking going on between the batter and the catcher. Tommy Louden was one. He was the New York Cubans catcher in the 1940s, and he was a real chatterbox. He would ride you so much that he'd distract you. Josh would do that too. Josh had fun playing baseball. He would talk to you when you came up to hit—anything to kind of get your attention off what you were doing. That's the way he got a lot of good hitters out. Josh would say, "I know you're not ready for this good curveball." Then you've got to guess with him that it's going to be a fastball after he's been talking about a curve. Or maybe it really would be a curveball. I'd just laugh at him and try not to lose my concentration.

Now when Josh'd come up, I'd talk to him and try to distract him. It didn't bother him one bit. "Well, you'll know if I get anything to hit," he'd say. "If you get anything in here, you'll never see it no more." He'd just kid like that.

The Elites had one boy, Henry Kimbro, who didn't allow nobody to say nothing when he was going bad. It would look like he was angry at the world. I remember once Josh talked to him when he was up to bat during a slump, and Kimbro didn't like that. He drew the bat back to hit Josh. He didn't want you to try to rub him while he was hitting. Some guys were that way. It's like this. If you're on the golf course, golf etiquette is for you to be quiet when somebody's fixin' to do something. Baseball doesn't work that way, and you'd better be able to do your job and not worry about a line of talk. I didn't care if somebody was talking, I'd just go ahead and hit the ball as best I could because I'm concentrating on one thing. If you let Josh get your attention behind the plate, you wouldn't hit the ball.

It was while I was catching in Maryland that summer that I finally got to see one of the great power hitters of all time. I'd played with Willard Brown and Turkey Stearnes, played against Josh and Buck Leonard but never seen the one they called Mule. Mule Suttles was a big right-handed hitter who was with the Newark Eagles and New York Black Yankees that summer. He would have been in his early forties then and didn't move too well, so they'd moved him from the outfield to first base. He wasn't a great first baseman, but he knew whether a guy was gonna pull the ball or hit it straightaway and would move to the right spot. That helped him around first base. Mostly though, he was just standing over there for his bat. When he'd come up to bat, the people would yell, "Kick, Mule!" They say he hit quite a few home runs, although when I saw him play, he was easy to get out. Still, he could hit the ball out of the ballpark if you threw it where he was swinging it. He was awful strong and hit the ball a long ways when he did hit one. After he retired, he umpired for the Newark Eagles for a long time. You couldn't compare him with Willard Brown or Josh because he didn't hit as many home runs. But then I never did get to see him play in his prime. In fact, when you get right down to it, you couldn't compare Willard Brown with Josh. Josh was in a class by himself.

One day in August the Monarchs came to Sparrows Point for an exhibition game, and I watched from the stands. Only this time some of the Monarchs saw me, and after the game I couldn't resist going to the Monarchs bus to see the guys. They were happy to see me, and I'm sure they didn't know I'd jumped the Monarchs contract. They were my friends, and even if they had known, it wouldn't have mattered to them. When it came to money and contracts, everybody minded their own business. Dizzy Dismukes, the old submarine pitcher who had moved to the Monarchs front office, was sitting next to the bus driver and spotted me. He got out of the bus, walked up behind me, tapped me on the shoulder and asked, "How long would it take you to get your clothes and everything and get ready to be with this team when it leaves here tonight?" Even though I'd been away from the Monarchs the entire 1941 season and more than half of that 1942 season, Dismukes wanted me back. And that's what I had to do.

I told him, if that's the way it was, I could be ready when the team leaves. He said, "You better be ready when the team leaves or else Wilkinson will blackball you." He said I was still under contract to the Monarchs and hadn't gotten a release. As far as they were concerned, I wasn't supposed to be playing with no other team. They might have let it slide except that Joe Greene had hurt his finger. They probably wouldn't have come lookin' for me if it hadn't been for that. See, they didn't have but just the one other catcher in Frank Duncan. And Duncan was the manager at the time. They knew that they still had me under contract and they needed help with the catchin', so they came lookin' for me. It wasn't that

I didn't want to go back with the Monarchs, just that I liked Baltimore better. So I went back with the Monarchs, and the guys kidded me about my year-and-a-half "vacation." Dr. Thomas never did get into the league.

I'll never forget my time in Baltimore for another reason. I became a father when my son, Luther, was born to my girlfriend. Luther's mom and I didn't stay together too long. Being a ballplayer with all the traveling didn't help being a father, but I loved Luther and tried to see him whenever I could.

So I had to play the last month of the 1942 season with Kansas City. The Monarchs hadn't changed much while I was in Baltimore except that Lefty LaMarque replaced Lefty Bryant who was in the Army. LaMarque had an excellent curveball, a good screwball, and could throw hard. He also had a very good pickoff move. The Monarchs had already won the pennant when I rejoined the team, and we had to play a bunch of AAA teams like the Toledo Mud Hens and Buffalo and around like that until the season ended. I missed Norman, but it *was* great to be back with Satchel and the Monarchs. And if I hadn't gone back, I would have missed catching Satchel in another no-hitter. This one came on a Sunday in that last month of the 1942 season when the Monarchs played a semipro club in Detroit that hadn't lost a game that season—they'd won everything. I guess they wanted to play us to see just how good they really were. Well, Satchel pitched a no-hitter against them. The following night we played the AAA Mud Hens in Toledo. And Satchel pitched the first four innings of *that* game, giving up one run in the second inning, before a pitcher by the name of Dave Barnhill was brought in. When's the last time you saw a pitcher throw a no-hitter and start again the next day? Sometimes I wonder what Satchel would have been like if he actually had a couple days rest between starts.

Anyway the Mud Hens had been having a pretty rough season and were happy to see the last of Satchel. It didn't bother them at all that Barnhill wasn't a regular member of the Monarchs. J. L. Wilkinson had borrowed him from the Cincinnati Clowns and had him waiting for us when we got to Toledo. They were even happier when they saw Barnhill take the mound. Barnhill stood about 5'7" but looked even shorter after a couple of at bats against Satchel who was about 6'4". As a matter of fact, they were so happy to see Barnhill they began to holler, "We'll get our runs now off this youngster." So I called for a fastball, and he threw it right past the first batter. What they didn't know was that despite his size, Barnhill could throw as hard as Satchel. They quit hollering and said, "It's Satchel with his legs cut off." They didn't get any runs off Barnhill who pitched the final five innings, and we beat them 3-1.

Satchel was pitching some of the best baseball of his career in 1942, but as great as Satchel was, I knew some guys could hit him. Good as he could pitch, they could hit him. One was Jim West, the first baseman for Philadelphia. Hit him like he wanted to hit him. And another was a boy by the name of Ameal Brooks, who used to catch for the New York Black Yankees and the Brooklyn Royal Giants. Brooks was an alcoholic—he'd drink all the time—but he could hit Satchel. This guy Brooks could even take Satchel over the fence. West and Brooks just seemed to know what Satchel was gonna throw, and they'd sit on his fastball. Then they wouldn't take a vicious cut, just swing at it and make contact. Somebody else who was hard for Satchel to get out was Charlie Gehringer, the Tigers second baseman. They called him Eagle Eye, you know. You were gonna throw him strikes to get him out. He could let a ball pass just an inch off the plate. He wasn't a bad ball hitter. You had to throw him a strike. Satchel couldn't hardly get those three guys out.

As for pitching matchups, if Satchel said, "I'm going all the way today," he was going to beat somebody. I only knew one guy that he couldn't beat, and that was Slim Jones. That's the only pitcher that Satchel couldn't beat. Slim Jones was tall—about 6'6"—and skinny like Satchel, and he could throw the ball as hard as Satchel. He was a left-hander who pitched for the Philadelphia Stars, and Satchel just couldn't beat him. And on top of that, they both went with the same girl in New York. And if losing games to Slim wasn't bad enough, Satchel lost the girl to Slim too. But this boy Slim didn't take care of himself, hurt his arm, drank, and died in his mid-thirties. Other than that, I'd put Satchel up to pitch against anybody when he was in his prime. You couldn't beat him.

And just like certain hitters gave Satchel trouble, there were some pitchers that Josh couldn't hit. One guy with the Philadelphia Stars called Rocky Ellis comes to mind. He threw pretty hard. He wasn't that big. He was about 5'11" and weighed about 170 pounds, but he got Josh out consistently. You could pick up the paper and see where Josh went 0-4 against him. He was a sidearm fastball pitcher, and he just gave Josh fits. It was just like those couple of guys that could hit Satchel. How can you explain these things? It could be they found some little weakness; it could be psychological. All I know is that this boy Ellis could get Josh out pretty good. But I don't know too many others got him out.

Since the Monarchs were the Negro American League champions in 1942, we got to play the Homestead Grays, who had dominated the Negro National League, in the Negro World Series. Joe Greene's hand had gotten better, and since he had been with the club all season and was the first-string catcher, he came back to do the catching for us in the Series. We had that great infield of Souell, Williams, Serrell, and O'Neil. And our pitching staff was the best in baseball and one of the best ever with Satchel, Hilton Smith, Connie Johnson, Jack Matchett, Booker McDaniels, and Lefty LaMarque. The Grays, on the other hand, were one of the greatest hitting teams of all time and had beaten up just about everybody that season. They were a solid team built around the power of Buck Leonard at first and Josh Gibson behind the plate.

Buck Leonard had learned baseball from a couple of the masters—Ben and Candy Jim Taylor—who had played with the great Indianapolis ABCs teams of the teens. He was the best fastball hitter in the league. Buck Leonard was. He would take the ball out of the park. And you couldn't throw him a curveball too fast because if you did, he'd get wood on it. You had to go to school on him. You had to slow the ball up on him, or he'd kill you. He could hit any fastball pitches you threw, but if you just walked it up there, changed up on it, you could get him out. He'd slap it

Buck Leonard was a lucky guy—lucky he didn't have to play first when Buck Leonard was at bat. Courtesy of the author.

From Kansas to Baltimore and Back

up or something like that. But you couldn't let him know when that change-up was coming so you had to throw him fastballs too and that's where you could go wrong. If you were lucky, he'd pull it foul. Otherwise, he'd just pull it over the fence. But if you could walk it up there without him looking for it, you could get him out. Easier said than done. Buck was always a quiet man. He'd talk with you if you talked to him. Cool Pape Bell was the same way. You'd talk with them and know right away that they were churchmen.

What you couldn't do to Buck Leonard was pitch around him because after Buck you'd get Josh, and the greatest hitter I ever saw was Josh Gibson. Josh was powerful to look at it with big arms. If you threw anything across that plate, he could reach it. And when he hit the ball, it would go. They taped a lot of his home runs. He didn't have a weakness. You might throw him a pitch, and he'd swing at it and miss and look bad on it. But you'd throw it again, and he'd hit it out of the ballpark. The only way you could get him out was to watch the way he moved at the plate. You'd see whether he crouched or stood straight up; then you could try to keep him from getting the big end of the bat on the ball. Sure as he gets the big end of the bat on it, it's going out of the park. Now if he leaned over too far, you could pitch high and tight on him. Most times that's a brushback pitch. Move him off the plate. But he didn't care where you pitched him. If he's crouched or leanin' over the plate like, you try to pitch him up. By the time he straightens up, he can't get all that bat on the ball. And if he kind of stands straight up, you can break the ball down and away. Let him go down and away. That was about all you could do with Josh was to pitch to spots—inside, outside, high, and low—and hope the umpire was in a generous mood. Just keep him guessing and hope you can make a strike out of that pitch. That's the only way you could try to get Josh out.

Since Josh and Buck Leonard were both power hitters and both played for the Grays, and since you could get Buck Leonard out with off-speed pitches, some pitchers figured they could get Josh the same way. It didn't work because Josh was strong enough to just manhandle the ball, whether you let up off it or not. Didn't matter to Josh. And he didn't take no vicious cut either. A lot of times he'd just stand back in the box, wait

Josh Gibson. If he raised that foot, he was gonna swing that bat.
Courtesy of NoirTech Research Inc.

From Kansas to Baltimore and Back

until that ball was almost in the catcher's mitt and had done whatever it was going to do, and then he'd hit that ball nine miles. He had such quick wrists that he could just wait on the ball. That's why Josh, I believe, had a chance to hit all those home runs. He could wait. A whole lot of times you'd have to tell the umpire to draw a line back there for Josh's rear foot. Otherwise he'd back it right up in your lap. He could wait and he'd break his wrists. That was the secret to Josh's success.

The only other guys I saw that had wrists like that were Marvin Williams of the Philadelphia Stars, Ernie Banks who would play for the Cubs, and a guy I would eventually play with named Lester Lockett.

Marvin, Ernie, and Lester all had quick wrists, but Josh was more powerful. Of course, there is one other guy whose quick wrists were legendary. Fellow named Hank Aaron. And just about everybody can remember what he did to baseballs. If you want to picture Josh, don't think of Ruth, Mantle, or McCovey. They had longer swings. Think of Hank Aaron, short and sweet.

Josh used a 40-ounce bat, and he had different models. His bat had a big head on it and a solid handle where he could grip it good. I'm quite sure they made a bat for him with his name on it. When you'd see Josh coming to the plate, he'd have four or five bats in his hands, swinging them to get loose. It was a sight you'd never forget.

Josh could run for his size, but he wasn't much of a threat to steal. But then Josh hit very few singles. When he hit the ball, it was either up against the fence for a double or out of the ballpark. He didn't hit too many singles. He did get a lot of intentional walks—*a lot* of them. He'd hit 55 home runs and be walked 75 or 80 times. They'd walk him because they knew this was one way to keep him from hurting your ballclub. And when Josh did hit one out of the park, the fans would go wild. That's what they come to see was those home runs.

Norman told me about one day in Baltimore when he was playing third base and they went to pitching Josh low so he couldn't get the ball up to get it out of the ballpark. That was fine except that he started hitting line drives and ground balls so hard that it made a couple of the infielders sick! It made them sick! Remember that those infields weren't very good, so you could expect a ground ball to take a bad hop and with Josh that could cost you your front teeth. Norman told me that these guys got in front of the ball and it shook them up some kind of way. Pee Wee Butts was playing shortstop, and Roy Campanella was catching. The second baseman was a utility man. Norman said he caught a ball off of Josh that he *had* to catch. If he doesn't catch it, it's going to hit him. He said it kind of shook him up. Any time Josh hit the ball on the ground, it was on you so fast. Of course I found out later that Norman had ulcers. I don't know whether Josh gave him ulcers, but he could certainly upset your stomach. Josh was hitting the ball so hard that it made Norman and Pee Wee sick in the stomach. I don't think they were afraid of getting hit by the ball so much as it was what you'd call a nervous stomach. At least that's what they told me.

I think Josh could have had a whole lot of infielders drinking milk if he'd have been a groundball hitter. But he very seldom hit balls on the ground, and I played against him quite often—sometimes two and three times a week. Most balls he hit were in the air. He hit the ball so hard that, if he hit it on the ground and you weren't standing right in front of the ball, you couldn't knock it down noways. It was just like when Ted Williams hit the ball. If he hit it on the ground towards you and you didn't get down real fast, you ain't gonna touch it. He was just that strong.

Josh and Buck weren't the only Grays who could hurt you. They had another boy called Howard Easterling and he could hit something like Buck. Easterling was a great, great ballplayer. He was a good defensive third baseman and he could really hit. Easterling was one you didn't want up late in a close game. He had a little drinking problem and that's what finally ruined him. Easterling was a line drive hitter, and he could hit it so hard it'd look like it'd bend when it left the bat. Where Josh would hit it over the fence, Easterling and Buck Leonard looked like they wanted to hit it *through* the fence.

Sam Bankhead, who played outfield and shortstop, was another one of the Grays that could hit. He was one of three brothers that played. Sam was one that you would underestimate. Guys would say, "He ain't gonna hit nothing too much." But you'd look up and he'd mess your ballgame up. You'd underestimate what he could do. You make a mistake on him and Sam could cost you a ballgame.

The Grays also had Vic Harris in left. Jerry Benjamin, who had been with the Grays for a long time, was in center. Lick Carlisle was playing second base. Pitching, they had Raymond Brown with his great curveball and the two Roys—Welmaker and Partlow. Both lefties. Both with excellent control. They also had a fine right-hander by the name of Wilmer Fields. Fields was such a fine athlete that when he wasn't pitching, you'd find him in the field.

So this was what we were up against when we opened the 1942 Series against the Grays at old Griffith Stadium in Washington. We were confident but knew that things could quickly blow up in our faces if we weren't careful. It was a Tuesday evening in September. The night before the Boston Red Sox had played the Senators before a crowd of about 12,000. Despite cold weather and a light mist falling, our game doubled that number and filled the stands with several thousand more standing in the aisles. They had to turn away people because they didn't have seats or standing room for them. That packed house in bad weather shows that people would turn out for good baseball no matter what color the players were. Even though we couldn't play the major league players on the field, we could compete at the box office. It goes to show you that our teams were drawing, and our owners were making money.

When we arrived at the park that evening, the Red Sox and Senators had just finished their day game. As we went past the Grays' part of the clubhouse to get to our dressing area, Cool Papa Bell was wrapping his legs up. Cool hadn't been with the Grays very long. He always seemed to have a contract that let him move as he pleased, and it seemed like he was always popping up where a catcher least wanted to see him—in the other team's locker room taping his legs up. This was in his later years—he must have been about 39—and he'd tape both legs. He'd want you to think that he was slowing down. And if you asked him how he was feeling, he'd say, "Feel pretty bad tonight." And then he'd steal you regular as soon as he got out there. He wasn't fooling nobody by telling you that he was hurting. He could run and you'd better be careful.

Josh's locker was next to Cool's, and Josh was sitting there pulling up his pants when Satchel walked up, dropped his bag in front of Josh, and said, "Well Josh, the time has come. I told you about this a long time ago. We're on different teams now. You're trying to beat me, and I'm *going* to beat you. Your batting average is going to be .000 when this Series is finished." And Josh just looked at him and smiled. He didn't say nothing. Satchel always tried to use psychology on people.

The Grays were putting their ace lefty, Roy Partlow, up against Satchel. In that first game Josh faced Satch three times. He struck out once and then he hit the ball to the outfield, but he didn't have much bat on it. He just hit it out there kind of soft and they caught it. Just popped it up— that's what he did. They had gone to pitching him in, out, high, and low. If he stood up straight, they'd pitch him low. If he crouched, they'd pitch him high. High and tight, they called it. All of our pitchers had gone to school on him. Satchel had worked with the pitchers and told them how to pitch to him. Josh went 0-3. Satchel went the distance and shut them out 8-0. Willard Brown's home run and Bill Simms's triple off Roy Partlow down the right field line were all we needed. Didn't too many Grays get on that night.

After the game we got our first real clue that we were getting beat out of a lot of money. It turned out that somehow J. L. Wilkinson couldn't take anymore gate money. If he did, he had to turn it over to the government. So in the locker room he said, "You boys, cut this money among the different players." We couldn't believe how much money there was. We knew that we had played to crowds like this before, and we knew that our salaries were low. They just didn't pay that much. So that was when we first started to suspect that we weren't getting our fair share. Nobody complained though. We always said, "Beats pickin' cotton." And that's what we went by.

Game #2 was the following Thursday night at Forbes Field in Pittsburgh. Only a few thousand turned out for this game, but people still talk about it. The legend has it that Satchel was pitching, gave up a single, and then intentionally walked the next two Grays just so he could pitch to Josh with the bases loaded. Then, as the story goes, Satchel slipped a curveball by Josh for a called strike three. It's a great story and Satchel loved to talk about it, but I'm sorry to say it didn't happen—at least not in that Series, and I saw every game from the dugout. Satchel never even appeared in that game. Our starter was Hilton Smith who pitched a complete game, and we won 8-4. Look, if it happened the way the story goes, wouldn't it have made headlines in the Negro papers? No such story was written in September 1942 because no such a thing happened. And besides, Satchel wouldn't pull a stunt like that in a World Series game. But that story gets told all the time because he *was* noted for doing things like that—just not in a big game. *Never* in a big game. I'm not saying that something like that between Satchel and Josh never happened, just that it definitely did not happen in the '42 Series.

We moved to Yankee Stadium for Game #3 on Sunday before a large and noisy crowd that included Joe Louis and his wife Marva and the actor James Edwards. We won again, 9-5, behind Jack Matchett. This game was the first of a doubleheader with an exhibition game following. In the exhibition game we had Lefty McKinnis pitching, and he shut the Grays out. The game didn't count but that didn't stop the Grays' Sam Bankhead from chasing a ball from his shortstop position into the stands and banging up his ribs in the process. The next game in the Series would be back in Kansas City on that following Sunday, and we looked forward to playing in front of our hometown fans. After sending Jack Matchett, our Game #4 starter, on ahead to Kansas City to rest up, we played several games against the Cincinnati Clowns.

Meanwhile, Cum Posey, the Grays owner, was granted permission to replace Bankhead and went shopping for another shortstop. Things would have been fine if he had stopped with the pickup of Bus Clarkson, Newark's shortstop. But Posey's team was down three games to none and the temptation to slip in Lennie Pearson, Ed Stone, and Leon Day with Clarkson proved too much. Or maybe Posey just figured that Clarkson would be lonely without some familar faces. These guys from Newark weren't just throw-ins. They were some of Newark's best players. Pearson was the Eagles first baseman and had excellent power. Ed Stone was an outfielder who'd make you pay if you tried to take an extra base. And

Leon Day was a right-handed pitcher with a fastball that helped him set strikeout records in just about every league he played in. Day was only about 5'7" or something like that, but he was such a great all-around athlete that when he wasn't pitching, you could expect to find him pinch-hitting or playing the field. Leon was simply one of the greatest ever, and in 1942 he was in his prime.

While Cum Posey was wheeling and dealing with Mrs. Manley, the lady who ran the Eagles, we barnstormed our way home—the whole time believing Jack Matchett was resting and waiting in Kansas City. It turned out that instead of Jack staying in condition, he was out there drinking and would have gotten more rest pitching in our barnstorming games with the Clowns. So when the Series resumed on Sunday, the Grays were surprised to see Satchel Paige warming up. But they weren't as surprised as we were when Leon Day started getting loose for the Grays. Frank Duncan, our manager, who was catching this game was very upset. And while J. L. Wilkinson wasn't happy that we had to face Leon, a good crowd had turned out and he liked the idea of refunds even less. So we played. Satchel was kind of tired and Day beat Satchel 4-2, but Wilkinson's protest about the "Gray Eagles" was upheld and the game was thrown out. So it was on to Chicago to replay Game #4.

It was now October and we ran into sleet and snow in Chicago so we got back in the bus and headed for Philadelphia. Shibe Park was drier but almost as cold. There is a story told about this game and Satchel that I also remember differently. The story is that Satchel was scheduled to pitch this game but was slow in leaving the company of a pretty young lady in Pittsburgh. In his rush to get from one end of Pennsylvania to the other, he was stopped for speeding and held up at a Lancaster, Pennsylvania, traffic court while the judge got a haircut. He finally arrived in the fourth inning, so the story goes, just in the nick of time to bail out Matchett who was getting it hard on the mound. It's a popular story because rushing from a girl to the mound with a speeding ticket in between sounds like Satchel, sounds *just* like Satchel. Like the showdown with Josh, it may have happened some time but not in the 1942 Series. And none of our pitchers got hit hard in any game of that Series.

What did happen in that final game at Shibe Park is this. Satchell pitched five innings and Hilton Smith pitched four. The Grays went with Roy Partlow. Josh, who was hitless in the Series, finally got a bloop hit over the shortstop off of Hilton, but it was too little and too late as we beat 'em 9 to 5 to sweep the Series.

Josh never did get a hit off Satchel in that Series, and Satchel's boast to Josh at the opener in Washington that they'd gone to school on him and his batting average would be .000 came very close to the truth. Not to take anything away from Satchel and our other pitchers, but something was wrong with Josh. You could tell by looking at him. He *looked* different. The reason I noticed something was wrong was because Josh was always jolly, laughing, kidding, and full of fun. Always saying, "Come over here man. Come here and tell me something funny." Always mingling with the ballplayers and a happy-go-lucky guy. Whenever I saw him, whether we were getting ready to play or sitting around at the hotel, we'd talk about different things and have a laugh. He made people feel good, and they loved to be around him. He even got along with umpires. But when I saw him in this particular Series, he wouldn't say nothing to nobody. Not even to his teammates. He was quiet and kind of segregated himself. He'd just sit there, quiet like. He would just catch and when his time would come to bat, he'd come to bat. Something changed inside of him. No, he wasn't at hisself in that 1942 Series.

Josh was mixed up in several different things. They said that his wife, in a lawsuit, had taken both of their homes. Then he went down to Mexico and Puerto Rico and played down there, and something drove him to use that reefer. Eventually, he got so bad that we heard he got drugged up while playing winter ball in San Juan, Puerto Rico, took off all his clothes, and it took half of the police force to try to put him up because he was so strong and powerful. They said that they put him in a straightjacket, and he broke out of it. The police said they knew who he was and didn't want to hurt him, but they had a problem trying to take him to where he could get a little help. They said he had been smokin' some kind of dope, but I never heard of marijuana changing you like that.

Following winter baseball he'd been with the Grays all of that 1942 season but something was wrong. He wouldn't have nothing to do with you. He'd just sit. He wouldn't talk much, wouldn't joke around, he'd just lost that spark. I think he knew that we'd heard about his troubles. After he come back to the States, he'd just changed his personality altogether. Josh was jolly all the time, but starting in 1942 he didn't say nothing to nobody, and he never was quite the same after playing winter ball south of the border. Never was.

Despite winning that final Series game at Shibe Park, I wasn't in the mood to celebrate. That's because right during the game a girl brought me a letter from the draft board saying I must come or they'd be coming after me. That was the last baseball I saw for a long time.

5

War

I went from Philadelphia back to Baltimore where I was living and reported to the draft board. In the space of a week I went from wearing a Kansas City Monarchs uniform to one that said "United States Navy." At least in my new uniform there was no color line. I went through basic training in Virginia and advanced training in Gulfport, Mississippi, and from Gulfport went to San Jose, California. My next stop would be some island out in the middle of the Pacific. I had no idea what to expect.

I remember going to see Andy Kirk's band with Mary Lou Williams the last night I was in the States. They were playing in Los Angeles at a night club called the Club Alabam near the Broadway Hotel, right across from Bill Robinson's theater. Kirk had a singer with him, and they played our song from the Monarchs, "I Know That You and I Will Never Meet Again." I was sitting there by myself, having a drink, thinking about my family and friends, and that song really hit me. I just tried to not let it get to me because what's got to be is got to be.

We shipped out on the USS *Bloemfontein*, a Dutch transport that had about 2,700 men on it. And we went from San Jose to Guadalcanal, and then they had us go to Banika in the South Pacific. That's where we unloaded, Banika Island. We stayed there about six months.

I was a bosun's mate first class on a personnel attack boat, PA-199 and was attached to the 1st Marine Division, 5th Regiment. These were the Marines that invaded, the first ones to hit the island. We were trained to do certain things to help the Marines there. Then we left Banika and went to Emirau, a small island northeast of New Guinea. We had to invade the island, but it wasn't too bad. We secured everything in about three days. From there we joined the 58th Task Force, which was part of the U.S. Fifth Fleet. Then they sent us to Guadalcanal on maneuvers, which was followed by a stop in Leyte. That's an island over in the Philippines. They let us go off the ship there in Leyte for one day. There wasn't much to do there but stretch your legs and drink a beer if you wanted. That was the lull before the storm.

Once back on ship, we were sent on an invasion of a little group of islands about 500 miles east of the Philippines and 500 hundred miles north of the equator. The Palaus, they were called. They were pretty rugged— nothing but coral, volcanic rock, sand, and a thick jungle. The temperature could climb as high as 115 degrees, and the mugginess and clouds of mosquitoes made you miserable the whole time. This was in September of 1944. We hit the larger island, Peleliu, and the Army hit Anguar. And Babelthuap, the largest island of the group was sitting over there too— they said with another 100,000 Japs.

The idea was that if you could control the Palau Islands you had a base to take the Philippines. And once you had the Philippines, you could move on Japan itself. The Palau operation was run by Admiral Halsey who was commander of the Western Pacific Task Forces.

Because Peleliu was well fortified, the U.S. Third Fleet and Air Force bombers from New Guinea shelled the island for eighteen days before we went in. We had a lot of support because there were aircraft carriers, the heavy cruiser *Portland*, the battleships *New Jersey, Missouri,* and *Alabama* and a bunch of destroyers out there to help us. The shelling destroyed a lot of the trees and aboveground buildings on the island, but the Japanese were safely dug in and waiting for us. It turned out that the island was full of caves which the Japs had connected with tunnels. They had also constructed fortified block houses and pillboxes. It was very dangerous because they could sit back, wait to see where you were, and then pick you off.

I was in charge of thirty-two men, black and white, and we were to be part of a big invasion. We got our orders to get off in a Higgins boat, form a circle, and when everybody was off, advance up to the amphibious tank line. Our job was to take the island's airstrip. I think we went in on the twenty-first day of the operation. The morning we hit the island was sunny and calm. We got out of the Higgins boat and into the amphibious tank because they would run on land and water. The first seventeen or eighteen tanks was put out of commission by direct hits. When we got to the beachhead, a Marine captain told me, "Have your men take cover. It isn't fit for a dog over there." Then our air power began to move 'em back by bombing and strafing so we could advance. We went halfway to that airstrip that day, but they counterattacked that night and pushed us back, almost into the ocean. One attack after another. When those mortars got near you, they didn't kick up dirt and dust like in the movies. They'd explode and spray pieces of coral and sharp volcanic rock at you like shrapnel. Then the next day we had our airpower right back, and we could advance again. They had told the guys not to bunch up, just two men to a foxhole. But on the second night about five guys out of Chicago wanted to stay together. They shared a foxhole that took a direct hit from a mortar. Killed every one of them. I was about two foxholes over from them. It could've hit my foxhole, but it hit theirs and killed every one of them.

As you can imagine, it was chaos and we found ourselves having to do something over there that we hadn't trained for. It got that bad and we had to do it. It was about the third or fourth day we were on the island that Company C went too fast, missed a flank movement, and found themselves exposed to enemy fire. They got banged up pretty bad, most of them got wiped out. A Marine unit, trained for rescue operations, refused to go in and bring back the wounded. We heard they were later court-martialed. Somebody had to go there and get some of the wounded. They assigned me to the detail. I was to take some men, go in there, and try to bring the wounded back to safety so they could go to the hospital ship. We weren't trained for this, but those were our orders and we had to do what they said. We had to go. You couldn't just leave those men in there. We had a scout with us, so I took about seven guys and we followed the scout in. We stayed in no-man's land about six hours and managed to bring ten to fifteen of the wounded back to safety. The only thing that bothered us were a few snipers. The Japanese would have guys chained to the trees up there shooting at you. Whole lot of times I'd think those guys would just shoot at you to kinda put doubt in your mind, scare you. Because they could've hit some of us. I know they could've. But that detail was one thing that happened over there that I thought was kind of bad for people because we wasn't trained for that. The men that was trained for it refused to go.

One day we were all sitting around, and one Jap popped out of one of those tunnels and sprayed bullets at us. He shot one of the boys, but we got him and tried to make him talk. We turned him over to a Marine captain who told him, "You're gonna talk or else." I don't know what they did to him. I never saw him again.

We worried that some kind of way those 100,000 Japs on Babelthuap would be comin' through one of those tunnels. It went on this way for weeks before we secured that island. When we finally did secure the island, there were about twenty-five old ladies, a bunch of kids, and a bunch of old men. They had also captured two white ladies. We didn't know who they were or how they got there. They put them all in a stockade and what became of them, we never heard. That information was strictly for the big wheels. We were supposed to take Peleliu and Anguar in thirty-eight hours. We were seventy-two days taking them. It was pretty rough and I wasn't sorry to leave Peleliu. I always heard that Peleliu was one of the bloodiest battles of the war, and based on what I saw it would be tough to argue.

After Peleliu we were sent to Iwo Jima, but I never made it there. They decided I had served enough time to get a thirty-day leave. And it was a good thing I didn't go to Iwo Jima because the Japanese messed up a whole lot of people from the United States. The first assault wave made the beach OK but the Japanese were dug in and opened up their artillery and mortars on them. They had water behind them and no cover. Lot of our boys died there. Anyway I got to come to Honolulu on a heavy destroyer, and then I got to come home from there.

When my leave was up I was to report back to Pier 92 in New York, but I found out that I had already gotten enough points to get out and didn't have to go back. They wanted me to reenlist. They asked me to go back over there and go from the rank of bolsonmate first class to chief petty officer, but I'd had enough. I knew if I went back over there, I might die. I don't know when I might have got back. I wanted to play baseball, not shoot and be shot, so I got out.

It wasn't long after I got back to the States that Truman had that bomb dropped and the Japanese signed the peace treaty. I don't know whether they should have used the atomic bomb or not, but I do know if they hadn't, they might still be fighting from island to island. It wasn't like over in Europe. Over there they weren't fighting from island to island. But right near Japan you might have to hit an island today and hit another tomorrow. You'd never know when the war would end. I think when they dropped the bomb on Hiroshima, it scared them. It just wiped out whatever fight they had left.

Some of the ballplayers that I knew got to play some while in the service. Leon Day had a team with Willard Brown in Europe. They even beat a team with Ewell Blackwell and other major leaguers. I didn't get to play except for a little softball to keep in shape and have a little fun. I met a ballplayer that played for the Baltimore Elite Giants over there. His name was Charlie Bayhard, and although we didn't know it at the time, we would soon end up as teammates on the Elite Giants. He was a center fielder and we got along together for a while. But to play baseball, I think we only played two games—both against the Army. We had the best softball team over there. We won everything in softball.

6

The Color Line Falls

I got out of the service on October 20, 1945, and headed to Baltimore. Luther wasn't but three years old and I hadn't seen much of him, so I took him home to Oklahoma to meet my mother. She was excited to hold her grandson and see me in one piece. A lot of mothers with sons in the war never saw their boys again. There was a lot of catching up to do with family and neighbors, and it had been a long time since I'd had my mother's cooking, so those were very happy times. We had a nice visit but I had to get back to Baltimore after a couple of weeks. Luther needed to get back to his mama, and I wanted to move to Maryland to be around Norman who had been playing for the Baltimore Elite Giants.

I hadn't been out of the Navy but a couple of days when the news broke. Jackie Robinson, who had just finished his rookie year as a shortstop with the Kansas City Monarchs, signed a contract with Branch Rickey to play in white baseball.

Looking back on Jim Crow and baseball's color line, I'd have to say that segregation was just something I'd gotten used to. I was brought up this way. I was used to it, and it didn't bother me. As long as I could get along, it didn't bother me. I knew this was just one of those things—the way it was. I knew it wasn't fair, but you had to accept it. There wasn't anything you could do about it. I'd played a number of times against all-white teams in Texas, Oklahoma, and Mexico. I played 'em and the fans seemed to enjoy it. It *could* work. I figured it was just a few people who didn't want to see integration happen. I didn't think everybody felt that way. When Jackie Robinson signed with the Branch Rickey, I just said, "So well and so good."

After the war it seemed like major league baseball was in trouble. They weren't drawing like they had been, and baseball was dying out. That's the reason, I believe, Branch Rickey wanted to integrate the majors. He could see ahead at times. He knew that if he brought Jackie Robinson in, the audience was gonna increase. He knew that. And he felt that if he didn't give the black ballplayer a chance . . . Well, this kinda rested on his mind. "If I can give him a chance, I'll give it to him and I won't have this to think about." So I believe this is another reason he wanted to see the color line broken.

There were players on the Monarchs—such as Bonnie Serrell and Jesse Williams—that, really, Jackie couldn't carry their glove. So I think most of us were a little surprised that a more established player wasn't chosen, but we were very happy for Jackie. And Jackie Robinson wasn't the first guy Rickey scouted. The first man that he scouted to take this spot was Silvio Garcia. Garcia was a Cuban shortstop who could hit for both average and power. He was a good ballplayer, but they just seemed to think he was too hot-headed. Rickey knew that Garcia couldn't take what Jackie was gonna take. When Rickey finally checked the history of Jackie Robinson, he saw that Jackie was smart. He had been to college. He'd been in the Army. He was both a great ballplayer and a strong person. Then Rickey gave Jackie a good talking to. Rickey was pretty straight about what Jackie was looking to confront. Rickey told him what he was gonna have to face and that he couldn't fight back—except when he was at the plate. Jackie said he'd be fine. After he talked with him, Rickey knew that if there was anyone that would be able to take what was gonna happen, Jackie would.

The year 1945 was also the year that Gus Greenlee, the Crawfords' owner, tried to make a comeback. Gus's luck had gone bad in the late thirties, and he had to get out of baseball. Gus reorganized in '45 and put together a new team with nineteen good ballplayers that included Roy Campanella. When he tried to get back in the league, the other owners turned him down. Cum Posey. Mrs. Manley. And Vernon Green who had taken over the Elites since their owner Tom Wilson had got sick. They turned him down. I can't say for sure if J. B. Martin, the owner of the

Catching Dreams

Chicago American Giants, voted against him or not. This vote was just before Campanella went up to the Dodgers' farm team. Gus Greenlee never did get back into baseball. They just voted him out. I think it was because they felt he treated his ballplayers better than they did. That he treated ballplayers too good.

When I got out of the service, I didn't feel like I was at full strength, so that winter of 1945–46 I just relaxed and rested and worked at odd jobs. I spent the evenings going to nightclubs with Norman. It was at one of the nightclubs that I met Catherine—a pretty Baltimore girl. She took to me about as fast as I did to her, and we got married later that year. It wasn't a big wedding. Norman was in Cuba playing ball, so even he wasn't there. It was just a few friends and some of her family.

Going into 1946 I was a little worried about being ready for spring training since I hadn't played any while I was in the service. I decided to join a few guys from Baltimore's Nashville club—second baseman Frank Russell and outfielders Jim Zapp and Art Hefner—who were going to barnstorm with a Jacksonville, Florida, team against the Indianapolis Clowns who had moved from Cincinnati. We played the Clowns because the Clowns were a drawing card and we were on a percentage. It was just a little extra money we could pick up before the regular season.

The Clowns had been barnstorming for years but didn't officially join the Negro American League until 1943. They had three or four clowns. King Tut was one. He was a good clown, that's all. He played a little but not regular. Goose Tatum was the regular first baseman, and that was Tut's position too. Goose was taller than Satchel, so with his clowning and size it was no surprise that he also played for the Harlem Globetrotters baseball and basketball teams. Pitcher Peanuts Davis was one. And Juggling Joe Taylor, who didn't play a position, was another one. Anyway they'd get out there like they were in a boat fishing. And we'd have to be sitting there watching that. To be honest, most of us didn't think too much of their clowning. For instance, if they were leading you and went into their act, you would have to just wait until they had finished clowning. They'd stay out there thirty or forty minutes clowning. Meanwhile your hitters wait, and your pitcher gets cold. It was true people would laugh at them, but it wasn't helping our end of the deal. And a whole lot of times when you get cold, you've got to almost warm up again. That doesn't do you no good. They finally cut out a lot of that clowning and wound up having a pretty good team. I played down there in Jacksonville until I returned to Baltimore later that winter.

By the spring of 1946 I felt pretty good so I decided to go with Norman to the Baltimore Elite Giants training camp. For several seasons the Elites had had solid catching from Roy Campanella. He wasn't always the great catcher people remember though. He came up with Baltimore in 1937, and at first Campanella's work behind the plate was pretty wild. Roy was liable to throw the ball over everybody's head into center field, but lucky for him it was also Biz Mackey's first year as the Elites manager. In his day, Biz Mackey was the best defensive catcher in the game, and when he saw the problems Campanella was having, he went right to work with him. Mackey worked with Campy until he got him kind of straight.

I know how lucky Campanella was to have a teacher like Biz because later on Biz worked with me some. Biz Mackey was just an outstanding receiver. He studied hitters and he was the best foul ball catcher I've ever seen. When the ball would pop up, he'd know which way to turn just by watching which shoulder it went across. Now Josh and Mule Suttles used to hit some of the highest pop flys in the game. You had plenty of time to get under them. Sometimes you had too much time to get under them, and that could be a problem. Drop one of those and you'd look real bad. "Now look," Biz told me, "When you look up at that ball, you look up once and see where it's at. Don't you keep looking up there. Take your head down. It'll come down soon enough. Look up, then take your eye off it and look back down so you can move to your spot. Then look back up. Because if you stare at it you'll start going around in circles and you'll miss that ball." He showed me how to do that. He showed me how to block the plate. "Don't try to catch everything that's down in the dirt," he said. "If you've got runners on, just keep the ball out in front of you. Block that pitch." He was just an outstanding catcher and was very generous

Catching Dreams

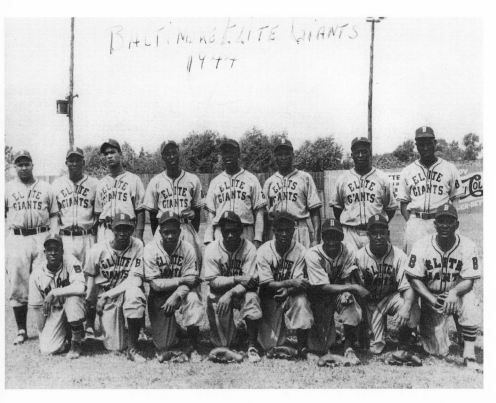

The Baltimore Elite Giants, 1944. *(Standing left to right)* Roy Campanella, Lester Lockett, Donald Troy, Thomas Glover, Laymon Yokeley, Doc Dennis, Bill Hoskins, Andy Porter. *(Kneeling left to right)* Unknown, Felton Snow, Bill Harvey, Henry Kimbro, Norman Robinson, Pee Wee Butts, Frank Russell, George Scales. I was in the Navy and rejoined the Elites in the spring of 1946. Courtesy of the author.

about passing along the tricks of the game. That's who straightened Campanella out, and Roy was always good about seeing that Biz got credit for showing him how it's done.

Young catchers need good coaching because there's so much to learn to play the position the right way. As a young catcher, Josh was kind of rough around the edges too. Early in his career Josh would tend to throw the ball down all the time, and he dropped a lot of balls too. But he finally got to where he stopped dropping them. But even if Josh dropped the ball, he would keep the ball in front of him. And when that happened, you'd better not run because he'd just pick it up and use those great wrists to snap a throw to second or third. He was that strong. Yes, sir. He had a throwing arm. And he could throw you out when his arm was sore too. The boy that was a backup catcher to Josh—his name was Gaston, Rab Roy they called him—was a better defensive catcher but he couldn't hit. He would catch the second game of a doubleheader, and Josh might stand up on third or first for his bat.

Josh and Campy weren't the only ones with great throwing arms. We had several other good catchers. Guys like Bill Perkins and Frank Duncan. But the strongest throwing arm of any catcher was attached to Bill "Ready" Cash. Ready Cash played for the Philadelphia Stars, and he was both very fast and very accurate—and he knew it. He loved to throw. The runners would be almost standing on the base, and he'd try to pick them off. Bill Cash. His claim to fame was throwing the ball.

In the winter of 1946 Branch Rickey saw what a great catcher Campanella had become and signed him. Rickey sent him and Don Newcombe to Nashua of the New England League. They became the first black battery in white baseball since the color line. Later on they went to Montreal and then the Dodgers. I have no idea why Campanella had to fool around in the minors because he was more than good enough to catch in the majors, but that's what they did.

Anyway I knew the Elites needed catching help in 1946 because their backup catcher, Robert Clarke, was a pretty good receiver, but he couldn't hit nothing. This time I talked to J. L. Wilkinson before signing with Baltimore. While I was in the service, the Monarchs had signed Othello Renfroe. Chico Renfroe, they called him. They say he was a pretty good little hustlin' catcher, but I never did get to see much of him until years later when I was in Canada and he was playing for a team out of Minot, North Dakota. After baseball, he moved to Atlanta and became a sportscaster and worked for a newspaper. But with Renfroe behind the plate, the Monarchs were pretty well fixed for catchers so J. L. Wilkinson told me that he didn't want to hold me to the Monarchs contract if I wasn't happy. He said he'd hate to see me go but wished me luck in Baltimore. He was a kind man.

I opened the 1946 season with Baltimore. My salary in Baltimore was the same as it was in Kansas City, $325 a month. I never did question what they wanted to pay me. Never did negotiate a salary. If they said I had to accept this kind of salary, then I'd have to accept it. That's the only thing I knew to do.

The Elite Giants was a very good team. Felton Snow was a playing manager that season. He mostly played third. Felton was always a good third baseman. He was mainly a line drive hitter and played until his health went kind of bad on him.

Over at first base was Johnny Washington. Johnny hit from the left side with good power and always had a high average. He was a bad ball hitter. He was just like Yogi Berra. Any bad ball you threw, he could hit. He'd hit it where you throwed it. He was about 6'3" but with short legs. He was all upper body and arms. That gave him a huge strikezone and you'd think he'd be happy just to cover his strikezone, but he'd chase and connect with balls way out of the strikezone. You'd never know where to pitch to him because he might go and get it.

We had Junior Gilliam playing second and Pee Wee Butts playing shortstop. Junior Gilliam came out of Nashville, Tennessee. He was always just a hustling ballplayer. You never did see him loafing or nothing like that. George Scales worked with him a good while. George Scales was one of the better ground ball fielders I've ever seen. He worked with Gilliam and got him to where Gilliam could field ground balls with the best of 'em. When Junior finally went up to the Dodgers in 1953, everyone that had watched him knew that he could play. That's the reason Jackie said, "If this man can hit .260 or .270, he's our second baseman."

This boy Pee Wee Butts that played alongside Gilliam was just a great little ballplayer. It's pretty hard for a little ballplayer to go that far, and Pee Wee wasn't too much of a hitter except that he could trick bunt. He was a great one for dropping the bunt when the infielders least expected it. But in the field, anything he got to, he caught. I don't care where it was because he had those kind of hands. Scouts said he had the greatest hands since Honus Wagner. He had that kind of grip in his hand. Like Josh would hit the ball to him and sometimes he'd back up on Josh, back up all the way to the grass, and it might even turn him around, but he'd throw him out. A lot of times he and Junior Gilliam played together so that when Pee Wee was down on his back, he'd flip the ball to Gilliam and Gilliam would throw somebody out. This is the way they played; they hustled all the time. When you hustle, you might get to a whole lot of balls that you thought you couldn't get to. He was just a great little short-stop. Drank beer all the time. He sure did, but he was great out there. He

The Baltimore Elite Giants outfielders, 1946. *(left to right)* Henry Kimbro, Canena Marquez, Felo Guilbe, Norman Robinson, Jimmie Armistead, Bill Hoskins. Henry, Norman, and Bill were the starters. Courtesy of the author.

helped make Gilliam a better ballplayer. He could play, and the two of them were just outstanding on the double play and our pitchers sure did appreciate that. Pee Wee and I got along real well, and he was my roommate the whole time I was with Baltimore. It was pretty important that you have a roommate that you get along with because there were a lot of times on the road where you'd have to share a bed. I don't think major league players have to do that anymore.

One other Elites infielder that I should mention is a boy called Frank Russell. He was a utility man but played a lot at third base. And just like Bonnie Serrell was the guy on the Monarchs who was always getting caught breaking curfew, Russell was the fellow on the Elites who'd forget how to tell time when the sun went down. He drank that beer and he'd stay out too late. They'd catch him and they'd fine him. That'd stop him for a while but then he'd go do the same thing again. Seems like there's one on every team.

By the time I went to the Elites, they had lost their best outfielder for good when Bill Wright decided to play in Mexico. He was big and fast, a switch-hitter who could make contact or go over the fence. Bill played in a bunch of All-Star games and might lead the league in batting or stolen bases and still be one of the top home run men too. On the basepaths, Bill was just like Josh; you better not get in his way or you'd get hurt. He was a quiet guy and would kind of stand off to himself. Bill was one of the best outfielders to ever play the game.

Even without Bill Wright we had a solid outfield. In addition to Norman, our other outfielders in Baltimore were Henry Kimbro, Canena Marquez, Felo Guilbe, Jimmie Armistead, and Bill Hoskins. They were all good all-around ballplayers with Norman just a cut above because of his hitting. By this point in his career, I think Norman had become one of the best switch hitters in the league.

On the pitching staff we had Jonas Gaines, Andy Porter, Bill Byrd, Enrique Figueroa, and Joe Black. Gaines was a southerner who went to college in Baton Rouge, Louisiana. He was a left-hander and had quite an assortment of pitches including a very good screwball and an excellent pickoff move. He was with the Elites a long time. Andy Porter was a right-hander, big and fast. Bill Byrd was an old-timer who had been pitching since the early thirties. He was past his prime and got by on a variety of knucklers, spitters, and big looping curves. Enrique Figueroa was good left-hander.

Joe Black was going to Morgan State College when he came to the Elites as a shortstop in 1943. The only problem was that Pee Wee Butts was at short, and he was one of the greatest in the league. They liked Joe's arm so they decided to make a pitcher out of him. He was big and strong and he could throw pretty hard, but it took him four or five years to develop his control. Joe never did have an outstanding curveball. Joe Black's curveball—what he called a curveball—broke just a little. That's called a slider when you get to the big leagues. A curveball has more break on it. So Joe had a slider something like Satchel had in the early days.

I caught Joe Black for several years before he went to the Brooklyn Dodgers in 1952. He had a terrific season in '52, was the Rookie of the Year, and became the first black pitcher to win a World Series game when he beat the Yankees. A lot of people didn't know it, but Joe couldn't raise his index finger. It was stiff and he had to raise it up to get it on the ball. I remember watching him in that World Series game, and you could notice it. I knew it but I don't know if other people knew.

Joe was big and strong and I think the Dodgers overworked him after they started using him in relief. You can only put so much strain on that arm if you haven't been trained to be a relief pitcher. A relief pitcher has to get ready in a hurry, and he has to be a man that can throw strikes when he comes in there. Every time you looked up, Charlie Dressen had that ball in Joe's hand. So he didn't stay up there as long as he could have.

Our other catchers were Robert Clarke, who had been Campanella's backup, and Luis Villodas. Villodas was a left-handed catcher who came to us from from Puerto Rico with Felo Guilbe and Enrique Figueroa.

Even though I was thirty-six, I did almost all the catching and that included doubleheaders. The reason I was doing most of the catching was that our manager told me he wanted me to catch most of the games because he didn't trust the other guys. One day, an umpire, Crush Holloway, who had been a great leadoff hitter in his playing days, took me aside. He said, "Robinson, you're doing all this catching. Doing all this work. Why don't you go in the office and tell the man to give you some more money?" I told him I just didn't see any point in complaining about a salary. When they were ready to pay me, they'd pay me. I just hate fussing with people. So I just went on and caught and didn't complain because I knew that eventually Vernon Green would raise my salary. See, Tom Wilson was now president of the league, and Vernon Green was the man that Tom let have the team. Vernon Green took the team over so naturally he was gonna handle the salaries. I just let it go for a while.

I finally did talk to Tom Wilson, who had originally set my contract. My offical salary didn't change, but Tom started giving me extra money anyway. He did it under the table so that the Elite Giants front office didn't know. I could call him and ask him for money, and he would let me have it. And when I'd offer to pay it back, he'd say, "Forget it." Tom did several of his players like that. So I wasn't worried about that contract. If you let Tom know you weren't satisfied with what you were getting or you would have to have extra money, he wouldn't say a thing. He'd just put his hand in his pocket and give it to you. He was a nice fellow, nice guy. Tom wasn't perfect—he liked young women—but he was good to his players, and people loved his company.

Just like in Kansas City, with the Elites I called all the pitches. We never did have no manager sitting in no dugout looking around and calling pitches. That was considered the catcher's responsibility. If the pitchers we had out there didn't like it, they'd shake you off. Joe Black was one that would shake you off periodically. Now Bill Byrd was a good pitcher, although he did throw a spitball—used that slippery elm—and a lot of times he might shake his glove for another signal. If he had thrown you two of those spitballs and they moved, he might throw you a fastball down the middle. And you can't get ready for that. It didn't matter where you set up, his ball moved all the time. When you'd caught Byrd nine innings, you'd kind of know you'd been in a ballgame. Because when the ball moves, you've got to shift so much. He almost always called his own game because you'd have to let those guys that were dopin' the ball call their own shots. Whatever they want, just so long as I know what's coming. It wasn't right but my job was to catch what was thrown. Still, I didn't like it one bit when I had to hit against those kind of pitchers.

We had one game that season where the Grays had Alex Radcliffe's big brother, Double Duty, pitching. Double Duty had gotten his nickname from Damon Runyon because in his younger days he would sometimes pitch the first game of a doubleheader and then catch the second. The game was moving right along when my brother Norman doubled with one out and I came up.

Josh, who was in his last season, grinned at me from behind the plate. "Big brother's trying to get little brother in." That's the way he talked and went on. He kidded with me, I kidded with him. I didn't mind him talking. It was just Josh's way of jiving you.

So Radcliffe threw me a pitch, and it looked funny. It acted funny. Fred McCreary was the umpire. I turned to him and said, "Hold on. Fred, look at the ball."

He looked at it. It was cut. I said, "Man, this man's cuttin' the ball. Why don't you tell him something?"

McCreary threw the ball out but didn't put Double Duty out. He just told him that everytime he'd scratch it, he'd throw it out. All Double Duty would say was "I don't throw nothing funny. I'm not going to throw you nothing but the fastball." That's Radcliffe. I didn't like him too well. He threw something and I hit the ball to straightaway center and he got me out. The fact is Double Duty would cut the ball. It wasn't any secret. This is called cheating. A cut baseball is extremely tough to hit because if the pitcher throws it a one way, it'll sink and if he throws it another way, it'll sail. You'd wait to hit it, and it would either drop or jump and you never knew which until it was too late. It was an illegal pitch.

When Josh kidded me about trying to get my brother home from second, I was glad to see him happy because he usually didn't talk to you the way he used to do. One night a little later on that season, the Elite Giants were playing the Grays in Wilmington, Delaware. Josh was coming to bat and George Scales, who was managing that night, told Andy Porter, "Go on and pitch to him. He's not at himself." And this boy Porter

Catching Dreams

threw Josh a fastball. The last time I seen it, it was leaving the park. But Josh didn't say nothing. He'd usually have something to say after he hit a home run, so I guess he really wasn't at himself.

Another game that I'll never forget from 1946 was one that I attended. The Brooklyn Dodgers' farm club from Montreal was in Baltimore to play the Orioles who were also in the International League. Montreal was where Branch Rickey sent Jackie Robinson to get him ready for the majors. And those of us on the Elites were very familar with the Orioles because we played them a lot at the end of the season and most always beat them badly. So a bunch of us on the Elites went out that night to see Jackie. We caught up with him before the game and asked him how he thought it was gonna be. He said that he thought it'd be pretty hard but he believed he could take it. Jackie got a chance to prove how tough he was right away.

Just before the game started, while Jackie was getting ready to go to the on-deck circle, a guy carrying a black cat jumped out of the stands and ran toward home plate. This guy dumped the cat on home plate and as he ran past the Montreal dugout he yelled, "There's your mate, Jackie." Jackie's response was to go three for four that night and steal two bases. Now how could there be any question in your mind that Jackie was going to make it? Anybody that doubted Jackie didn't know how determined he was to succeed. Nothing else on the field mattered. And Jackie was smart; he was always thinking of how he was gonna get an edge. If you weren't up to par, if you slipped up or made a slight error, Jackie would take advantage of you. When you combine Jackie's physical skills, his intelligence, and his determination, that's a pretty powerful combination.

I played about half the 1946 season, but I wasn't at myself. It looked like I had lost something by being in that hot weather in the south Pacific. I just wasn't as strong. So Tom Wilson, the owner of the Elites, told Vernon Green, who ran the team, to send me down to Nashville and let me finish down there for the rest of the year. That's the way I went to the Nashville Black Vols. Played down there the rest of the season. Our manager down there was Tex Burnett who had played with a bunch of teams beginning in the early twenties. We played in the AA Nashville Vols ball-park which was a sweatbox. It had a hill all around the outfield so it looked like the diamond was down in a hole. That's the reason it got so hot down there. Also, like most of the ballparks in the south, it was seg-regated. We didn't play too many games there. We were mostly on the road at Atlanta, Asheville, and other cities in the south.

Right from the start of 1947 things would never be the same. In January, Josh, who was at home in Pittsburgh, got a bad headache one evening. He went to lay down and didn't wake up no more. They said it was a stroke. He was only 35. He never lost hope that he might play major league base-ball. It wasn't meant to be. He didn't even live long enough to see Jackie Robinson put on a major league uniform that spring. And Jackie *was* the big news that spring. How would Jackie do? How would his teammates treat him? How would other players treat him? What would the fans and the press say? Would the majors take more of our players? If you knew the answer to that first question, you'd know the rest, but going into the season nobody knew for sure. That's a lot of pressure for a youngster.

That 1947 season I was back with the Elites and glad of it. I hadn't cared for Nashville and was happy to be back in Baltimore near my son and playing on the same team as Norman.

The 1947 team was mostly the same as 1946 but there were a few changes. We picked up a couple of solid outfielders in Butch Davis and Lester Lockett. Both Butch and Lester were good hitters, but I'd give Lockett the edge. He had a very quick bat. Here's how quick Lester Lock-ett was. One night in 1948 the Elites were in Chester, Pennsylvania, to play the New York Cubans. Pat Scantlebury was pitching for the Cubans and Lester was standing at the plate with the bat leaning against him. And as he was standing there with the bat just propped up against him, he was waving at someone in the stands—knowing Lester it had to be a woman—completely ignoring Scantlebury who was into his windup. Pat threw a fastball and do you know that Lester picked that bat up that quick, snapped his wrists, and hit it over the fence!

Catching Dreams

One guy who didn't come back in 1947 was one of the Puerto Ricans, Enrique Figueroa. I'd have to say he was in the wrong place at the wrong time. I heard that at the end of the '46 season some fooling around in the locker room got out of hand. When the guys were taking their showers, Luis Villodas snapped a wet towel at Joe Black. It stung Joe and he whirled around and knocked Villodas out. When Figueroa saw Villodas, his friend from Puerto Rico, laying there, he came after Joe. And when Junior Gilliam, who was a good friend of Joe Black's, saw Figueroa going at Joe, Junior come after Figueroa. Some kind of way Junior cut Figueroa's pitching arm, and Figueroa never did come back to Baltimore. The other two Puerto Ricans, Villodas and Felo Guilbe, left after the 1947 season.

Felton Snow had gone to Nashville to manage the Black Vols while the manager of the Nashville Cubs, Wesley Barrow, came up to manage the Elites. Barrow was a superstitious guy, and I remember when the Elites went on a twelve game winning streak, he wouldn't change his sweatshirt until we lost. After a few days we had to stay away from him.

Tom Wilson, the Elites owner, died that May. He'd been sick for a couple of years. Vernon Green who'd been running the team for Tom took over. They called Vernon "Fat Daddy." Well, Wesley Barrow was Tom Wilson's man, and Fat Daddy didn't think too much of Barrow. Barrow was gone by late summer, and the new manager was Hoss Walker who stayed on through the '48 season.

Another late summer change in '47 was Ed Finney who replaced Frank Russell at third with Russell becoming a utility man. Ed was from Akron, Ohio, and grew up near my brother Edward G. So Ed had heard about me from my brother, but I didn't meet him until he came to the Elites. Ed was built like a fireplug and had played all kinds of sports in high school—baseball, football, basketball, tennis. Despite his size, he was quite an athlete. He was a good third baseman and would usually hit around .300 and steal you a few bases when you needed it.

So the Elites had a good team in 1947, and I liked our ballpark much better than the Nashville park where I'd finished up in '46. The park in Baltimore, Bugle Field, was owned by the owner of the team and that meant we had our own clubhouse. That wasn't something you always had. See, when we'd go to Griffith Stadium in Washington, we'd all dress in the same clubhouse. Both teams did. But when we'd go to Yankee Stadium, we'd dress in separate clubhouses. At Shibe Park, Philadelphia, separate clubhouses. At some of them, both teams had to use the same dressing room, but it was usually large enough. That's the way it was. So Baltimore was just a nicer park, a nicer clubhouse, and a better place to play baseball. Also seating at Bugle Field was integrated. Everybody sat where they wanted to sit. We'd get around 6,000 into that park and another 1,000 S.R.O. Overall, I'd have to say my favorite ballparks were Bugle Field, Shibe Park, and Forbes Field in Pittsburgh. They're all gone now.

Another park I liked a lot was the Polo Grounds. It was a good hittin' place for a right-hander because that fence was around 315 feet. Yankee Stadium was a good hittin' place for a left-hander. When we played at the Polo Grounds or Yankee Stadium, they'd book four-team doubleheaders. Like you might see the Newark Eagles, the Philadelphia Stars, the Baltimore Elite Giants, and the New York Cuban Stars. They'd draw a lot of people.

They weren't all hitter's parks, though. You had quite a few pitcher's parks. Several places moved the fences back. Like League Park in Cleveland was a good pitcher's park. When the Buckeyes won the World Series in 1945, it was because of speed and pitching. Sam Jethroe supplied the speed, and Willie and George Jefferson supplied the pitching. Willie and George were the brothers that had grown up near me in Clearview, Oklahoma. We'd played ball as boys together. They pitched like the Dean brothers for a couple seasons with the Buckeyes. The best hitter on that team was the manager and catcher, Quincy Trouppe, and he hit more for average than power. League Park was a pitcher's park, and the Buckeyes took advantage of it.

Bugle Field was pretty friendly to pull hitters but you'd have to hit it over 500 feet to clear the fence in dead center. And "dead" center was just what it was, a graveyard for long fly balls. The other thing about that outfield was that instead of a warning track like you see today, the last eight feet rose up and you had to run uphill. Right and left fielders would run up that hill and jump to try and keep that ball in the park. Center fielders didn't have to worry, it was just too deep.

This is how deep it was at Bugle Field. One time early in 1947 we played a home game against the Eagles. This was after Leon Day had left Newark and moved on to a team in Mexico. Newark was still a great team with Larry Doby at short, Lennie Pearson at first, and Monte Irvin at second. We had Bill Byrd pitching, and Newark had Max Manning. Max had won a lot of games for Newark over the years. He was very tall and wore these very thick glasses. I think his toughest pitch was his curveball. When he started to get his curveball over, you were gonna get out because you'd have to give a little. He kept right-handed hitters kind of off-balance because he stepped to third base on you all the time. When he stepped over there, it looked like the ball was coming right dead at you. I'd just stay and wait until it'd do what it was gonna do and then try to hit it. If the ball is coming in at your left side, you'll start moving out of the way, and his ball would break over the outside corner. You'd give away to his pitch. He was hard on right-handers. Left-handers didn't pay him no mind.

At the time I could hit the ball almost as hard as Josh, and that's what I did this game. I hit a ball off Manning as hard as any I ever hit, and when it sailed over Jimmy Wilkes' head in center field, I thought I'd finally done something I'd never seen even Josh do: hit one out of dead center at Bugle Field. Josh hit plenty of 'em over left field but never center. Do you know that ball went over 500 feet, and it *still* hit the top of the fence and didn't go out of the ballpark! I had to settle for a triple. My next time up, I got a hold of *another* of Max's pitches, hit it hard to dead center and thought, "Well, I know I got it out this time." Only this one hit the top of the fence and bounced back in for another triple. I wound up going 4-4 that game and we run 'em pretty bad, but I couldn't get it out of dead center. After his shower, Max came up to me and said, "You lit me up but good today." Now that was high praise because Max Manning was one fine pitcher. I saw him at the 1993 Negro Leagues reunion at the All-Star Game in Baltimore, and we were laughing about it. Max pitched for Newark for a long time, and then he finished his career down in Mexico.

The one guy who finally did hit one out of dead center at Bugle Field was a big fellow off of the Grays named Luke Easter. I never saw anyone else do that. But Luke did it. He must have hit it pretty close to 600 feet.

Hit it off Joe Black. You could get Luke out, but when he hit one—look out! That ball would land in places where baseballs just didn't go! Luke was that big and strong.

In fact, I'd have to say that the longest home run that I ever saw was one that Luke Easter hit off Joe Black at the Polo Grounds. Luke hit it to dead center field where we'd come out of the clubhouse. We had to come out and around the left field wall to get to the dugouts. He hit one up there. Hit it about ten rows up. He was that strong. It almost went out of the park except for the way the park was built. That was the longest home run I've ever seen. They say Luke hit the longest home run ever hit in Cleveland when he was with the Indians. I don't recall who he hit that one off, but it wasn't Joe Black. Joe was safe over in the National League. Luke happened to swing and hit those two off Joe Black, but Josh hit them off everybody. Josh hit them to all parts. And a lot of 'em. And in all ballparks.

Now Josh hit one at Bugle Field in Baltimore that went 570 feet, but I don't think that's the longest home run he hit. They say the longest one Josh hit went out of Yankee Stadium, and no one had hit one out of Yankee Stadium. I don't know where it went.

The size of a particular ballpark was just one of the things you had to keep in mind when pitching to a particular batter. There wasn't any kind of scouting like they have now, so the catcher would have to kind of memorize how to pitch to different guys—the good hitters. So we had to kind of go to school on those big guys. When they hit the ball that far, we'd start to make them hit it out with their own power by changing up on them. From a change-up, if they hit it, they'd have to hit it out with their own power. So there were a lot of times you had to try to set 'em up to get 'em out. Or make 'em hit the ball to the infield where somebody else could help get 'em out. That's the only way you could do it. No, we didn't have scouting in our league, but we did play smart baseball.

Just like I always knew how to get Luke Easter out. You'd get Luke Easter with change-ups. You'd have to set him up. Or pitch him tight up near the shoulders. Sometimes he'd swing and foul them off. Any left-hander with a good curveball could get Luke out. All you had to do was pitch him up tight and then break one of them curveballs off over the outside corner and you got him. Luke thought he could hit better than what he could. He hit pretty good when he went to the majors, but we had guys who could get him out. But if he should happen to guess with the pitcher, he might hit it a mile.

I didn't know anything about Luke Easter until he came to the Grays after Josh died in 1947. He had been with a team out of Cincinnati before the Grays got him. The first thing the Grays did was to give Luke Josh's number 20. We thought it was disgraceful to put Josh's number on Luke. They should have gotten another jersey. They should have retired that number. Luke was one of the highest paid guys on the Grays. I think they gave Luke $1100 a month when he first came to the Grays. Only Buck Leonard and Josh had been paid more, and a lot of Josh's money had come under the table. They'd pay you a salary and if you did all right that year, they'd give you some more money under the table. Extra money.

Now Luke Easter was the sort of a guy that liked to pin flowers on his shoulder. He believed he was a great player, and he wasn't bashful about telling you. About all he'd talk about was how much better a hitter he was than everyone else. Well, he didn't hit too much in the two years that I played against him, but that didn't keep him from talking. You hear that talk from him enough, and you start to get sick of hearing it. So I would always tell him different. I'd say, "You can't hit. You can't hit your weight. You may get lucky and hit something every once in a while but you're not that hot." "And," I'd say, "you got no business wearing Josh's number." I'd tell him something like that, because he would boast about what he could do and I'd try to shut him up. That is, I'd try to shut him up, if I had a good left-handed pitcher in there. Like a Jonas Gaines. I'd talk to him like that, and I must have got the best of him talking like that because he said, "If ever I come to home plate on a close play, I'm gonna break your legs."

"You can't steal first base," I told him. "You've got to get on to get me in a close play at home."

We'd have words like that—not fighting words—but not friendly words either. I talked to him like that, and pretty soon we just stopped having anything to say to each other until he went to the Cleveland Indians. He was like that though. He was a guy that thought that every-thing he had or did was better than everybody else. This is the type of guy he was. One time he hit a home run, again off Joe Black, came home, looked at me and said, "I'm the greatest—ain't I?" That was Luke. Other than that, he was all right. I didn't have too much problem with him. He was just hard to take on the ballfield. Once we quit playing against each other, everything was fine. But when we were playing, he wanted to win and I wanted to win. And it came between us for a time.

While the World Series was a big event for the two teams that made it, the East-West All-Star Game held every year at White Sox Park in Chicago was a big event for everybody. The crowds were huge, people talked about it, and reporters wrote about it. If there was a bigger black event anywhere, I can't think of what it would be. When it began, back in the early thirties, they let the fans choose the players. They got away from that in the later forties, and the owners started sending who they wanted off their club. Mrs. Manley was especially good at convincing the other owners to put her players on the All-Star team. That's not to say that she didn't have some great ballplayers in Newark because she did, just that she wasn't shy about letting everybody else know.

The 1947 All-Star game would be the first one in years where Josh wasn't catching for the East. I was having my best season ever, hitting .348 by the All-Star Game, and should have been chosen to go. Instead, our other catcher, Robert Clarke, who wasn't hitting nothing, begged Ver-non Green to let him go. Green chose the guys off of the Elites. Clarke was a good receiver, a good man handling pitches, but he couldn't hit you if you run the ball by him. What I mean is he couldn't hit nobody. And if he did somehow get on, he was so slow he'd clog up the basepaths. He was a defensive catcher and that's all. Here I was 37 years old and had been around for a while myself, but Clarke, who was four years older than me, convinced Green that he should get one last chance. I was healthy and could have gone but they picked Clarke. When it came to the other own-ers, they passed over Clarke and picked Johnny Hayes off the Black Yankees and Louis Louden from the New York Cubans to do the catching for the East. Biz Mackey was on the East team too, but he must have been about fifty and was used only as a pinch hitter. They had something like 49,000 people there at White Sox Park. I would have liked to go but circumstances wouldn't let me. I suppose I could have argued with Green about it, but I don't like fussin' with people. Besides, you should be chosen because you deserve it, not because you argue for it. It turned out that 1947 was the only year that I know of that I was considered for the All-Star Game, and here Green backed Clarke who didn't even stick with the Elites for the rest of the season. Clarke retired and went on back to his home in Richmond, Virginia, and that was the last I saw or heard of him.

Now Norman went up there to the All-Star Game in '51 or '52, and the only way he got up there was because he complained about it. What happened was that some reporters come and asked him why he had never been in an All-Star Game. He said that he'd never hit under .300 in our league since he been in it and he wondered too. Norman made a big beef about it, and they sent him. He went two for four and I think he scored the winning run that year. Norman could hit, run, steal bases, do everything, and he had to complain to get to one All-Star Game.

The talk at that 1947 All-Star Game, the talk that entire 1947 season, was about Jackie Robinson. With Jackie breaking the color line in the majors that season, the fans and sportswriters started paying a lot of attention to how he was doing. *We* were paying a lot of attention to how he was doing.

We knew that when Jackie broke the color line that this would change baseball. We didn't know that this would begin to change society too. When I think back to segregation, I remember a wall. As a black man, I knew that there were places you couldn't go and things you couldn't do. You might look over the wall, but you couldn't get over the wall. And the first cracks I saw in that wall were caused by Jackie Robinson. And from Jackie those cracks in the wall spread throughout baseball. And from baseball to other sports and from sports to hotels and the rest of society. But it started with Jackie. How many black players were there in organized basketball before Jackie? How many were there? Wasn't any. How many football players? None. So when Jackie went up and broke the color barrier, everybody started getting blacks to play sports. And after people saw blacks playing sports, the walls in other areas started to come down. This is the way it worked. Before Jackie there was none of this. Jackie was smart enough to follow Rickey's advice. Rickey had told him what he was looking at, what he had to face, and that he shouldn't retaliate. Rickey told him if he kept cool, the Dodgers would do what they could to help him. Like when they went to Atlanta to play, the hotel didn't want to let Jackie have a room. So Rickey told them, "Then you don't want this team. If he doesn't go in here, then we don't stay." And they had to accept this. And that forced them. They had to take Jackie, or Rickey would move the team.

And I think Satchel deserves some credit too. Before Satchel Paige there was Smokey Joe Williams. The old-timers I talked with said he was as fast as Satchel. Today everybody knows Satchel's name, but very few have ever heard of Smokey Joe Williams. I think this was because Satchel came along later than Joe Williams. Joe Williams came along at a time when he knew he couldn't go any farther than where he was at. Satchel come along when he thought he could change things, so he started to push. And to a certain extent, Satchel could have been one of the reasons Jackie Robinson had a chance to go to the majors.

Satchel, when he was doing his barnstorming, was helping pave the way. Because Satchel proved that the black ballplayer could play major league baseball by barnstorming against all those white teams. Now Dizzy Dean, who had barnstormed against Satchel, helped Satchel a whole lot because Dizzy Dean made a statement when the Cardinals were in the World Series. The Cardinals only had two good pitchers, Dizzy and his brother Paul. And they asked Dizzy, "If you had a choice, who would be your pitcher to work the third game of the World Series?" He said, "None other than Satchel Paige." He and Satchel become great friends. People saw that the black ballplayers could play, but they didn't know when they were going to get a chance to play. That's what I think. Satchel loosened up things. Satchel and Josh and guys like that. All this kind of helped Jackie Robinson to get in.

Catching Dreams

With Jackie doing so well with the Dodgers in 1947, the major league teams began scouting our games, looking for players to follow Jackie. Mrs. Manley had put together a great team with guys like Monte Irvin, Max Manning, Lennie Pearson, and Larry Doby, so it wasn't surprising that the majors were looking closely at her players.

In early July we played the Newark Eagles in Trenton, New Jersey, and Larry Doby had noticed in the morning paper that Johnny Washington, our first baseman, was hitting .398. So before the game Doby kidded Washington, "Johnny, you ain't hitting that much." Johnny said, "I'll show you tonight." Newark started a right-hander named Rufus Lewis and relieved him with a left-hander they had named Jimmy Hill. Right-

Larry Doby and Luke Easter as Cleveland Indians. Courtesy of AP/Wide World Photos.

hander, left-hander, it didn't make any difference to Johnny Washington. He went 4 for 4 that night, and we run 'em pretty bad. Larry got, I think, one hit. Larry couldn't have been too upset with the evening because in about the seventh inning they announced over the intercom that he had just been sold to the Cleveland Indians. After the game Johnny congratulated Larry, but couldn't keep from reminding him of his perfect night at bat. *"That's* the reason my batting average is where it's at."

If Larry knew what was coming that night in Trenton, he never showed it. I guess he knew about it because they'd probably talked to him about it but he never said anything before the announcement. Larry was very quiet. He was one of those quiet type of ballplayers who did his job and stayed in top shape. Larry was always in great shape. He didn't do too much talking to too many people. I can't say that we were surprised that Larry Doby was chosen to break the American League color line. Most of us figured it would be Larry or Monte Irvin. Larry hit quite a few home runs in our league, and he was a good, young ballplayer. Somebody had to be the first to go to the American League, and Larry was an excellent choice.

Larry talked to me one night when he first went to Cleveland. He wasn't hitting the ball too well. He was having trouble with breaking pitches. We talked for two or three hours before he went on back to his hotel. He was determined to make good, and it drove him nuts that a AAA player named Pendelton was tearing up curve balls. He wondered why he couldn't do that. And I told him, "You're taking blind cuts." It looked to me like he was holding his bat too high and when he'd go to swing at it, he'd have to drop his arms, and that was causing him to take his eye off the ball. Danny Tartabull does the same thing today. He's got that bat way up in the air, and he's got to drop his arms to hit. I don't see how he hits either. I also thought it might help Larry if he moved off the plate a little. Whatever it was, he got it straightened out.

I always thought that Monte Irvin would be the first to leave Newark and go to the majors. Monte was just a great ballplayer, but I think the war hurt him. Monte went into the Army at the same time that Larry and

I went into the Navy. But Monte came out kind of shook up. They called it combat fatigue, but I've since heard it was some kind of inner ear problem. Whatever it was, he really wasn't at himself for a while. So he started back with Newark, and he played there for a while until he got back into the shape he was in before he went in the service. And after that, couldn't nobody get him out. He was such a good hitter. And he played his position well. He was a complete ballplayer.

They said Mrs. Manley got $15,000 from Bill Veeck, the Indians owner, for Larry Doby, which may not sound like much, but when Branch Rickey went after Monte Irvin he didn't want to pay her a thing. Rickey tried to embarrass her by making it look like she would be the cause of Monte not getting his chance in the majors. She called Rickey's bluff and spoke up and squawked that the major leagues were trying to take her ballplayers without paying for them. They were treating Negro League players like they were free agents. That got Rickey to back off, and Monte got a tryout with the Giants and made the team right off. But Mrs. Manley only got about $5,000 for him.

While all of this was going on with Monte, Mrs. Manley was in the process of selling the Eagles to some guys who moved them to Houston where they became the Houston Eagles. She sold the team, the uniforms, the bus, the whole works. I think she figured it had been a nice ride while it lasted, but it was time to cash out because the end was near.

7

A Ballplayer's Life

The Elites had only a fair season in 1947. We were better than .500 but not much. I hit the ball pretty well that season—hit pretty well my whole career. I didn't hit like Josh or Buck Leonard, not too many guys did, but I hit for a good average and helped my team. There were some pitchers I hit very well, like Henry Miller of the Philadelphia Stars and Alex Newkirk of the New York Cubans. As a matter of fact I hit most left-handers good but old man Tiant. Anybody that threw overhanded like this was easy for me to hit. I'd see it all the way. But if you come kind of sidearm, it's kind of hard to pick up the ball. That's why I always had a little trouble out of old man Tiant—that's Luis Tiant, Sr.—the daddy of Luis, Jr., who pitched for the Indians and Red Sox. Daddy threw a change-up all the time. And he threw a screwball. Old man Tiant's screwball was the best I saw in our league. That was his bread and butter pitch. He'd throw you a screwball just to get you set up. He could get you going for that screwball, get you looking. Then he'd throw a fastball down the middle of the plate and you wouldn't be ready for it. He gave me a lot of trouble. That's the only left-hander I know of gave me trouble like that. He could get you out. His boy was just like him with that herky-jerky delivery and junk he'd throw. That really frustrates a batter. So I had trouble with him for a while. Another guy that threw that screwball was Verdell Mathis of the Memphis Red Sox. I played against him quite a bit. He was a left-hander and a good pitcher all-around. He'd use that screwball on right-handed batters and, just like Tiant, it'd keep you off stride. The other thing that Mathis did that reminded me of Tiant was fool runners with a very tricky pickoff move.

Another pitcher I used to have trouble with was a guy out of Philadelphia called Ricks, Bill Ricks. He was a right-hander with the Stars in the forties. He had three or four curveballs that he'd throw you. Never throw you the same curveball twice. You had to try to outguess him. And I had trouble trying to hit him. It wasn't just me though; Ricks struck out a whole lot of batters.

One of the New York Black Yankees pitchers gave me some trouble too. Neck Stanley. He was a spitball pitcher. When he threw that wet ball, the bottom would fall out of it. I had a little trouble with him but those three—Tiant, Ricks, and Stanley were about the only three I did have trouble with.

I caught Satchel for several seasons and knew him quite well for more than forty years but the one thing I never did was hit against him. But I believe I could have hit him because although he threw the ball fast, I knew he was gonna throw the ball over the plate and wasn't going to throw at me because he was a good friend of mine. Satchel didn't ever throw at people except for that one time against the House of David. You could kind of dig in on Satchel. The reason I think I could have hit Satchel was that Max Manning was very similar to Satchel. Max was also a right-hander, was taller than Satchel, and could throw hard too. Max was a good pitcher, but there were times I hit him pretty well, like that time I hit those long triples off him. The Kansas City Monarchs had a boy who threw as hard as anybody named Gene Richardson. I hit him like I owned him. And when I was with the Satchel Paige's All-Stars, we had a right-hander named Bill Barnes, and he threw as hard as anybody I've ever seen. I hit him just like he was my brother. Unfortunately, I never got to hit against him in real games—just squad games and batting practice. With fastball pitchers I'd take a short swing, just punch at it.

In my travels with the Elites I saw a whole lot less of Jim Crow than I had in the past because the Elites very seldom went south. They stayed in the east when I was with them. They started out as the Nashville Elite Giants, then moved to Baltimore in 1938. When they became the Baltimore Elite Giants, they mostly played the Homestead Grays, the Newark Eagles, the

Philadelphia Stars, the New York Black Yankees, and the New York Cuban Stars. These were the teams that played in the east in the Negro National League. When we did go west, we played the Kansas City Monarchs, the Memphis Red Sox, the Birmingham Black Barons, the Chicago American Giants, the Indianapolis Clowns, and the Cleveland Buckeyes. They were the Negro American League. These were the teams left in both leagues after the war. After the regular season, the winners in the east would play the winners in the west. The only way we would go south is when we didn't have a chance to win the division. Then we'd go south and play those teams.

Because we were mostly in the east, we could usually find a pretty decent place to stay or cafe when we needed one. We had a special place where we'd eat when we made the trip to New York City. It was between Wilmington and New York and looked like just another diner from the outside, but you'd go inside and have yourself an excellent meal and piece of pie. We'd stop there just about every time we went to New York. Down south it was rougher. We used to stay at the Traveler's Hotel when we went to Memphis and the food was all right, but in other little towns you'd have to get sandwiches and things like that.

With the Elites I mostly hung around with Norman and Pee Wee Butts, our shortstop. We might play cards all day. In Kansas City, Jesse Williams was the club card shark, but we didn't have any sharks in Baltimore. We'd just play Trump and Rummy. That's where you get five cards and you try and get as low as you can. You try and get down to one if you can. And then a whole lot of times, if you played your last card and somebody else had a one, you'd get caught. And if you'd be playing for a dollar, you'd pay double if you got caught. That's the way we played, but we never played for much money. We were just looking to pass some time until the next game.

Sure there were some rough spots on the road, but I enjoyed traveling with the team. It was nothing like that movie they made with Billy Dee Williams, *The Bingo Long Traveling All-Stars*." If they were trying to say that this was what the Negro Leagues were like, they were wrong. We never slipped out of a hotel. Never in my life have I done such a thing.

We didn't have to because the owners paid our expenses on the road. We had the best that they had to offer in the way of rooms and food and stuff like that. They said second rate, third rate. They can say whatever they want to say, but the owners did the best they could for us. Now a whole lot of times it wasn't great because of the way the people would let it be run down, but that wasn't because our owner was being tight. It was because he didn't always have a lot to choose from. But slip out on a hotel bill? Never. When we'd get out of that bus, we'd go and check in. And that was it. The business manager was standing right there when we checked in. He made reservations a week or two ahead, so we had rooms for all the men that we had on the ballclub including the business manager and staff. All we had to do was go and check in when we got there. That movie made it seem like we were traveling con men, and it's wrong.

When the Elites went to New York, we stayed at the Woodside Hotel. The Woodside was a famous hotel because that's where a lot of jazz musicians stayed. There was even a song about it called "Jumpin' at the Woodside." It was a favorite of Count Basie's band. You couldn't pass through that lobby or walk those hallways without bumping into a musician. You'd see Lionel Hampton. He was with us up there in New York a lot. And you'd see Coleman Hawkins. And Charlie Yardbird Parker would stay at the Woodside. Chu Berry, this boy Lester Young, my friend from Oklahoma, Oscar Pettiford, all them big guys stayed there.

They had a nightclub right there at the Woodside, so you could stay there and then go see the show that evening. To tell the truth we didn't get to see too many full shows. We'd get to go down and pick up a set of jazz, especially if a couple of guys were really blowing at each other. Then we'd go over to the bar for a beer or something like that, but usually we couldn't stay too long. We always had a curfew. The ballplayers had to get out of there. Those musicians would stay up until morning.

Of all the musicians I met, my favorite to talk to was Nat King Cole. He was a nice guy. Another one I liked was Gene Ammons. Jug, that's what everybody called him, was nice to talk to. Lester Young was all right too. All those guys were regular guys. They knew that without the people, they wasn't nothing. You had to support them too. They felt the same way about us. The only one that wasn't very friendly was Louis Jordan and that's not firsthand. That's from a friend of mine who had a little fuss with him. But for the most part they were regular guys.

My other memory of the Woodside is the bedbugs. They got so bad at the Woodside that I'd sit up all night in a chair with the lights on. They'd bite if you didn't leave the lights on. I wasn't about to get in bed and get those bugs on me. Whenever I hear "Jumpin' at the Woodside," I think of bedbugs because if those bedbugs were in bed with you, you were gonna be jumpin'. It got so run-down that eventually we moved to the Wilshire Hotel.

We didn't get to too many other clubs in New York. There was one that wasn't quite a half block from the Woodside on the same side of the street, around 137th and Lenox Ave. It was called the Victoria Bar. It was a big place, and they had live music in there. The Victoria's where I saw the sax player Illinois Jacquet, Count Basie with a small combo, and other small acts like that. It had a small stage, so they wouldn't get no big bands in there. Sometimes they'd just have piano and drums. It was a pretty popular place with ballplayers, and I'd usually run into guys off the New York Black Yankees or New York Cubans. We'd stand in there a while and listen to the music. If we was playing hard for a championship, we wouldn't stay too long. We might have a beer or two and go on back to the hotel and get to bed.

Another of our favorite nightclubs in New York was the Cotton Club. We'd be sure to go there if we didn't have a game the next day or something like that. We'd go there or the Apollo Theater when I was in New York. Washington had some nice clubs too and we'd always stop in to hear the music. When I was playing ball, I didn't like to dance that much because it was hard on your legs. You can't dance all night and catch all day. I couldn't anyway. Baseball came first. They paid me to catch, not dance. In the wintertime, I'd go and dance up a storm.

We stayed at the Wilshire in New York a long time and gradually it was run down to nothing. Then from there we went to the Hotel Theresa in Harlem and soon it went down. This is all they had to offer and we had to stay somewhere, so we had to put up with it.

                                                        Catching Dreams

After his show at the Comedy Club, Redd Foxx and I would walk up and down Edmondson Avenue in Baltimore and go catch a couple sets somewhere else. We'd usually end up at the Edmondson Club to hear big Arthur Prysock or Billie Holiday. Courtesy of the author.

Now when I was at home in Baltimore in the late forties I never had trouble finding somebody to go to the nightclubs with me. I had a bunch of friends that would go. Pee Wee Butts would go. Sometimes Norman would go. We'd go hear Lionel Hampton, Louis Armstrong, boy called Johnny Sparrow. Johnny Sparrow was a tenor saxophone player. He played with Louis Armstrong a long time and he came out of Baltimore. There were several good musicians out of Baltimore. There was that boy that Hampton picked up, a tenor player called Bill Swindell. He was out of Baltimore. And there was Jimmy Scott who was a vocalist. He came out of there. Brought a girl out of there and she sung too. Oh, there were a bunch of them and you couldn't hardly see them all.

We liked to go to a place over on Edmondson Avenue, that nightclub where big Arthur Prysock and Billie Holiday played. The Edmondson Club. A couple times me and Redd Foxx walked over there together. I knew Redd good. A lot of times I'd go hear Redd do his show, and then we'd go catch a couple sets somewhere else. Redd'd play two shows a night at the Comedy Club. And then Pearl Bailey was a block away at the Alhambra. And right across the street was the Casino. All those places were run by the same guy, Willie Adams. All on Pennsylvania Avenue. Another place we'd go to on Pennsylvania Avenue was the Royal Theater. That's where we'd hear Duke Ellington. It's hard to believe now but for 75 cents you could see the whole show of the greatest acts in the country. Sammy Davis, Jr., Moms Mabley, Lionel Hampton and all those big bands came to the Royal Theater for shows. Entertainers like that all up and down Pennsylvania Avenue. And all them people knew me. All I had to do was walk up the street and they'd say, "There's Robinson. He catches for the Elites." They knew that I caught for the Elite Giants, and I didn't have no problem with none of them. There's no more Pennsylvania Avenue—not the way it used to be.

The Royal's also where I first saw Peg-Leg Bates. Peg-Leg Bates was a dancer. Tap dancer. He had a wooden peg leg and he had a tap on that peg. With just one good leg, he still tapped as good as anybody. You don't believe that? Well, you get an old *Down Beat* or something like that, and

To Lanny Page
Working With You Really
Grand I Wish You much luck
and Happiness.
sincerely. Peg Leg Bates

Peg-Leg Bates tap danced with one good leg and a wooden peg. The ballplayers loved to go see his show. Courtesy of NoirTech Research Inc.

you'll see he was one of your greatest dancers and he had a peg leg. One leg but you couldn't tell the difference between Peg-Leg and a man with both legs. I heard he lost his leg in an accident when he was a little boy, and they replaced his leg with a peg. He learned to spin on his peg and do little tricks like that. That's how he started performing. When I saw Peg-Leg, he would be tappin' and steppin', coming down on that peg. He liked to dance right to the edge of the stage, balance himself on that peg, wave his arms around, and lean towards the crowd. It looked like he was gonna fall off the stage and land right in the front row, and the audience would go to hollerin' and jumpin' out of their seats. They'd be scared for him. At the last second, when it looked like he was gonna go off the edge, he'd pull up and say, "I scared the hell out of you, didn't I?" Then he'd go on with his act. And when he changed clothes between acts, he changed pegs too. If he came out to dance with a white tux on, he'd have a white peg leg. If he come out in a black tux, he had a black peg. He had a different peg for every time he changed clothes. He must have had a dozen of them pegs. Oh, could that man dance!

Peg-Leg Bates was very popular, and I didn't have any problem finding people to go with me to his show. A lot of the boys from the ballclub would go whenever Peg-Leg would come to town. Sometimes Redd Foxx would go with me. Redd was just starting out. He hadn't gotten no breaks. Then when this boy Slappy White came through town, he joined up with Redd. They were just starting out, trying to make a little money.

Lionel Hampton was a big baseball fan, and he liked to come to the park and work out with us. Lionel was a great performer. He really worked his band hard, and we'd get a thrill just watching him work. Lena Horne's father ran numbers from above Gus Greenlee's Crawford Grill, so a lot of the guys knew Lena. I saw Lena several times, but I never liked her singing that much. I liked Sarah Vaughan. I'd go see her every chance I'd get. And Ella Fitzgerald. I liked jazz more than I did anything else except baseball.

The Elites finished the 1947 season in the middle of the pack, and only a few changes were made for the 1948 season. They brought Butch Mc-Cord up from the Nashville Black Vols to play some outfield and give us another bat from the left side. And they brought in a couple new right-handed pitchers, Apples Wilmore and Leroy Ferrell. Both of them had good fastballs with decent changes and curves.

Our best games in the middle to late forties were with the Grays, the Cubans, and the Newark Eagles. Things had finally gotten to where one team didn't dominate. The Grays had dominated beginning in the late thirties up to the war. They dominated like the Yankees did in the fifties.

After Newark built their team in the mid-forties around Leon Day, Larry Doby, Don Newcombe, and Monte Irvin, things got kind of shaken up, and the Grays couldn't win all those games anymore. The Grays had to scuffle to win games. Then the Eagles started losing guys to the majors and they sank.

The Birmingham Black Barons had a good team too with guys like Pepper Bassett catching, John Britton and Piper Davis in the infield, Ed Steele and Jim Zapp in the outfield, and James Newberry and Alonzo Perry pitching. And they picked up a guy from Baltimore in the second half of the 1947 season who'd always try to get under your skin. My brother. Norman was always hustling, always trying to get an edge, always looking to beat you, just like he had back when we were playing the House of David or when we were kids. He played hard against everybody, played hard against his brother, and I played hard against him. Norman would talk to you during the game to try to shake you up so you'd make a mistake. Once we were leading them 3-2 in the seventh inning, and Norman came up and told me he was gonna be running when he got on. Sure enough, he hit one of Jonas Gaines' screwballs for a single and right away started dancing off first base. He jumped up and left on the first pitch, and I threw him out by forty feet. They had it in the paper the next morning, "Brother Against Brother." That's the way we played. We played against each other hard.

Norman *(left)*, with a couple of his teammates on the 1947 Birmingham Black Barons, pitcher and first baseman Alonzo Perry and right fielder Ed "Iron Man" Steele. Steele should have been made of iron because he wouldn't give much at the plate and was always getting hit by the pitch. Courtesy of the author.

Another time Norman tried to take that uniform off me in a game. He'd hurt his sister if she got in his way. What happened was that the Elites were leading Birmingham 2-1 in the late innings. Norman was on second base when somebody hit the ball to straight away center and Norman rounded third and headed home. Our boy was playing shallow, and he threw the ball to me and it got there a little ahead of Norman. Norman tried to take it out of my hand by spiking me. He was noted for that. He was like Ty Cobb that way. I tagged him out and said, "Man, I'm your brother." He looked at me, kind of shrugged and said, "You got the wrong uniform on." I didn't say anything because that was his business. If he wanted to get the ball out of my hand, that was his business to try to get it out. Mine was to keep him from getting it out. After all, *he* was the one with the wrong uniform on. That's the way we played the game.

Catching Dreams

If it wasn't Norman giving you a hard time during the game, it was Birmingham fans giving you a hard time before the game. There was one game with the Barons where we were a little late getting into Birmingham. We were out there practicing and one white guy came up and said, "Hey boy!" And George Scales, our batting instructor said, "Ignore the guy, Robinson. Let him go." So I did ignore him, but he kept on saying, "Hey boy!"

Finally I said, "Yes?"

And he asked, "Where you boys hail from?"

"Different parts. Some of them from New York. Some of them from Illinois and around."

"I don't believe that."

See, he was calling me a liar and trying to start something. I didn't say anything more and he kept on, "You guys think you're going to beat our Birmingham Black Barons, don't you?" I didn't say anything. He said, "You're going to have to play to beat us." I already knew that because of Norman playing for the Black Barons. I knew from Norman that they had a good team. For the whole warm-up this guy was standing there talking as though he wanted to start something. Finally, I just walked away from him. I'll bet he wasn't none too happy when we won that game.

Now in 1948 Baltimore won both the first half and the second half in the Negro National League, and they *still* made us play the Grays for the League championship. What was supposed to happen and what they did in the past was to have the winner of the first half play the winner of the second half for the League championship. If a team won both halves, then they were the champs. A team that won both halves had proven themselves during the regular season and shouldn't have to play a second place team. Here's what happened. When Tom Wilson died in '47, they chose a minister, a big time minister from New York, the Reverend John H. Johnson of St. Martha's Episcopal Church in Harlem, to be the president of the Negro National League. I'm not sure why he was chosen to be president because I don't believe that man knew home plate from a collection plate. Now when Cum Posey died in 1946, his money partner, a numbers backer from Homestead named Sonnyman Jackson, took over the team.

And at the end of the '48 season Sonnyman complained to Rev. Johnson who forced us to have a playoff with the Grays. We knew it was wrong. I mean we went to our owner and asked how could they make us have a playoff with the Grays when we done won both ends of it? Vernon Green said, "Well, I don't know how they did it, but this is his ruling." Vernon felt that this was the league's ruling and we'd just have to live with it. I think that Sonnyman had got to Johnson some kind of way.

Anyway, we had to play them off in the best three out of five. Here's the way it was. We were down two games to one going into Game #4 before a big crowd at Bugle Field in Baltimore. If we won, Game #5 would follow as part of a doubleheader. Well, we did win that fourth game thanks to some fine pitching by 41-year-old Bill Byrd and big hits by Henry Kimbro and Lester Lockett. I helped the cause with a double and a triple. So that tied the series at 2-2 and forced a fifth game.

For the nightcap we went with Jonas Gaines, a left-hander who, along with Byrd, had been one of our best starters. The Grays went with Big Tom Parker, a right-hander who had returned to the Grays in 1948 after eight years with other teams. Now Bugle Field didn't have lights and along about the sixth inning, with the score tied, we noticed that it was getting dark fast. The top of the seventh inning, they run about three runs on us. Now this is the rubber game, and we saw that we weren't going to be able to get the entire game in. So I threw the ball to right field instead of throwing to first base and let 'em run. We let 'em run all the runs they wanted to run just so we could prolong the inning into darkness. Well they did call the game on account of darkness and, by rights, the game would revert back to the last complete inning because we couldn't fin- ish—tie score after six. But when we took the field the next day, there was the Grays' Jerry Benjamin sitting on first base, Luke Easter sitting on sec- ond base, and Sam Bankhead sitting on third. We looked up at all of those Grays sitting out there on the bases and said, "What is *this*?" The bases were loaded with nobody out. It was that Rev. Johnson that made us put those men back on base. And that's what they did. They put the Grays back on the bases, and when that inning finally ended the Grays were five runs ahead. Now you know by rights they were supposed to revert that inning back because of the curfew. But they wanted that game to start from where it stopped. Our owner said if that's the way it is, let 'em have it. Just give it to 'em. We wouldn't play. Joe Black, Junior Gilliam, and I went up to the office to try and find out what happened. There was nothing to find out. They gave it to the Grays when we forfeited it to 'em. Let 'em have it. That was the last playoff game of 1948. That's the way it was.

The Grays got to go on and play the Birmingham Black Barons, who had defeated the Monarchs in the Negro American League playoffs, in the World Series. That Barons team was led by infielder-manager Piper Davis. Piper was a tough one with a bat in his hand and the game on the line. It seemed like he always got the big hit in a ballgame. Norman had been playing excellent center field for Birmingham and batting leadoff since joining the Barons the season before. In May of that 1948 season, Norman was chasing a fly ball in the outfield, stepped in a hole, and broke his leg. Norman's spot in center went to a youngster just out of high school from the Birmingham area. His name was Willie Mays. When Norman came back later in the summer, Piper sent Norman to left field rather than back to center where Willie was playing. Piper said that although Norman was faster than Willie, Willie had the better arm. Norman and Mays in one outfield is a lot of speed. If you were playing Birmingham in 1948, you'd better hit to right or hit it out.

Willie's father was an outfielder, you know. They called him Kat Mays, and he worked with Willie a long time before he came up to Birmingham. Willie could play the outfield, but I didn't know how far he would go because he looked like he stayed in the bucket when he hit—kind of run up and hit. Mays was always a bucket hitter, but he finally learned how to hit that way. I guess Leo Durocher helped him out a whole lot when Willie got called up to the Giants. He stopped him from running up on the ball as much. He kind of stayed in there and started hitting. That was the only weakness he had when he went up there because he could play the outfield and he had a good throwing arm. And then Mays was smart enough to study hitters too. By knowing the hitter and watching how he was being pitched, he had a very good idea of where the ball would go if the batter made contact. He'd position himself and if the batter didn't hit it out of the ballpark, Willie'd just take two or three steps to make the catch. He'd know when to come in on a guy and when to back up off of one. He was just outstanding like that. He learned how to play that way by paying attention. He was plenty fast, but he didn't want to rely on that. He'd use that speed to bail himself out, as anybody that saw the 1954 World Series knows. Willie Mays could do it all.

Unfortunately for Birmingham, even Willie Mays wasn't enough for the Barons in the 1948 Negro World Series, and it was the Grays in five.

Willie Mays was just one of the great outfielders we had. Harry "Suitcase" Simpson of the Philadelphia Stars could throw. So could Willie Grace from the Cleveland Buckeyes. He had a good arm. In Baltimore, Lockett knew how to throw. All those guys had powerful arms. Guys wouldn't take that chance if the ball was hit straight to them. Like you singled straight to them with a guy on second base, your runner wouldn't take that chance of scoring. Then there were guys like Henry Kimbro. Kimbro had a good arm. He just didn't know how to throw. Instead of throwing it so it would hop and give the catcher a chance to field it right, he'd throw it right up on you. You'd have to trap it to get it. And while you're trying to trap it, you've got a guy running down that line. You have a good chance of getting hurt.

You also had some Cubans that would throw you out. There were some good Cuban outfielders. Martin Dihigo comes to mind. He was with Alex Pompez's New York Cubans, and he had an outstanding arm. Actually everything Martin Dihigo did on the the ballfield was outstanding. Throw, pitch, hit, run, field—there wasn't anything he couldn't do. He could play every position but catch. He wasn't just a good-hitting pitcher or a hitter that could pitch a couple innings from time to time. He could do it all. Eight Martin Dihigos and a catcher could beat anybody. I only saw him the last year he played in our league. He'd gotten old then, but he still knew what to do out there. He just couldn't execute like he had before. He was the greatest ballplayer to ever come out of Cuba and one of the greatest ever. He was one of the big Cubans. He was tall—a little over six feet and weighed about 205 or 210 pounds. After he retired he went back to Cuba and never did come back. I never did see him any more. He's in the Hall of Fame in Cooperstown now, and I'll bet very few of the people visiting there have ever heard of him. Too bad. The majors have never seen a player like Martin Dihigo.

And of course the guys with speed were good outfielders. The Grays, as great as they were in other areas, really didn't have anybody that made you worry about taking an extra base, although David Whatley wasn't bad because of his speed. Sam Jethroe was very good before his eyes started going bad on him. He could play it.

A couple of guys could show you that number on their back and go get that ball. Cool Papa Bell religiously did that. I'd have to rate Cool Papa Bell as one of the best outfielders that I saw. Cool and this boy that played for the Baltimore Orioles. Paul Blair. He was good too. He played a short center field. He played behind second base. If you hit the ball and you didn't hit it out of the park, he'd go back and catch it. Cool was the same way—just like he did me in that game in Louisville in '41. That boy Charlie Biot was another one that could run a fly ball better than anybody but that's all he could do was run that fly ball. He couldn't hit and couldn't do nothin' else. He played for the Elites in 1941.

You didn't have to have a great arm or even be all that fast to be a good outfielder. Some guys really studied hitters. One of the smartest was Gene Benson. Benson played for the Philadelphia Stars long as I knew him. He could hit the ball real well, but he wasn't that fast. He made up for this in the outfield by paying attention to where the hitter was likely to hit the ball. Despite his lack of speed, he was good enough to not have to make those way-out catches. You seldom saw Gene Benson have to make a desperate lunge for a ball. What he lacked in his legs, he made up for with his head. Like Lockett. Lester Lockett, my teammate in Baltimore. He studied hitters too. He knew just about where you were gonna hit the ball. And I already called Mays as one who studied hitters.

These three outfielders, Willie Mays, Gene Benson, and Lester Lockett, really worked at their game. They studied hitters and they knew how you were going to be pitching to a man. If you were pitching a man inside, they knew just about where he was going to hit the ball. Are you gonna pull the ball, or are you gonna hit it straightaway or hit it to right field?

If he's a good pull hitter, they're not going to pitch him inside. They may pitch him outside, and he'll hit the ball straightaway most of the time. The only hitters that could trick them were hitters that could go with the pitch. Like if they threw it to the outside, the batter'd step that way and hit it. Don't try to pull it, hit it that way. Wasn't too often that these three got fooled though. They'd watch what pitch you had and break with the crack of the bat. They knew how to play the hitters.

Although I only saw him play that one time back in 1936, from what everybody told us the best outfielder ever was Oscar Charleston. All-around. Field, run, throw, hit, Oscar could do it all. He managed for a long time and for several different clubs when his playing days were up. Oscar Charleston was as hard-nosed a manager as he was a player. He especially didn't like to hear a ballplayer complain. If the umpire called a bad strike or something like that (and you know how ballplayers usually do), well, you'd get no sympathy from Oscar Charleston. I saw him one time when he was managing Philadelphia, and they had a pitcher in there by the name of Bill Ricks. Ricks complained about a couple balls that he thought should have been called strikes. And he was out there kicking and carrying on, and Charleston went out there and talked to him. Charleston was pretty short-tempered, and you could tell he was getting hot. Then he snatched the ball out of Ricks's hand, turned his back towards home plate, and threw the ball to his catcher as if to say he could beat him pitching backwards. And I'll tell you, the catcher didn't have to shift too much to catch that ball. He was just that way. Can you imagine Cito Gaston or Tommy Lasorda doing that today? The players wouldn't stand for it. Once Charleston felt that you were overdoing it and complaining too much, he just told them, "This is a game that you're supposed to play and play it rough and you ain't got no business complaining." He just figured you weren't supposed to be no baby out there. He wanted to know, was you a crybaby or was you a man. He was that type of manager. He was nice to talk to, he just didn't back down from nobody. He knew baseball.

Catching Dreams

After the 1948 season, the Negro National League folded. The Baltimore Elite Giants and the other N.N.L. teams except the Grays and the New York Black Yankees joined the Negro American League. The N.A.L. had to expand into Eastern and Western divisions to make room. At this point six players from the Negro Leagues—Larry Doby, Hank Thompson, Willard Brown, Dan Bankhead, Roy Campanella, and Satchel—had followed Jackie to the major leagues.

Not all of these guys were a big hit in the majors. The St. Louis Browns picked up Hank Thompson and Willard Brown from the Monarchs, but when neither guy knocked the cover off the ball, the Browns released them after about a couple dozen games. Didn't send them down to AAA, released them! Now how can you judge a player in less than a month's worth of games? It should never have been that way in the first place. First, you have to remember that while Hank and Willard weren't the first black players in the American League, they were only a week or two behind Larry Doby. So they were going to cities that had never had black major league ballplayers before. And on top of this, the Browns players didn't exactly welcome them with open arms. The Browns should have laid some groundwork with the white players, help them accept this. The black ballplayers had enough to worry about trying to hit pitchers that they've never seen before without the white guys making it rougher for them. That's a lot of pressure, more than just the usual pressure that a new guy has to face. The Browns didn't prepare their white players for what was coming. Second, Hank and Willard probably should have spent a little time in AAA before going up to the big club. You couldn't just run some guys out there. Branch Rickey didn't do that with Jackie. He didn't even run Campanella out there without some time in AAA, and he probably could have. Now Bill Veeck sent both Larry Doby and Satchel right to the Indians. But Larry was a very mature, serious guy, and Satchel was a veteran who could take any kind of pressure you could throw at him. Satchel loved pressure and pitching out of jams. Sometimes he'd even create a jam just so he could pitch his way out of it. But not every black player could walk right out on to a major league field and do the job. Not every white player could do that. You had to look at the indivdual ballplayer and decide what would work best. Branch Rickey understood that. Bill Veeck understood that. The people running the Browns didn't get it. Maybe that's why Rickey's Dodgers and Veeck's Indians won so many games and the Browns were usually in the cellar. Willard Brown never did get another shot at the majors.

Hank Thompson didn't have an easy road to go either. He'd come to the Monarchs at the age of about 17 and Kansas City sat him on the bench about a year before he started playing. He was a good little ballplayer, good hustlin' ballplayer. He could hit the ball out of the park if he caught a hold of one right, but he mostly hit line drives. He was a good base stealer, good runner, good with the glove. And Hank was a good clutch hitter. He could play infield and outfield. After the Browns let him go, he went back to the Monarchs, hit very well, and eventually signed with the Giants. He started the 1949 season with Monte Irvin in the minors at Jersey City, did fine, and got called up to the Giants. I think Hank would have been up there in the majors long before he got up there except he had a little something against him. It goes back to when he was with the Monarchs in the early forties.

This is what happened. We were on our way to spring training, and the Monarchs let Hank stop in his hometown of Dallas to see his sister. After he saw his sister, he was to come on and meet the ballclub in New Orleans and start training. That night in Dallas he happened to carry his sister and his brother-in-law out to have a few beers and visit. I'm not sure what sort of a place this was, it could have been a nice nightclub or it could have been a bucket of blood, but while they were sitting at their table, Hank saw four guys sitting over at another table. Hank thought he'd be a nice guy and told the waitress to get those guys another round of what they were drinking and tell them it was on him. Those guys took it all wrong. Here he bought a round, sent it over to them, and they taken it as an insult! One of these guys asked the waitress, "Who sent this over here?" The waitress pointed to Hank and said, "That fella over there." This guy knew that Hank was a ballplayer and that he was from up Kansas City way. He said to the waitress, "Oh, that big shot from up north. Tell him we'll be over to see him." That's what he said. Hank and his sister and her hus-band were just sitting there drinking and thought no more of it. In a few minutes that guy came over and jumped up on the table waving a big knife in his hands. He looked at Hank and said, "I'm gonna show you what we do to smart-alecs." Thompson told him to stop because he didn't mean no harm, but the guy kept coming after him with the knife so Hank pulled out a gun and shot him off the table. Shot him dead. He had bought this gun at that old pawnshop right there on 18th and Vine in Kansas City, right across from the hotel we stayed in. See, Thompson was a little guy and because he lived in Dallas, he knew Dallas was pretty rough at the time. He might have just bought the gun to have in the off-season. It just so happened that night when he went out, he carried it with him. And Thompson knew this guy. Thompson knew that this guy had cut up several people there in Dallas, so he knew that he was in danger. And that's what happened.

It took the police a while to sort it all out. Hank called J. L. Wilkinson. Wilkinson was the best friend a ballplayer in trouble could have and that's who finally got Hank out of trouble. From then on, even though it was self-defense, Hank said that that guy was always with him. He was with him when he played with the Monarchs, he was with him when he played in the majors, he was with him everywhere he played. He never could get rid of that. It always bothered him that he killed that guy. It was always on his mind. He felt that was why things didn't work out for him. I think that was part of it because after that he started drinking big. I re-member he went down to Mexico or South America to play, married a girl down there somewhere, and when he came back, he was still drinking a lot. He drank all the time after he killed that guy. He drank when he was playing with the Giants. No telling what kind of major leaguer he could have been.

Years later, in 1976, a similar sort of thing happened to Sam Bankhead, the shortstop. His best friend shot him and killed him. Sometimes you hear people talk about it as being an accident, but they didn't tell me nothing about it being an accident. They said they was drinking and ar-guing and some kind of way this guy shot him.

I never did carry no gun or nothing like that, and most of the players that I knew didn't fool with them either. Now Satchel carried a gun but that was later on. He didn't carry it when he was playing baseball. Satchel was a gun collector, and after he'd retired he carried a gun because he did some detective work. At least he said he was doing detective work. I don't know how serious he was about it, although he did run with a sheriff in Kansas City for a little bit. But guys would never have a gun with them when they were with the team. They didn't do that. This was a rare thing for a ballplayer to have a gun, it just happened that Hank Thompson had one with him that night in Dallas.

Matter of fact, the only other player that I remember that regularly carried a gun was Othello Renfroe. He bought a gun, and then Goose Tatum went out and bought one. The problem was that Renfroe and some other guys were pickin' at Goose because Goose played basketball and baseball and they seen that he was making more money. You know how guys do. So Goose got a gun for his own protection. That's the reason, I think, why Goose finally quit playing baseball. On account of these guys, like Renfroe and few others, being nasty to him. Renfroe, they said, was a little rude, a little agitator, but I didn't know him too well. I figured if Goose was picking up a little extra cash, good for him. It wasn't like he was taking it from anybody. It was money that he earned, and it wasn't nobody else's business.

In 1949, Minnie Minoso, Don Newcombe, Monte Irvin, and Luke Easter all got their chance in the major leagues and they made the most of it. The better these black players did, the more Negro League players the big league clubs wanted. It even got to the point where major league clubs were fighting each other to sign our players. That's how quickly things changed, and that's what happened to Art Wilson, the shortstop for the Birmingham Black Barons. He was in a dispute about not going to the right team. In February of 1949 the Indians had him, and the Yankees said they talked to him first. Commissioner Chandler had to settle things, and Wilson went into the Yankees farm system.

Other guys came so close to making it in the majors but were just a little too old. Guys like Ray Dandridge. He was an *outstanding* third baseman, the best I've ever seen. He mostly played for the Newark Eagles or down in Mexico. I know many of our players say Ray Dandridge was the greatest player ever. That's tough to say but he was certainly the greatest third baseman ever. He was bowlegged and squat, but he could do it all around that bag. And this was at a time when they didn't always take such good care of the infields the way they do now. We had plenty of bad hops. Defensively, I don't know who else would rate with Ray Dandridge. Maybe Newt Joseph. They'd stand right in your face if they thought you was fixin' to bunt the ball. They were fearless. And Dandridge was a smart hitter too. He'd smack that ball all over the field. He'd get his share of home runs, but he was known for having a high batting average. Dandridge could have played anywhere. The New York Giants scouted him and sent him and Dave Barnhill to the Minneapolis Millers of the American Association in 1949. Barnhill didn't set any records up there, but Dandridge was terrific. Unfortunately, Dandridge was 36 and that's as far as he went. He must have felt a little like Moses going all the way to the Promised Land but, in the end, having to look in from the outside.

Since I'm on the subject of great third baseman, there's one other that I should mention, although I never got to see him play. That's Judy Johnson. He retired a couple of years before I hooked up with Satchel's team, but guys talked about him as one of the greats. They said he had very good hands, a strong arm, and never seemed to make a mistake out there. At the plate, he was a solid line drive hitter who hit for a good average. He mostly played for the Hilldale ballclub and the Pittsburgh Crawfords. They say he was one of your great third baseman. Both Judy Johnson and Ray Dandridge are in the Hall of Fame.

Anyway, losing all these players to the major leagues and their farm teams was taking its toll on our clubs, and a lot of the owners were hurting. There was nothing we could do but play baseball and wonder which player would be the next to go and which team the next to fold.

When Tom Wilson died in 1947 my extra money stopped. I kept waiting for a raise, but I never did get a raise from Vernon Green. Green wound up dying of a heart attack in 1949 and his assistant, Dick Powell, took over as general manager. I never got more money from Dick either, but by then I knew the team was having serious money troubles.

Despite all the off-field distractions in 1949, I was having a solid year, and the Elites as a team were playing good baseball.

That 1949 team may have been the best of the Baltimore teams that I played on. There were two reasons for that. First, the Elites got Lennie Pearson for Johnny Washington when Mrs. Manley sold the Eagles to Houston. Lennie came to Baltimore and became our manager and first baseman. Lennie was a good power hitter, only he didn't have the best arm so he played first base. He had hurt his arm playing football in high school, and it never did get better. Today they'd do some kind of surgery

The Baltimore Elite Giants, 1949. *(left to right)* Ed Finney, Henry Kimbro, Johnny Hayes, Leon Day, Pee Wee Butts, Vic Harris, Butch McCord, Junior

and you might be back in a few months or even weeks, but back then if you got hurt, you might stay hurt. And you'd learn to play with it or find some other line of work. So Lennie threw the ball underhanded. Even on a double play, even trying to cut down a run at the plate, he'd throw it underhand, but he'd have something on it. He was pretty accurate with it too. To second base, third base, home—didn't matter, that's the way he threw.

Second, Baltimore picked up the best pitcher I'd caught since Satchel. That was Leon Day. After he was discharged from the service, Leon had returned to Newark before playing in the Mexican League for a couple of seasons. Leon Day was a good guy and, boy, could he pitch. He believed he could get you out with his fastball. And he could because if you got

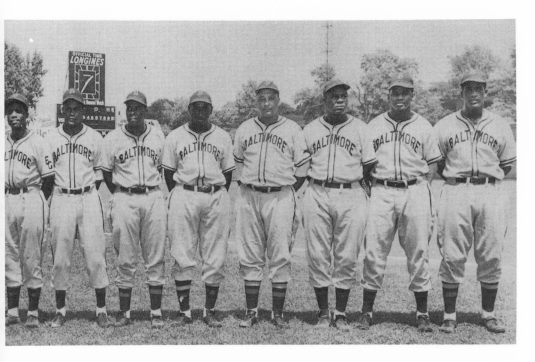

Gilliam, Bob Romby, Frazier Robinson, Al Wilmore, Jesse Walker, Butch Davis, Bill Byrd, Lennie Pearson, Leroy Ferrell, Joe Black. Courtesy of Ed Finney.

Leon Day, teammate, friend, Hall of Famer. Courtesy of Lee Milazzo.

too close to that plate, you was gonna get hit. He wouldn't let you dig in and get buried. He had such good control that he'd move people off the plate and then hit that inside corner. Very seldom could you extend those arms on him. If he let one slip and get out over the plate, you might get to hit it. But after he'd been pitching you tight, you wasn't gonna get all the bat on the ball. As a youngster, Leon watched Laymon Yokeley pitch, and that's where Day kind of picked up some of his habits. But he didn't learn to pitch tight from Yokeley. I don't know where he got that from. He could have developed that himself. That was his way of staying in the league, throwing the ball close to people. This meant I had to move with the ball. He was a great pitcher but he made you work. And he had a reputation all around the league. Guys would go up to him and say, "Day, don't you hit me!" And so he wound up being successful pitching like that.

The other thing about Leon was that he didn't have no windup. He had an unusual delivery. What he would do was bring the right hand up, and it would look like the ball was coming out of his ear. He'd throw it from there. He never did go up and come down with the ball. He'd just go up with the ball and here it comes and you best be ready. It'd look like he'd shortarm it, but he threw with his whole body and got a lot of power out of his legs. That's what was doing it. It was those legs. As you can imagine, with no windup it was hard to steal on Leon. Plus he was quick and had a good pickoff move. And then when he did turn the ball loose, he'd have the ball in the catcher's hands before the runner had three or four steps. That's the kind of pitcher that a catcher loves to catch.

It's funny. I caught two Hall of Fame pitchers, both with excellent fastballs. One, Satchel, was very tall and was known for having a long windup, so long that sometimes he'd even hesitate before letting go of the ball. And Leon, the other one, was a little man and was known for not having any windup at all. Leon would never hesitate but got rid of the ball and looked like he had a train to catch. The only time Leon would change up on you would be to show you he had a change-up. If you hit Leon, you were gonna hit his best pitch. That was that fastball and he had one. Day had a fair curveball (it was just a little curve really), and he wouldn't throw it to certain hitters. Those big hitters, he never would throw 'em no curveball. In a close game he would tell you, he won't throw no curveballs. And he wouldn't. There'd be no need for a curveball. He knew they wasn't gonna be ready for his fastball the way he was gonna be pitching.

Leon was pretty smart, and I never did see him get very mad out there. He didn't have a temper because he very seldom questioned balls and strikes. And that was because he was around that strike zone all the time. So if the umpire missed one, he just missed it. Leon wasn't the type to fuss. He was just a good, hard, hard ballplayer. You didn't hear him argue too much.

And like most of the pitchers that I saw, Leon would pitch start to finish. That's one of the biggest differences between baseball today and our game. We had the kind of pitchers that would say, "This is my ballgame." We just didn't have too many relief pitchers. You might have a guy like John Markham who could throw a knuckleball or an old-timer like John Donaldson who would pitch a little relief but that was about it. We didn't have too many relief pitchers because Connie Johnson, Lefty LaMarque, Booker McDaniels, Jack Matchett, Satchel on days when he had only one game, Dick Bradley, Lefty Bryant, Byrd, Leon . . . all these boys would go the distance just about every time. The only reason why you would use another pitcher was to pinch hit for one of them. If you were trailing by a run or two you might yank your starter to try to get the game tied. But that move wasn't automatic because a lot of these pitchers could hit. LaMarque could hit. Hilton Smith could hit. Matchett could hit. Gentry Jessup could hit. Bill Byrd could hit. Satchel said he could hit, but he couldn't hit nothing. Connie Johnson couldn't hit good. Double Duty hit sometimes but he talked more than he hit. And Leon? Leon Day could do it all. Leon was the most complete ballplayer I ever saw. He could hit. Play any position you'd put him in but catch. He'd go to the outfield, play infield, and could hit. Flat-out hit. You just can't imagine how a guy like that can help a ballclub.

Leon was just a great athlete and one of the best fielding pitchers I saw. Yeah, Day was beautiful out there. If you were going back up the middle on Day, you'd better get it over his head. There were several pitchers that could field their position. Jack Matchett was one of the best they had up there. He could field. Hilton Smith could field it. Lefty Bryant could field it. When Lefty Bryant was on the mound, if the batter hit it back anywhere near the mound, he was right there. Then there was Lefty Gaines. He could field it. Schoolboy Walker could field that position too. He was a good fielder all the way back in the TOL when I first saw him. Quite a few could field their position. You didn't drop that bunt on 'em too often. They could catch them balls like an infielder'd catch it. Now Jack Matchett would be on that ball just like a cat. Some of the big guys, like Joe Black, were a little clumsy. Their size cost them some quickness, and you've gotta have quick feet to get to first and get your foot on the bag when the first baseman fields the ball. But having Leon Day out there was like having a second shortstop right in the middle of the diamond.

And Leon Day could sing. Although we never got a singing group together like in Kansas City, some of us would sing on the bus. It was mostly Leon, Pee Wee, Lennie, and me. One of my favorites that we'd sing was a Louis Jordan song called "Don't Steal My Wheel McNeil." Ed Finney and some of the younger guys heard that song so much that they started calling me "McNeil." To the older guys, the ones that knew me from the Monarchs, I was still "Slow."

Not everybody I'm afraid liked our singing on the bus. Now Henry Kimbro was one, if he was in a slump, he might go out and just get drunk as he can get. He'd party all night to try to break that spell. So on top of being angry at the world, he'd be drunk or hungover. One night that season we were on the bus coming back from a win in Philadelphia. Kimbro didn't get a hit that night, but I'd gone 4 for 5 so I was in a pretty good mood. Me and Pee Wee Butts were sitting toward the back of the bus, right in front of Kimbro. And we started singing a little song. And in this song Kimbro's first name was mentioned. It was a song that Nat King Cole used to sing all the time. Saying, "We're going to have a party, We'll eat some meat that's rare, And at the hitter's table, Will please brother Henry share." And as I was singing you know he jumped up, yelled "Robinson!", and pulled a knife on me! I said, "Man!" And I just git. I had nothing else to say to him. He was angry because he was in a slump, and I done got four out of five that night. Later in the season I had him over to my house to a little get together. Lennie Pearson and Leon Day and some of the guys were over. Kimbro brought a girl with him, had a couple of drinks, and he just got out of control. Commenced to cutting the furniture with that knife. We just put him out. "Man you go home because you ain't right." And that's the way he was when he'd get in a slump. You couldn't get close to him. He was a good hitter—he'd won a batting championship down in Cuba—but when he'd go on those slumps, he'd go crazy.

Speaking of slumps, Pearson was another one that wasn't himself when he went in a slump. He didn't want you sayin' nothing to him. A slump is something everybody goes in and you just have to wait. There's no point fussing with your teammates or the umpires. Just be patient.

I never did have too many problems with umpires until I come east to play for the Elites. There was one time we went to Pennsylvania to play the Chicago American Giants. This was when this boy Candy Jim Taylor was managing Chicago. Fred McCreary was our regular umpire and used to travel with us. Well, Fred called a third strike on a boy called Junior. His real name was Clyde McNeal. This kid was a good ballplayer—a shortstop—but he was awful hot-headed, and he just turned around with the bat in his hand and stared at Fred. That was all it took. Fred changed his decision. I couldn't believe it. I didn't really argue with him, but I did question why he changed his decision. He said he just missed it. The next pitch and the boy hit it over the fence. The game was over after that boy hit the home run. Now I'm mad. I wanted to know why he changed his decision. Here he'd been riding with us and knew us. We'd always gotten along. What had we ever done to him? I couldn't figure it out. Afterwards, I went to our manager, Leonard Pearson, to see if he knew what was going on. "Fred changed his signal. Why did he chicken out and change his decision?" He told me that Fred had lost his nerve. As he had gotten older, he'd become afraid that somebody would hurt him. He didn't umpire long after that and died shortly after retiring.

That 1949 Elites team had all the other teams I played for beat in one category. We had some guys who could *really* eat. Butch Davis was one.

He would order a big steak, as big as he could get with all the trimmings, and polish it off in no time. You've never seen so much food disappear so fast. You had to see it to believe it. Leroy Ferrell was the only one that could keep up with him. These boys were a little tamer at home because the club only paid for road expenses.

Late in the '49 season things were going very well. I had caught just about all our games, and we were well on our way to winning the Eastern division title. At the end of a long road trip, we pulled into Des Moines, Iowa, to play a four game series with the Monarchs. They had a pretty rough diamond out there in Des Moines, and things could go wrong in a hurry. We were happy when we went up two games to one and were anxious to wrap things up and go home.

I'd bought me three bats when we were in Birmingham because that was the only place I could get them. So when I got to the clubhouse that last night, Lennie Pearson said, "Robinson, go on and use one of your new bats. We're trying to win this game." I said, "O.K.—no use saving 'em."

Like the first three games, this last one was pretty rough. Gene Richardson, Kansas City's hard-throwing little left-hander, hit Butch Davis. Hit him in the head slightly. We saw what they were doing. They wanted to win that game. They didn't want us to beat them. Late in the game I came up to face the Monarchs' Lefty LaMarque with Junior Gilliam on second base representing the go-ahead run. I doubled off the left field fence and Gilliam came on home. On the next pitch LaMarque threw the ball low and the catcher, Earl Taborn, blocked it over to the left of the plate. I started for third base and when I went to slide, I saw I was going to spike this boy Herb Souell. He was a friend of mine. He had been with Kansas City when I was there. I tried to keep from spiking him, got too close to the base, and my foot went under the bag and popped my ankle. They had those upraised bases that were anchored to the ground. Broke my ankle to keep from spiking Herb Souell.

So a broken leg kept me out of the playoffs. They picked up another catcher after I got hurt. He was a Cuban boy called Earl Ashby who had played for the New York Cubans. Our regular backup catcher that season was Johnny Hayes, and he handled the catching during the Negro American League Championship with the Chicago American Giants. They had my leg in a cast so the guys would come by and pick me up and take me to the games. I knew Chicago didn't have a chance, because we had the best team that year. And they *didn't* have a chance no way. We wound up beating Chicago four straight to win the Championship.

It was typical of the way the business was going that the owners didn't make any money on that series because the games weren't played in the right parks. For some reason they couldn't play in Chicago, so they had to spot the towns they played in. And Chicago shouldn't have been in the playoffs in the first place. They were the second place team in the Western division. Kansas City won the division, but by the end of the season the Monarchs had lost so many players to the majors that they had to skip the playoffs.

When Gene Richardson hit Butch Davis with a pitch in that game in Des Moines, nobody thought anything of it. And we didn't even have helmets to go on your heads when we batted. If you didn't know how to dodge you'd get hurt. Lot of guys *did* get hurt. Our pitchers believed in making you respect them by throwing to the inside of the plate. In the major leagues they call it, "pitching tight." In our league, people would be throwing at you. You couldn't get a toehold up there. They'd throw at you. One thing a batter didn't do in our league was go deep and expect to get away with it. If you hit for power, you could expect our pitchers to throw at your head and legs. Willie Mays didn't become a power hitter until he got to the major leagues because our pitchers wouldn't have stood for it. Lot of our pitchers would just as soon knock you down as look at you. They'd move you back. And they weren't shy about moving you back more than one time. And see, they'd get you thinking about stepping back. Anyway, you had to keep your head out of the way because you didn't have no helmet.

The meanest were Dave Barnhill, Chet Brewer, and Dick Bradley. Barnhill had started out with the Clowns but spent most of his time with the New York Cubans. Brewer was a big right-hander who played for several teams including the Monarchs. He had a good fastball and very good control. If Chet hit you, at least you knew it was no accident. I'd caught Bradley with Kansas City, and he'd never hesitate to come inside with his fastball. Another of the Monarchs' pitchers, Connie Johnson, was kind of mean about doing things like that. You take Leon Day. Leon was one of the best for throwing at people. Others who wouldn't hesitate to move you off the plate were Terris McDuffie and Rufus Lewis. Both pitched for the Newark Eagles in the forties. That McDuffie was something else. He was a great pitcher. He kind of knew it, and he boasted about it. He was also a very flashy dresser. He'd back you right off that plate. Don Newcombe was another Eagle that would come inside.

Lot of times guys got hit. I remember one time my brother Norman went 4-4 on Newcombe, and Newcombe told him he was gonna knock him down. And you know that button on top of a baseball cap? Newcombe knocked that button off his cap the next time he come up. Norman was lucky enough to get out of the way. Those guys would throw at your head! Now Chet Brewer wouldn't throw at your head. He'd throw at your hands, or he could hit your legs and get you back. But guys like Newcombe would throw at a person's head. Don wasn't the only one that would do it. You could put a person out of baseball by hitting him in the head—especially if you ain't got a helmet. I remember when Goose Gossage hit Ron Cey in the head. If Cey hadn't had that helmet, Gossage would've of killed him. It was rough but it was their way of pitching.

Some guys never threw at a batter. Satchel didn't have to throw at anybody to get them out. And you had a boy there in Hilton Smith who could get you out with his curveball, and he wouldn't have to throw at you. He'd set you up with different pitches and get you out. Joe Black wouldn't throw at you. Joe didn't throw at nobody noway. It wasn't his style. Joe just believed in muscling the ball by you. Also, when Joe come along there wasn't as much of this going on. It had died down some. A lot of times a pitcher would have to throw at a batter because the other guy was throwing at his teammates. But when these guys like Chet Brewer and Leon Day came up in the twenties and thirties, that's the way they told them to do. In a close ballgame and a good hitter up, knock him down. They was taught to do that. There were plenty of guys that'd knock you down.

So we had to play under those conditions and if we told the umpire a man was throwing at us, he wouldn't warn them. He would just say, "Best get out of the way then." The umpires were a mixed bag. We had some white ones and we had some black ones. In the east, they had about four white ones, and all the rest were black. They called the game to the best of their ability, but none of these umpires, I don't think, had been to umpiring school like in the major leagues. In the majors they have to go to school for a certain period of time before they become umpires. We didn't have that. Some of our umpires were retired ballplayers, and they would call 'em as good as they seen 'em. But to warn a pitcher like they do now about throwing at batters, our umps just wouldn't do that. Today if you're warned the first time about throwing close to a guy and you happen to hit somebody next time, you're going out of that game. That's the way they do in the major leagues. But in our league, during that time, a guy could throw at you as much as he wanted to throw at you. Some of the pitchers would tell you, "I'm not going to let you make my game hard. Get back."

If you think this led to fights, you're right. Some guys just didn't like getting hit, and they'd take off with a bat after the pitcher. I remember when a boy called Rayford Finch of the Cleveland Buckeyes kept throwing at some Cuban ballplayers because the Cuban ballplayers were noted for losing their nerve when you threw close to them. They were hotheaded anyway. Most Cubans were quick tempered about fights. But Finch kept on throwing until he hit one and those Cubans, led by Minnie Minoso, grabbed bats and headed for the mound. Finch took off for center field with a gang of angry Cubans right behind him. Other guys broke it up before the Cubans could get to him. If you liked to pitch inside, it paid to be fast.

All in all, we didn't have too many fights down there. Not the players. Sometimes when you'd get a rotten call from the umpire, people out of the stands would wanna start it. But the players didn't get into it too much. That's one thing that's really changed. Not like they do now, we didn't get into them kind of fights. Guys would mess around, get hit, get mad, and want to fight about it. But afterwards we'd laugh about something like that. See we knew them pitchers were gonna come inside. They'd tell you. You'd know it before you come up there. They was sure gonna throw at you. That was Day's claim to fame. He would get you off the plate. No doubt he'd get you off of there. Chet Brewer would too. When you go up there, you'd just give 'em enough of the plate so they wouldn't have to throw at you. These guys today crowd the plate. That's fine but don't act surprised when you get one in the ribs because that pitcher isn't in the business of making the batter happy. He's got to have a piece of that plate. Just like Bob Gibson and Don Drysdale were known for backing you off that plate, so were Leon and Chet.

Those were the guys that would come inside to make a point, and the batters understood that, but there were some guys that were just plain wild. Those were the guys you were really afraid of. That's the only way I ever got hit. One time we were playing in a town about thirty miles from where I come up called Muskogee. That was Newt Joseph's home. And down there in Muskogee they had a baseball park with a tin fence. The park also had lights, but the lights weren't high enough to shine down on the field to where you could see good. The Elites played the Buckeyes there in 1947 or '48, and Cleveland pitched Sam Jones against us under those lights. He was a big right-hander but he was wild at the time, very wild. He didn't have no control, no control at all. There was a man that they shouldn't even pitch him in the daytime, wild as he was. When Lester Lockett faced him, Sam hit Lockett on the arm. Lockett said , "Get me out of here. I don't wanna get killed." When I came up there, I just gave him all the plate. I thought, just get me out of it. Don't you kill me. Jones was wild for a long time, but he did help the Buckeyes get to the World Series in 1947. He didn't really settle down until he come up to the majors in the fifties. By then he learned to control his curve and that made him very tough on right-handed batters. He even pitched a no-hitter for the Chicago Cubs in 1955, although he also lost twenty games that season. There were a couple of seasons that he led the National League in strikeouts. The problem was that he also led the league in walks. It was the fellows like Sam Jones, not Day and Brewer, that really scared batters.

Now there were some hitters that didn't care about getting hit. They'd just get back up and crowd the plate again. Josh would get up, dust himself off, and get back in there. He didn't get angry, he'd just tell you you were throwing at him. Josh Gibson didn't scare worth a damn.

There was one other guy in particular that you could knock down, and it wouldn't bother him at all. That was a boy named Gal Young who'd been our right fielder on the Satchel Paige's All-Stars and later played for the Monarchs and Birmingham Black Barons. His real name was Leandy but we called him Gal. He'd come up and just stand on the plate until you throw it at him. And if you didn't throw it at the right place, he'd hit it over the fence. He'd get as close to the plate as he could get, and if you'd tell him to get back off the plate, he'd say, "Just throw it." And he might get hit by the pitch but next time up he'd be in the same spot. He was a bad ball hitter and was liable to hit it no matter where you threw it. He figured if he wasn't getting hit every so often he was giving away too much of the plate. I'd see him do a lot of pitchers that way, but I wouldn't stand up there like that.

When I went to Charlotte in 1950 for the Elites spring training and tried running, I could feel my ankle hurting. I knew then it was gonna take time, but eventually it got to where I could play on it. The team hadn't changed much from from '49 except we picked up a right-hander named Robert Preston. He had a pretty good curveball but never threw hard enough to get guys out regularly. By the second half of the season it was pretty obvious that we weren't going to win anything that year. Late in the season the Chicago American Giants came to Baltimore for a series. Chicago was managed by Double Duty Radcliffe who was then in his late forties. Chicago was short on catching and, when I noticed that Double Duty's fingers were crooked all the way around from foul tips, I knew he wasn't going to pick up the slack. So Double Duty caught up with our owner, Dick Powell, and asked if he could sort of borrow me for the rest of the season. At first he said no, but Double Duty kept begging him, and Powell finally let me go to the Chicago American Giants for the rest of the season.

Sometimes a ballplayer has to put aside personal feelings and play in situations he doesn't like. It's part of being a professional. Now I hadn't played too much against Double Duty other than a few games when he was with the Homestead Grays. He was a good catcher and he could pitch, but he would scratch the ball and I just don't go in for cheating.

To tell the truth, he and I didn't get along together noways. There were some ballplayers in the league that I had little or nothing to do with because of their character. They carried on in public, talked bad about women, and didn't act like gentlemen. That's not how I was raised. They had no kind of respect for women. I never did go for that. I wouldn't have my sister around nothing like that, and I *sure* wouldn't have my mother around it. It's a matter of respect for other people. You need to show people some respect. Well, Double Duty was one, and Willie Wells was another. Wells was one of the greatest shortstops we had, but he was just like Double Duty. With Double Duty, I'd see him, and I didn't see him. What I mean is when I'd see him setting up in the locker room, I'd go someplace else and sit. I didn't mingle with him. I didn't carry on with him. Nothing like that. He was my manager. I didn't have anything to do with him other than play ball for him, and that was it.

So I played with the American Giants that week, and when we got back to Chicago I had to catch a Sunday doubleheader against the Clowns at Comiskey Park, and I was 40 years old myself! And then we couldn't get together on a salary. After the game when I spoke with Dr. J. B. Martin who owned the Chicago team, he wanted to give me $50 less per month than what Double Duty had promised me. We were off to a bad start.

That evening, after I left the ballpark, I grabbed a bite to eat and, because the Indians were in town to play the White Sox, I planned to drop by the Indians' hotel to see Larry Doby. I didn't get to see Doby that day because when I stopped by my hotel, the desk clerk said I'd had four or five calls. I was told that Winnipeg of the Canadian Man-Dak League had been calling all day and trying to get in touch with me. The next day they finally caught up with me and offered me the catching spot on their team. I wasn't under contract with Chicago, and although Baltimore hadn't given me a release, they were gradually folding up so there was nothing to hold me back. I accepted the offer to go to Canada instead of staying on with Chicago. When Radcliffe found out I was headed to Winnipeg, he got angry with me for not staying with Chicago. But I wasn't going to stay there and play for the kind of money they wanted me to play for. So I was a member of the Chicago American Giants for a total of one week.

8

Canada

Winnipeg sent me a plane ticket, so I left my wife in Baltimore and headed to Canada. When I arrived in Winnipeg, the owner, a white fellow named Stanley Zedd, picked me up and carried me to the Mandalay Cafe. That's where he was based out of. Zedd went out of his way to make me feel welcome. He handed me a menu and said, "Get what you want." So I ordered and they waited on me. Then he said, "This is one of the places where you could eat. There are several places you could eat, but I think you'll find this is pretty nice." And then he said, "Whenever you come in here to eat, just sign the ticket. Sign the back of it 'Robinson,' and I'll take care of it." That's how he was. I'd just go in and eat, sign my ticket, and turn it over.

When I reported to the Winnipeg Buffaloes the next day, I learned that my old Elites teammates Butch Davis and Leon Day, who were playing for Winnipeg, had recommended me to their manager. That was great until I found out just who that manager was. The Winnipeg manager was none other than Willie Wells. As a player, Wells had been maybe the best shortstop around in the thirties. "The Devil," they called him. He would cut the palm out of his glove because he thought it gave him a better feel for the ball. The other thing that Wells did to his glove was to load the fingers with rocks. Then if you were sliding in to second, he'd step aside and slam you in the head with them rocks. He didn't just try to put you out at second; he'd try to put you out of the game. In the early 1940s he moved to the Mexican League and played several seasons down there. He was

I'd just gotten to Winnipeg when they took this picture. That dome, which was just beyond right field, was an ice hockey arena. Courtesy of the author.

Catching Dreams

a guy who played for a lot of different teams and even played with the Elite Giants while I was in the service.

In twenty years of baseball with several teams and many managers I had never had problems with a manager before Radcliffe cut a check that his owner wouldn't cash. I hoped things would work out with Wells but, like Radcliffe, he was another guy that I'd never had anything to do with. What I mean is that with a lot of ballplayers I'd fool with 'em, kid 'em, talk with 'em, and associate with them. But not Wells. I didn't like the way he acted, and I didn't have anything to do with him. Butch and Leon told me that Wells was OK to play for, so I went ahead and signed with Winnipeg.

Things started off pretty well but hit a little snag a few games after I arrived. As a manager, Willie Wells was like Candy Jim Taylor and Rube Foster in one respect. He absolutely did not want his pitchers throwing the first ball across the plate and told me so. That was fine as long as the pitcher felt the same way. But some pitchers believed that a few batters, knowing how Wells felt about first pitch strikes, were taking the first pitch and putting the pitcher in a hole. They just couldn't see wasting the first pitch, and when they'd start the batter out with a strike, Wells would get mad at me. What could I do? I wasn't throwing the ball, and to tell you the truth, I thought the pitchers had a good point.

Off the field, Canada was like no place I'd ever been. Never did I imagine such a place even existed. Living and eating conditions were very much nicer. I never ran into a restaurant or a hotel that wouldn't take me. Nothin' up there like that. Canada was like paradise. You could go to any cafe you wanted. There was nowhere you couldn't go, nowhere you couldn't eat, no nothin' like that. After playing in Texas and Oklahoma and in the south, it was as different as night and day. You went wherever you wanted to go, and nobody bothered you. People didn't even look crossways at you. Even the police didn't bother you. The police up there didn't even have no pistols on them. All they had was sticks. It was just like heaven.

In Winnipeg I roomed with Leon Day. We were good friends, and we looked out for each other. I always got along with my roommmates. I never did have no problem with nobody. Of course, it's easy to get along with guys like Pee Wee in Baltimore and Leon in Winnipeg. Leon and I lived at the YMCA with our third baseman, John Britton, and a great pitcher by the name of James Newberry. Newberry threw a curveball from over the top that drove batters nuts. He called it his "dipsy doodle." Both Britton and Newberry had played with Norman in Birmingham, and we became good friends and card players.

It was especially nice to be back with Leon because he liked to sing on the bus as much as I did. Me and Leon and Newberry even put together a little singing group on that team up in Winnipeg. We sang a cappella. On one of our favorite songs Day would sing: "There was an old shanty in old shantytown where the green grass grows all around, all around. With a room so small it touches the ground, yes, it touches the ground. Come out to the shack that sits way back, about fifteen feet from the railroad track." That's the way it goes. He'd sing the lead on several songs. He always had a good voice. One time we sang at a rugby game they were having up there. Rugby. That's what they play up there in Canada instead of football. They asked us to sing some songs in front of the crowd. We went on after the Canadian national anthem. We sang "Blue Skies", that shantytown song, and a few others. We sure had fun with that little group.

Even though the Man-Dak was an integrated league, the Winnipeg Buffaloes were an all-black team. That was because Stanley Zedd, the guy that got the Winnipeg team up, was the big shot of the town, and he had the money to get the good ballplayers, and that's the way he got the Winnipeg Buffaloes established real fast. All the players he got on that team were from the old Negro Leagues. That's the reason he had a good team, and that's the reason that I already knew most of the guys on the club when I got there.

I already called Willie Wells, our manager. He was an old man up there in Canada, but he could still play shortstop. And he could still hit; he might have hit around .375 up there. He'd play maybe one or two games a week, but that was because he was managing and playing. It'd look like he wasn't going to throw you out, but he didn't miss throwing out nobody. He played a shallow shortstop because his arm had lost a little

Jimmy Newberry and John Britton *(holding bat)*, my teammates in Winnipeg and neighbors at the Y, were the first black ballplayers to play in Japan. Courtesy of the author.

something. Sometimes it'd look like he was standing up there by the pitcher, playing shortstop. Even though I didn't care for his character, I still thought Willie Wells was a great shortstop.

Lyman Bostock was on that Winnipeg club too. He was a good first baseman and had played for Birmingham and Chicago a long time. Sometimes he played a little outfield. Lyman was an average ballplayer. He could hit you .300 at times. He was all right, a hustling ballplayer. He was a nice guy. I talk with him some time now. He was the daddy of Lyman Bostock, Jr., who played for the Angels until somebody shot and killed him.

Winnipeg also had Andre Porter. I'd caught him with the Elites. Spoon Carter was in his late forties and had pitched for just about everybody but still had a good knuckleball and several off-speed pitches. He was in Winnipeg too. Jim Hill. He was a little left-hander who had pitched for Newark for several years. There was Joe Taylor who was a catcher turned outfielder. He came to Winnipeg from the Chicago American Giants. He drank too much. Taylor Smith had started with Chicago too. He was a solid pitcher. Robert Preston had started the season with the Elites, and when they got rid of him he went to pitch in Canada. Butch Davis left the Elites and batted over .400 for us.

There were a lot of good players in the Man-Dak League. Winnipeg had another team in the Man-Dak, the Elmwood Giants, and they had a bunch of Memphis Red Sox ballplayers up there. They had Johnny Cowan, who was an infielder and solid glove man. They had an outfielder by the name of Bubba Hyde who was past his prime but had been one of the fastest men in the game when he played for Memphis. And they had Larry Brown who would have been in his mid-forties by the time he played in Canada but had been one of the toughest catchers in the game. They say that when he was a youngster, Brown caught Ty Cobb trying to steal five straight times in an exhibition game. The Elmwood Giants were managed by Wesley Barrow, my old Baltimore manager, and then by Double Duty Radcliffe, my Chicago manager of a few days. The Man-Dak rosters ran to about twenty-six men.

The Winnipeg Buffaloes were a good veteran team, and we had a great season in 1950. I remember one game against the team from Brandon where we faced a pitcher that had been signed by the St. Louis Cardinals. Brad Posen was his name. They signed him out of Canada when I was up there, and he was going to be sent to one of their farm teams. He was good but I hit four doubles off him in a row. He'd throw the ball in the same place everytime. After the game one of their other pitchers, Gentry Jessup, came up to me and said, "Hey, Robinson! You wouldn't of did me that-away. You kept hitting the ball against the right field fence, and he kept throwing the ball to the same spot."

We wound up playing Brandon for the 1950 Man-Dak League championship. The series came down to a final game, and Leon Day hooked up with a Cuban pitcher named Gardenia in one of the greatest pitching duels I've ever seen. Leon went the distance—seventeen innings—and we won it one to nothing. I caught all seventeen innings and my legs were almost as tired as Leon's arm.

That off-season Britton and Newberry signed to play in Japan. They were the first black players to go to Japan. Both guys found the Japanese to be very friendly, but James noticed one major difference. The Japanese players were smaller and made for a smaller strikezone. He said he had to work on his control and remember to keep the ball down. Now if it had been me, I doubt very seriously that I would have gone to Japan. It would have been a bad place for me because I just wouldn't have felt comfortable there. The war was still pretty fresh in my mind, but that wasn't the whole problem. I wouldn't have wanted to try to learn that language, so how would I have communicated with the pitchers? No, Japan just wouldn't have been up my alley.

After the 1950 season was over, the usual question popped up: now what? In the past I had played winter ball in Phoenix, Arizona. I guess I could have played with Satchel when the season was over because somebody'd always call him to get some games, get some players, and barnstorm. But when he'd get that together, if I was gonna play at all that winter, I'd already be gone to Phoenix or Texas or somewhere like that. I wouldn't wait around. I know several times in the past he played Dean's All-Stars and Feller's All-Stars. By not waiting on Satchel I missed the chance to play against Dizzy Dean, Bob Feller, and other major leaguers. In the past a lot of guys also barnstormed with a team Chet Brewer had in California. They played Feller's All-Stars too.

As it turned out I got an offer from Quincy Trouppe to play in Cuba. Trouppe had been a switch-hitting catcher and manager for just about everybody over the past twenty years and had spent a lot of time south of the border. He offered me $1000 a month. Was gonna put the money in the bank and there I'd go. I just said, "No, I'd rather stay in Canada." Quincy ended up getting the New York Cubans catcher, Louis Louden.

I wouldn't go to Latin American countries because I couldn't eat that food. It was just too nasty. I wouldn't even try to think about going down there, and I'd had many offers over the years. I had been to Mexico when I played in Laredo and Hobbs, New Mexico, several years before. I learned then I just couldn't eat Mexican food. It's funny how two boys that grow up in the same house can have such different tastes in food. That Latin food didn't bother Norman because he'd played for Almendares in the Cuban Winter League back in 1947. He'd been on a team with Jesse Williams from the Monarchs, Pepper Bassett from Birmingham, and Gentry Jessup, the pitcher from the Chicago American Giants. Dolf Luque, the old Cincinnati Reds player, was their manager. Norman liked Cuba and liked their food, but I'd just rather stay home and work rather than go down there. Most winters when I didn't play baseball, I'd just piddle around. A whole lot of times I'd work in a garage or just work an odd job with people I knew. You worked from around about October to February, but I never did get all that much.

Entering the 1951 season I was nearly 41 years old and didn't seriously expect to hear from a big league club. Still, a fellow couldn't help but wonder, and one day this boy named Parnell Woods called me. He had been a good third baseman for the Cleveland Buckeyes, but at this time he was one of the scouts working for the Washington-Homestead Grays. He asked me if I would consider moving to a major league organization. I told him I'd listen to most anything, so Woods had Syd Pollock get a hold of me. Pollock had been a promoter and booking agent in black baseball since the 1920s. He had owned the Clowns for a long time and knew who was who, and he acted as a kind of go-between for major league teams that were after black ballplayers. It was through Syd Pollock that Luke Easter got his chance. Easter had played for Pollock and Abe Saperstein's barnstorming Harlem Globetrotters baseball team. So Pollock knew all about Easter and gave him his chance. Easter and Canena Marquez, a Puerto Rican who could play most any position and seemed to hit in every league but the big league. Anyway, at the time Luke and Marquez were with the Grays, the Grays had a working agreement with the major

Catching Dreams

leagues, and it was Syd Pollock that helped them get their breaks like that. So, sure, I'd talk with Syd Pollock.

When Pollock talked with me, he said the Oakland Oaks of the Pacific Coast League needed a catcher. The Oaks had Piper Davis out there trying to catch. Piper was a good second baseman, but he was out of position behind the plate. I asked Pollock what was in it for me, and he said that he would get about $25,000 for me by selling me to Oakland but that if I didn't make it out there then I couldn't go to the majors. When I asked him how much of that $25,000 I was going to see, he said, "None of it." If I'd have gotten any of that money, I would have gone and taken the chance because I knew Piper Davis was no catcher. But I wasn't going to get anything out of it no matter how I did. What they were doing was selling the ballplayer for several thousand dollars, keeping the money, and then sending you on to sink or swim with some team.

So when Pollock asked me if I would accept a contract with the Oaks, I told him I wouldn't want to go to no AAA, and having problems with my ankle, try to make it to the big leagues. My ankle was still very tender, and even though I was wearing a brace, when I'd swing at a curveball, miss, and have to pivot, it would hurt like a toothache. I didn't want to go out there and look bad. I was just too old and too banged up to start all over again in AAA, so I just told him I'd rather not go. At 40 you're ready to fold up just about. You'd have to be somebody like Dave Winfield or Satchel to play much past 40 years old. Especially catchers don't make it that far, and I knew that my career was just about over.

If they would have come to me ten or fifteen years before, things would have turned out completely different. Now I don't mean to sound boastful, but I'm quite sure that I would have done well in the major leagues. Those boys in the majors had the best control. Just like Campanella said, "All you got to do is stand in there and wait." They had good control. There were some pitchers that I'd probably have problems with like Lew Burdette, Warren Spahn, and Johnny Sain. Those kind of guys. They had an assortment of pitches, and they say Lew Burdette doctored the ball. I don't know whether he did or not. He and Eddie Lopat. Lopat was another junk pitcher. I always had problems with junk pitchers. But the average pitcher I wouldn't have to worry too much about. As for Feller, I don't know whether I'd have hit him or not. Feller was fast *and* he had good control. In general though, the fastball didn't bother me that much. It didn't matter to me how hard a guy threw, because I'd adjust. You can't hit fastball pitchers by slugging at it. You kind of choke up and just wait and punch at it. You don't have to be taking no vicious cut to hit the ball noway. Anyway, I hit just fine in our league, and I believe I'd have done the same in the majors.

Norman was another one that I think would have done well in the majors. Norman could *run*. He practiced that all the time, always worked to stay in shape. He always seemed to know a way to get on base, and after he'd get on he was just like Cool Papa Bell. He was gonna be running. He was somebody that would get you two or three runs a game. Regardless. In any league. Norman played against a whole lot of those All-Star teams, and it didn't change his batting at all. His performance never changed.

I guess the real question is: How would the Negro League players have done if they had had a chance in the majors? I think they would have done great. I'm sure they would have hit. In the majors you don't have guys throwing at you intentionally. If they do, they get warned and they won't keep throwing at you. And our boys would have had more protection when they got to the majors. They'd have helmets and the umpire's going to kind of watch out for them. And if they'd had that kind of protection, these boys would hit the ball, and do what they wanted to do. It's just like Campanella said about our league. He said, "These boys could throw at you a couple of times, then the curveball would give you jelly legs." When Campanella went up to the Dodgers, he hit forty-one home runs one year. That just shows what you can do when you can concentrate on hitting and not on being hit. Anyway, when he was with the Dodgers, he said this is paradise compared to the Negro League he'd been in. It was.

Catching Dreams

And Campanella didn't have to worry about the little things either. For instance, he didn't have to worry about his uniform. All he had to do was pull it off and leave it. Someone would pick it up, and he'd have a clean one when he was ready to go the next game. He didn't have to worry about his equipment. All he had to do was get up there and give the pitcher a certain part of the plate, hit, go to the hotel, and then think about the next day. He played the game as well as anyone ever had. He just needed the chance.

As for fielding, I'm not saying that all or even most of our infielders would compare to players like Brooks Robinson and that shortstop the Orioles had, Mark Belanger. Now these guys had more talent than the average guy, and it's unfair to expect every one of our third basemen to field like Robinson and every one of our shortstops to field like Belanger. That Brooks Robinson, they called him the Human Vacuum Cleaner. But how many major league third basemen can play like Brooks played? Not too many. Every once in a while somebody comes along that played this way. For us, that was Ray Dandridge and Judy Johnson.

I don't know whether all of our boys would have been able to make it, but quite a few of them would have. I'd just say that the average ball player I knew could have played major league baseball. Could have made it then—could have made it in today's game. No doubt in my mind, they could have.

Anyway I got my chance but at the wrong time. I'd had a good career—one that I was proud of—and I decided I'd rather not go to some team and be a goat like that. So I just stayed in Canada where I knew I could play two or three days a week, help my team, and make pretty good money. As it turned out Syd Pollock's big find came the following year when he signed Hank Aaron to a Clowns contract—and then quickly sold Hank to the Braves for some easy money. Parnell Woods did OK too. Later on Syd Pollock made him the road secretary for the Harlem Globetrotters basketball team and Parnell traveled all over Europe with the team.

While I was enjoying my time in Canada, the Negro teams in the States were trying to keep their schedules and finances together without much luck. When Jackie first went up, I didn't think this would bother our league. Of course, nobody thought it would. What happened was that when he went up, the people that had been supporting us started slacking off and waited to see Jackie play with Montreal and Brooklyn. The Negro League teams weren't getting much press, and they weren't drawing close to what they needed to stay afloat. The whole thing was springing leaks faster than the owners could patch them, and naturally the league had to fold up. When the Elites folded up, they sold Joe Black and Junior Gilliam to the Dodgers and closed shop. Those were the only two, although Leroy Ferrell had a chance in spring training with the Dodgers but couldn't push himself away from the dinner table. Most of the players out of our league went to Canada. But some teams stayed in longer and kept playing without a league. Like the Clowns, they played longer. The Monarchs, they played longer. Birmingham hung around for a while. The Grays tried to hang on as a barnstorming outfit. When they folded after the 1950 season, their best player, Wilmer Fields, chose Canada over the majors. He played several seasons for Brantford, Ontario, where he was just a dominant pitcher, hit around .400, and won several MVP awards. The Grays' last manager, Sam Bankhead, went on to manage Farnham, Quebec, of the Provincial League. That made him the first black manager of a "white" team. Sam had Willie Tasby in the outfield and picked up Joe Taylor off our championship Winnipeg team to go with him. Both Taylor and Tasby made it to the majors for a few years. When Joe Taylor left Winnipeg for Farnham, I would have gone over there too, but the salary wasn't right. I talked on the phone with Bankhead about it, but I didn't go because I couldn't make what I was making in Winnipeg. In fact, they treated me very nice in Winnipeg, and I was quite happy to return for the 1951 season.

That spring I went to Winnipeg's training camp in New Orleans. When we broke spring training, we loaded up our bus and began to barnstorm our way back to Canada. We'd gotten as far as Marshall, Texas, which is maybe thirty-five miles out of Shreveport, Louisiana, and stopped for the night. There wasn't no big hotel in Marshall, so they got us rooms in different houses in the same neighborhood. A couple of us stayed at this lady's house. Her husband was the manager of the local team, and they had beaten everybody in northeast Texas and the area around Shreveport. After lunch we were layin' on the bus, just sittin' and relaxin' and waitin' to get back on the road. That's when a bunch of these young, black ballplayers from this local team came up to our bus, climbed on board, took one look at us—old, black ballplayers—and challenged us to a game. We were anxious to put a few more miles between us and Louisiana, so we shooed 'em off but they wouldn't stay shooed. They kept running up to our bus telling us, "We're gonna beat you fellows to death!"

We said, "Yeah?"

"Yeah. We'll bet y'all that we're gonna beat y'all to death!"

And everytime they said that, our manager Willie Wells would get angry. "Git on out of here. You mess around we won't let you do nothin'."

"No, we're gonna beat you!"

Since we wouldn't pay 'em no mind, they went and got a man—a big, rich, white fellow that I guess owned the team—and he said, "These boys are gonna beat y'all. I'll bet anything. Y'all got some money?"

We told him, "We ain't allowed to bet but lookit here, what are you bettin'?"

"I'll bet all the money you fellows can get or send for that my boys gonna beat you tonight."

We told him again that we weren't allowed to bet but said, "OK, you've got a game." Before they left they were talkin' about how they couldn't wait until we got out to that ballpark. This made Wells even madder. After they were gone, Wells stood up at the front of the bus, looked up and down the bus at us, and said, "You know what they did comin' up to the bus. Now what you gonna do?"

Nobody said nothin'. We knew what we had to do. Wells said, "All right. Now, Leon Day? You're pitchin'. Day, you pitch the first four innings." Then he said, "Newberry you come in next. And Taylor Smith? You come in after Newberry. They won't get nothin' that even looks like a score."

Of course, they didn't know who Leon Day was. Or Jimmy Newberry or Taylor Smith or any of us. They didn't know anything about any of us. They just knew we were some old ballplayers from somewhere up in Canada. They got a big crowd at the park that evening. It looked like the whole town was there. They figured them boys were gonna beat us easy because they had beat everybody down there. Well, we run 'em so hard, hittin' baseballs everywhere, that they looked like chickens with their heads cut off chasing after those balls. We had seventeen runs on 'em in the first inning. By the time Leon took the ball and went to the mound, the sun had already set and the lights wasn't too good nohow. So not only did they get Leon Day, they got Leon Day in bad light. Some of 'em would be swinging at the pitch while I was throwing the ball back to Day. And against Day and the other boys, they had two chances, that's slim and none. Leon Day didn't give up nothin', not a loud foul. And Newberry followed him, and they didn't get nothin' off him. Here comes Taylor Smith, and he was just as bad as all the rest of them. We shut 'em out seventeen to nothin'. We didn't say nothin' to 'em. We just got on the bus and went back to where we were staying. We were supposed to leave that next morning and do you know they begged us to, some kind of way, play 'em another game?

So we gave 'em another game. And we whupped 'em again, bad as the first. Like to run the shoes off 'em. When we left they all had their heads hung down. The lady that fed us said, "I don't like y'all because of the way you did our boys." She was a nice lady (and a good cook), and we tried to explain it to her. We told her what her boys had said they were gonna do to us. And then we told her that our manager made us go on and not hold back, go on ahead and play. We had a powerhouse team anyhow, and it would have been hard to not beat those guys. They didn't have a chance because no AAA team could beat us.

I had a good season in '51, and we won eighteen straight at one point. Nobody up there in Canada could touch us. When we were riding that winning streak Bill Veeck sent Winfield Welch to scout us. Welch had played for the New Orleans Black Pelicans back in the twenties and went on to manage the Shreveport Giants and the Birmingham Black Barons. Welch was very familiar with Negro players. He came up there, watched us play, and signed Leon Day, Butch Davis, John Kennedy, who had played second base on one of Willie Wells's Memphis Red Sox teams, and Charlie White who had played third base for the Philadelphia Stars. Welch signed 'em all to AAA, and Kennedy eventually made it briefly to the majors. Leon had been around quite awhile. He'd gotten his start in 1934—a long time before I got up there. As a matter of fact, I was still playing in the Texas-Oklahoma-Louisiana League when Leon came up with the Baltimore Black Sox. I was very happy that Leon was finally getting his chance. He went to Toronto of the AAA International League and pitched pretty good, but he was past the age. They waited until he got a little too old to send him any place.

Anyway, in return for Day, Davis, Kennedy, and White, Veeck sent us four replacement players and set up some kind of working agreement with our owner, Stanley Zedd, for future deals. You can't replace guys like Leon and Butch, but we were in pretty good shape heading into the 1951 playoffs.

What happened was that we had a game in Carman, Manitoba, which is about forty miles from Winnipeg. It was very cold that night, and Wells told us all that it was too cold to play and that we should come on off the field and go back to the clubhouse to change back into our street clothes. Well, I didn't hear anybody complain, but when we got back to Winnipeg, the front office told Wells he should have gotten permission before pulling the team off the field. They held Willie responsible and decided to fine him. When he refused to pay his fine, they decided to get rid of him as manager.

All of this was happening while the team was getting ready to go to Minot, North Dakota, to play Brandon, Manitoba, in the 1951 Man-Dak playoffs. The last thing we needed was a distraction before our playoffs with Brandon because they had a good team.

Brandon had my old teammate from the Elites, Ed Finney, at third. Ed was a good ballplayer, but he never did come up to his potential because the Elites was folding up in the late forties. And when he went to the Man-Dak League, he broke his ankle. I just hated to see him get hurt in Canada because he wanted to play so bad. Ed was just coming back from that injury for this series. They had Leonard Hunt, an outfielder who'd played for the Monarchs. They had Gentry Jessup who was a right-hander with a very good fastball. He had represented the Chicago American Giants in four All-Star games.

At first Brandon had Alonzo Perry. He was a good ballplayer. He could pitch, hit the ball, played outfield sometime. He had played for several years with the Birmingham Black Barons, played with Norman a little. He had pitched for Birmingham but was such a good hitter that they shifted him over to first. After Birmingham he went up to Canada looking to get some ballplayers. See, he would go to Mexico, and those teams down there would give him money to go get ballplayers. And he'd come up north looking for ballplayers. Perry always had a reputation of messing around, foolin' with that dope. And that's what happened to him. He fooled around with those reefer cigarettes, and that landed him in a lot of trouble south of the border. And it got to the point where they asked him to stop coming down there. He was a guy who always seemed to be one step ahead of the law. Good ballplayer, though.

Anyway Brandon had a bunch of guys out of our league, and I knew they were gonna be tough in the playoffs.

Just before we boarded the bus for Minot, Stanley Zedd, the Winnipeg owner, came up to me and said, "Robinson, until further notice, you are in charge of this team. Will you take the job?" And Wells was sitting right there! I think Wells always held this against me—as though I had talked to them about taking his job. The truth is I never said a word to them and was as surprised as he was. All I could think to say was, "Somebody gotta take it." As we got settled in the bus for Minot, Zedd's general manager, a guy named Jack Marshall, stood up and made the announcement. He told the players that whatever I said, go along with it.

I had very mixed feelings about the whole thing. It happened so suddenly and I didn't like the circumstances much. I wasn't even sure I really wanted the job. I figured I didn't have too many playing days left, and I didn't want managing to cut into my time behind the plate. On the other hand it felt good to know that the Winnipeg front office thought so much of me that they'd put me in charge of the whole team. I think Zedd looked at the way I carried myself and decided I was the man for the job. It was especially flattering because I wasn't the only veteran on the team. We also had Spoon Carter, Lyman Bostock, and a bunch of players who had been with the team long before I showed up. Zedd could have made any of them manager.

Minot's a two hundred mile bus ride from Winnipeg, so I would have plenty of time to sort everything out. But my first move as manager was to talk to a young left-handed pitcher that I wanted to start when we got back from Minot. This boy's name was O. B. Roberts. He was out of Baton Rouge, Louisiana, and came to us in that big deal with Bill Veeck. I told him, "You stay in. You get your rest. You don't have to take that long ride, but you be ready to pitch when we get back." Riding the bus to Minot I turned the whole thing over and over in my mind. I just added it all up and subtracted it down. When we arrived I stood up and talked to the ballplayers. I told them, "I believe this. We're all gonna get together and make this right. When we get back to Winnipeg, we'll pay Willie's fine, and he'll be the manager again because I don't feel like playing and managing." So they all agreed to put in and pay his fine. We beat 'em in Minot that night and got back on the bus for the long ride back to Winnipeg. It had been a very long day, and I slept the whole way home.

The following night O. B. Roberts was more than ready, and he beat 'em 11-0. After the game we all got together and paid Wells's fine. This satisfied Zedd so he made Willie Wells the manager again. I finished my managing career with a perfect record of 2-0 although we went on to lose the playoffs to Brandon.

When I think about my brief time as player-manager, I can see how tough it was for guys like Lou Boudreau and Frank Robinson. I'd been around long enough that I knew how to manage, but I didn't like to play too. Because that's a double responsibility. You've got to manage and try to play your position too. That's pretty rough. I was lucky because it just so happened that we had a couple of old-timers like Spoon Carter and

Lyman Bostock that went along with me and coached. That's the reason I got along. It was the help of the coaches because I had to play. We didn't have anybody else to catch but Wells, and they done fired him. That meant I had to do all the catching and manage the club. So I was happy to get the guys together to get Wells back. But despite all this Wells never did like me after that. I don't know why because all he had to do was ask any of the guys, and any of them could have told him that I was the one that helped pay his fine.

After the 1951 season was over, I got a call from a black fellow in Raleigh, North Carolina, who owned a cab line and did a little booking on the side. He wanted Pee Wee Butts, Frank Russell, Jim Zapp, me, and some other ballplayers to come to Raleigh in late October and play a couple games against Jackie Robinson's All-Star team. Even in an exhibition game, Jackie was always hustlin', trying to find an edge, trying to win. He did this in Raleigh by trying to force me into a mistake. He jumped off second and headed to third, and he knew if he kept on going, I was gonna throw him out. So he stopped. Stopped right between second and third. He was smart enough to try and get in a rundown. He thought I was gonna throw the ball to second or third. Now if I throw to third base, he'd get back to second. If you haul off as soon as you catch him out there and throw to second, he's going to third. So I just kept the ball and walked from behind the plate right up toward him. I wouldn't throw to any base. I made him decide which way he was going because either way he goes, I can throw him out. As long as I know which way he's going. He knew this and wouldn't make a move. He knew that a catcher's first reaction is to throw to a base. Think about it like a catcher. Most of the time something bad happens to you is when you don't get rid of the ball fast enough. Jackie knew this. He had the ability to put himself in the other guy's place and know what he was thinking. His only mistake was to forget that I was no youngster—that I'd had more than twenty years to get over that urge to get rid of the ball in every situation. I just walked up to him and tagged him out. He was smart like that. Willie Mays was another one who'd try to get you to throw behind him. For the runner, at worst he'd get back to his base. At best he'd steal that base and make you look foolish. They'd just walk off base and dare you to throw, and it was all you could do not to throw. But see what they were doing, was using psychology. They'd try and get you upset.

Jackie did something else that shows that he knew a little psychology. He wouldn't segregate himself when he went to the Dodgers. He would be with Pee Wee Reese and them boys. He didn't associate with Campanella and Newcombe. When we played against him down there in Raleigh, we asked him about Pee Wee Reese and he told us about Reese. When we asked him how he was getting along with Campanella and Newcombe, he didn't have anything to say. It was Jackie's determination to break the color line. That's what he was doing. He wanted to make friends with the white ballplayers and let them know that segregation with him was out. This came with a price.

When that boy off the Memphis Red Sox, Dan Bankhead, went to the Dodgers, he thought that Jackie would be with him all the time. This boy was raised in the south and came up that way. He segregated himself on the Dodgers, and he didn't stay up there long. He couldn't do nothing up there. Jackie didn't have anything to do with him when he was up there. Jackie went up there to break the color line, not to segregate himself. And that's what happened, because I talked with Newcombe and Campanella about it.

Before I'd left Canada, Stanley Zedd told me that he wouldn't have the Buffaloes no more. Winnipeg was going to fold it up and, since I was thinking of retiring anyway, I thought I wouldn't play no more. As much as I liked Baltimore there wasn't any real reason to go back. My wife and I had drifted apart, and we were starting a divorce. And my apartment had burned up in a big fire. I lost everything—clothes, family and baseball photos, everything. It was awful. And I didn't want to go back to the shipyard anyway. It was just too cold. I had a friend in Cleveland, and my older brother Edward G. was still in Akron, so I decided to move to Cleveland and start over.

That April I got a call from the man that owned the Brandon team in the Man-Dak League. I can't recall his name. He said, "I'd like to have you come up here. I was looking and you hit .342 up here last year." Then he said, "What are you doing?" I hadn't even trained. I told him I wasn't doing anything. He said, "Do you feel like you could play this year?" "Yeah," I said, "I could play." Then he asked, "Where can I mail you a plane ticket?" I told him, "You'll have to give me a week to get in shape."

So I went out there to Druid Hill Park, a city park near where I lived. They had two local teams out there, and I practiced with them. I ran and ran to get in the best shape I could. Then I went on to Canada.

On my third night in Brandon I was working with a pitcher who said he was practicing a slider when the ball sailed and hit me on the cheek. I was the only catcher they had up there so I had to keep on catching. Finally, they got a boy called Luther Clifford who used to be with the Homestead Grays to come up there and help with the catching. Brandon also went out and got Norman to come up from Birmingham. Him and a boy called Pee Wee Jenkins come up there. He was a pitcher, a knuckleball pitcher. I stayed up there with Brandon in 1952 and 1953.

I have very fond memories of playing in Canada. Both in uniform and out, the Canadians were very good to me. Don't get me wrong, I enjoyed my time playing in the Negro Leagues and was sorry to see them fold, but if that's what it took to break the color line, then so be it. I was glad that my teammates and friends were finally getting the chance to show that they could play major league baseball. I knew that I was past the age to play, and I didn't let that bother me. The only thing I wanted to do was find a place to play until I retired, and I finally found that place in Canada. In Canada I could play and still keep up with my old friends. I could even follow some of the young fellows in the minors because many of them, including Mays and Aaron, were sent north to play. Hank Aaron, when he first went up, was in Eau Claire, Wisconsin, and that wasn't too far from Winnipeg. Willie Mays went to Minneapolis of the AAA American Association in early 1951 and hit well over .400! This got the Giants attention and they figured, "Well, we've got to get this fellow now!" And that's when Durocher brought him to the Giants and Willie began his big league career by going 1 for 25. But Durocher was patient and Willie finally started to hit—and didn't stop for 22 years.

Catching Dreams

9

Too Old to Play,
Too Young to Retire

After the 1953 season, at the age of 43, I decided I was old enough to hang it up. I'd noticed during the season that I just didn't have the energy that I once had, so I decided to finish the season and not try to come back. I went back to Cleveland and got me a job at General Aluminum. At first they started me working with motors, then I got a job inspecting castings.

To tell you the truth, that job was the hardest thing to adjust to. Not that I was afraid of hard work, but it hadn't been that long since I could walk down the street in Baltimore and overhear people say, "There goes Robinson. He catches for the Elites." People knew me. And then it seemed like the next thing I knew, there I was in Cleveland, just another working man, and no spring training to look forward to. At first that really bothered me but later on I figured that's just the way it has to be. I can't do nothing about it. I can't change it.

When I was looking to retire from baseball, I thought I'd get into some kind of business, and I would have if I could have found the right person to go into business with. Then maybe I could have gone and done all right in business. As it was, I never did find nobody that I could trust that much so business was out. Of course, a job in baseball was out too. They didn't have jobs for black coaches. John O'Neil got a coaching job, but he was the only one.

Buck wound up scouting for the Chicago Cubs for a long time. He sent Ernie Banks up. And Gene Baker. Baker and Banks. Bingo and Bango. They both went to the Cubs in 1953 and became the first black double play combo in the majors. In 1962 Buck joined the Cubs as the first black coach in the major leagues. He used to come to Cleveland and ask me what ballplayers that he could talk with. I put him on to a young pitcher named Joe Philpott, and Buck signed him but he developed a sore arm that winter and never survived spring training. That was the beginning and end of my scouting career.

Buck O'Neil's job as a scout for the Cubs caused him a little confusion with Satchel. This come up after Satchel had finished with the Browns in the 1950s. Satchel was telling him that he still could pitch, and Buck knew that at Satchel's age he wasn't a good bet. Satchel believed that Buck could have sent him to Chicago if he wanted but Buck was just being stubborn about not giving him a break and was using Satchel's age as an excuse. Of course, Buck was right but it was never easy to convince Satchel of something when his mind was made up. They had some words about it at the time, but it eventually blew over. Buck never held a grudge, and they remained good friends until Satchel passed. That's about the only problem I ever heard of between Satchel and one of the guys, and it added up to nothin'.

Satchel didn't give up the idea of pitching in the majors when Buck turned him down. I think Satchel felt he still had something to prove and in 1965, when he was 59, he talked Charlie Finley into letting him pitch for the Kansas City Athletics. Satchel pitched three scoreless innings against Boston and while the Red Sox won, Satchel gave up just one hit— a double to Carl Yastrzemski.

But back in the early fifties a lot of our guys suddenly had to decide what they were going to do in life. After our league broke up, we all started looking for jobs elsewhere. Some of them were fortunate enough to get jobs playing up in Canada. Others just got jobs. Like Ed Finney. After baseball, Ed went back to Akron and got a job with my brother Edward at Goodyear. He was a young man and could have played longer but things were folding up, so he got a factory job. Cool Papa Bell went back to St. Louis and worked as a custodian and security guard for the city. You got what you could.

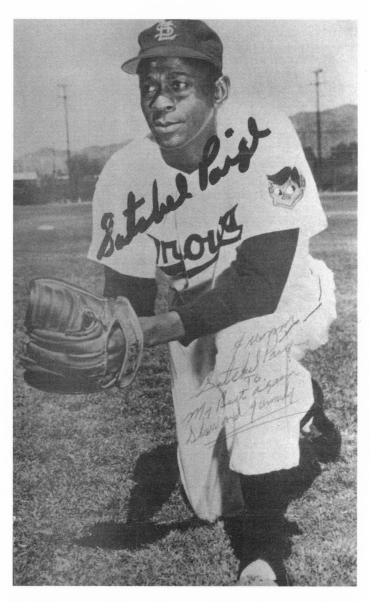

Satchel was out of the majors in 1950 but hooked up with Bill Veeck's St. Louis Browns in 1951. Courtesy of the author.

My son Luther and I had always gotten along. If he wanted something, he'd ask me and I'd give it to him. The only problem was that I didn't get a chance to see him everyday. So now that I was finally settled down in Cleveland, I sent to Baltimore for him. We'd always had a good relationship, and he was eager to come to live with me. He stayed with me for a few months but grew homesick for his mother and his friends in Baltimore, and we decided that he would be happier back in Maryland. I was sorry to see him go but knew it was for the best.

Early in 1954 a lady friend of mine introduced me to one of her girl friends. Wynolia Griggs. I still remember it was a Friday night, and we talked for quite a while. I was in my forties and she was very young. She'll say she was about twenty years old, but she was really about eighteen or nineteen. She had just gotten divorced and had a little boy and girl, Benjamin and Carolyn. She didn't know much about baseball, but she was certainly fun to be around, and I made sure to get her phone number before leaving that night. I saw her a couple of weeks later and asked her out to dinner. We were going to go to Luke Easter's cafe, The Majestic Blue Room. Luke had settled in Cleveland after he finished with the Indians. He had a lot of jazz acts at his club, and it was a pretty popular place in Cleveland. I used to go down there quite a bit, and I thought she'd like it.

We were going to leave from my place but when she came in, I saw the wind had blown her hair out of shape. I said, "You can't go nowhere with me until you fix your hair." She got mad at me, but I wasn't gonna let her go looking like that because all the ballplayers were gonna be there. Sam Jones, Luke Easter, and all of them. We laugh about it now, but she went and straightened up and we went ahead and had dinner. We had a wonderful evening together, and then I put her in a cab and sent her back home and I went on to work. I was working third shift at General Aluminum.

We started going out together from then on. Now Wynolia is an Indian name and that's what everybody called her, but I started calling her Winnie and she started calling me Bob. I guess you know it's serious when the nicknames you give each other stick. A big date for us meant we'd get all

Winnie and I in 1955, early in our courtship. Courtesy of the author.

Too Old to Play, Too Young to Retire

dressed up and go to a nightclub or something like that. I could hold my own out on the dance floor, and Winnie was a pretty good dancer too. We'd go along and pick up each other's steps. I was quite a dresser in those days and spent a lot on clothes. I guess I was dressing like this because Satchel and I used to try to outdress each other until it got to where he was going berserk. He'd go to Ben's Tailor Shop in Philadelphia and have them make him six and seven suits at a time. I remember one time he was buying shoes so fast he bought two left shoes. We laughed about that one all the time. Then Winnie and I went to having her suits made like my suits. We used to dress alike after we met and started running together.

We saw as much of each other as we could. What with me on third shift and Winnie busy with her children and her day job, we had to find the time to see each other. Winnie worked for Winkleman's and then Lerner's department store and supervised their big display windows. They had several stores in the Cleveland area. They'd pick a window and she'd pick the dresses or furs to put in the window. She'd give them to the girl to be pressed, and she'd go on to the next store and do the same thing. By the time she'd made it back from the other stores, she'd look at the garments, pin them to the mannequins, and dress the window.

Winnie and I went together for several years before we got married in 1960. We had a small wedding in Las Vegas. It was a second marriage for both of us. I just didn't think I'd get married again. My first marriage left me skeptical. I'd just traveled too much during my first marriage to make it work, so I was slow to marry the next time. Satchel married late in life too. Satchel believed in making every penny he could make, and every time he thought about marriage he felt his wallet getting lighter. He just didn't have time for marriage.

If Winnie married me because she thought that I was a little famous, it was for my singing in a group that I put together in Cleveland, not baseball. We sung gospel, that's what we sung. We didn't sing jazz at all. We had six guys and we sang a cappella just like Take Six. People couldn't understand how we'd blend our voices like that. We had a great group. Later on we added a little piano backing, and then one of the guys went to guitar school, so we had guitar and piano accompaniment. We were

Catching Dreams

called the Goldentones and sang together from '56 to '66 with five of those years on Cleveland TV. I forget the name of the TV station, but we had two sponsors, I.G.A. Fox, they sold Fox furs, and Shaw's Jewelry. They sponsored us as long as we stayed there. On radio, we were on WJMO, and we did something like two hundred programs for the March of Dimes.

We used to bring all the big groups in to sing, and we'd have a big program. We even brought Mahalia Jackson to town. She came to the biggest church they had in Cleveland, over on Euclid Avenue, and they had so many people they couldn't get in the door. The Goldentones sang about six or seven songs and then turned it over to Mahalia. She was something to hear. Another singer that we played different churches with was James Cleveland. Oh, we opened for a lot of the big time groups they had at the time. Like The Five Blind Boys and The Swan Silvertones. I don't guess most people remember The Swan Silvertones and their great lead singer, Claude Jeter, but if you've heard Al Green, you've heard a little Claude Jeter. That's because Claude Jeter's the singer that Al Green modeled his singing on. A lot of soul music comes right out of gospel music. You listen to Ray Charles, and you just know that boy spent a whole lot of time inside a church somewhere.

For a long time Winnie didn't know anything about baseball or me playing baseball. She knew I liked to coach a little with some of the local sandlot teams. And when we went to Cleveland Stadium to see the Indians, she got to the point where she knew to stand up and holler when one of the Indians hit a home run but that was about it. It was actually several years before I told her that I had played professional baseball in the Negro Leagues. Since she wasn't interested in baseball, it just never came up until she met Satchel. How do you explain Satchel Paige to your wife? I told her all about him. She'd never met anybody like Satchel because there wasn't anybody else like Satchel.

After I left Kansas City and Baltimore, I didn't have the opportunity to see a lot of the other old ballplayers as much as I did Satchel. Satchel was always going someplace, and he would sure come by to see me and Winnie when he was in town. Plus we talked on the telephone all the time.

If Satchel was headed to Cleveland, he would call me and tell me what time he'd be arriving, and I'd pick him up at the airport. Sometimes he'd stay a couple of weeks. One time, in the 1950s, he walked in the door, said "Hello," and handed $3000 to Winnie. He told her to send $1000 to his wife, Lahoma, and keep the change because, "We're gonna party with the rest." She's hadn't met him but once before, so she didn't know what to expect. He told her: "I'm not gonna work like a mule that plows the field all week and then pulls the carriage to church on Sunday." Winnie and I would laugh at him. We all got along swell. He used to send Winnie out to buy all of his shirts because he couldn't get them long enough. One time Winnie was in the hospital and Satchel sent flowers. When he called Winnie at the hospital and asked how she like the flowers, she told him to shove his flowers. He had sent them to the house, and she didn't know anything about them. Satchel was really upset, and the next day Winnie got an even bigger bouquet—delivered to the hospital.

A visit from Satchel meant we had to go find catfish. Satchel loved catfish. Winnie wouldn't eat a catfish, and I don't eat them either but Satchel liked them. He was sort of careful about what he ate because he used to get indigestion so bad. The other thing about fixing dinner for Satchel was that you never knew who might show up with him. Once when Satchel was performing with the Harlem Globetrotters basketball team in Cleveland, he showed up at our house with the entire team! Winnie fixed them all food, and those boys were what you'd call good eaters. That's the way we got along.

After retiring from baseball, Norman lived in Chicago for a while. We got to see a lot of each other then. He used to drive over to Cleveland and stay with me for the weekend, and then go on back to Chicago. Later on, he moved to California where a whole lot of old baseball players had found work. Guys like Theolic Smith, Sammy T. Hughes, Andy Porter, and several others. Norman was working for A.R.A. Services, a vending machine company, when he started getting severe stomach pains. His doctor told him he had a bleeding ulcer. I decided to see for myself how he was doing, so I took some vacation time and went out there. He was in a lot of pain and was worried that if something happened to him, he wouldn't have anybody around to take care of him. I was very concerned about his health, so when I got back to Cleveland I talked things over with Winnie. I told her that Norman needed me and that there wasn't any good reason to stay in Cleveland. After we'd been married for a few years, I'd gone to work at the Winkleman's clothing store in downtown Cleveland where Winnie had worked, and I wasn't making much money there. And it didn't hurt to remind her that it doesn't snow in southern California. We moved to Los Angeles in 1966.

Winnie had left Lerner's on good terms and when they found out Winnie was in L.A., they asked her if she'd dress the windows at their store on Hollywood and Vine. She said she'd give it a try for a couple of weeks and went right to work getting things straightened up. First, she made the girls wash the mannequins, and they weren't used to that. Second, Winnie wouldn't let a window get clogged up to where you couldn't get through, and it looked cluttered so she moved a lot of things out. This didn't sit too well with her supervisor, and when they couldn't get together on her salary, Winnie transferred to the shoe department.

Meanwhile, Norman got me a job with A.R.A. servicing vending machines. The vending machine people gave me thirty machines a day to do. That meant that I had to keep those machines filled with inventory and keep them clean. My first call was at St. Anthony's High School, and those vending machines were those kids only means of eating. There was no cafeteria staff, just me for that whole school, and I had to have those eighteen machines ready by 11 o'clock, so those kids could eat their lunch. Then I had to leave and go to Cerritos Hospital and service another twelve machines there. The problem was that they gave the other boys twelve machines a day and looked to me to get back from my thirty in the same time they did. I couldn't do it, and they had to pay me overtime— the union made them pay me overtime. They kept putting so much work on me that I finally gave it up and went to worked as a custodian for the L.A. School Board in 1967.

The Goldentones broke up when I moved to California and, later when I asked our manager for our tapes, they came up missing. Nothing but memories, just like all those ballgames, but what memories! When the Goldentones' instructor moved to California I thought I might get another group together. That was Napoleon Bruton who was Bill Bruton's brother. Bill Bruton played outfield in the fifties and sixties for the Milwaukee Braves and the Detroit Tigers. Napoleon pitched in the minors but never made it to the big leagues. Napoleon did get a little group up when he moved to California, but he had problems and it didn't work out. Napoleon had worked for the Liquor Board of Control, but the liquor he needed to control most was his own. He got to the place where he was drinking a lot, and that caused him a little family trouble. He wound up and drank himself to death, I'd say. Because he drank until he had a major stroke, and it blinded him.

I hadn't seen much of Redd Foxx since our Baltimore days but since he ended up in L.A. too, I decided to look him up when I moved out there. He wasn't scuffling like he was when I first knew him, but he still hadn't made no money. He had a nightclub on Wilshire Boulevard, near Hollywood. I think one of his problems was that his cover charge was kind of high, but he still usually had a lot of people in there. And they looked liked that class of people that a successful night club would usually have. Somehow it didn't work for Redd, and he had to get rid of it. Then he went to Las Vegas, and this comedian Buddy Hackett showed him a few things and that seemed to turn things around for Redd. You're probably thinking that Hackett talked to him about comedy or what clubs to play or which agents to see—show business advice. Nope. Hackett's advice was to recommend which keno numbers to play. Redd kept those same numbers all the time, and he caught the keno for $35,000. That got him over the hump. That money gave him a new start, and he started getting a few gigs around Vegas. He made his name and came back to Los Angeles and cut that "Sanford and Son." He made pretty good money off that for a while. It was very popular and they wanted him to shoot some more episodes, but he told them he wasn't goin' to shoot no more pictures until he got part of the action. So they gave him part of the action, and that's where he first got his big money. That's the way he started.

While Redd was making his way in show business, I worked hard at my custodian job with the L.A. School Board and made it up to supervisor by the time I retired after nineteen years. I didn't stay retired long before me and Winnie started our own business cleaning offices. It was good, honest work and I have no regrets.

My brother John's life, on the other hand, hadn't gone so well. He was the one that got into everything when we were kids, like the time he got those dogs to fighting on a Sunday. I don't know why he was always that way, but he was and he got pegged as the black sheep of the family. He was a chef and he cooked in a lot of different hotels. Eventually, he stopped working altogether, and then he started drinking a lot. In 1971 I went to Baltimore to get my grandchildren. I drove from Los Angeles to Baltimore, and I stopped to see John on my way back. He lived in Oklahoma City. John had married and had three boys by a lady, but he never did stay with no one person too long. He was kind of a drifter. Maybelle kind of kept him in check as good as she could. She was around him all the time because she lived in the family house in Okmulgee, and John used to come by and stay two or three days. Then he'd get up and go. He was drinking heavy, drinking that old wine and stuff. It wasn't long after that, must have been '74, that we found out he had passed. We kept in touch as good as we could. Maybelle kind of kept us posted on what he was doing. She passed in '78 or '79. She had married and taught school for a while, but she never had any children.

It wasn't long after Maybelle died that Norman's health started to get bad. He had been losing weight for a while. I don't know what was wrong with him. He had been to several doctors, and I don't think they ever told him what was wrong with him. Since he wasn't but twenty miles from me in Los Angeles, I could go to visit him, and I could see that he wasn't doing too good. We decided to go see our oldest brother, Edward, in Akron, Ohio. Edward was in his late eighties and getting pretty feeble himself. When we were going through the airport I noticed Norman kind of stumbling. It looked like he was drinking, and Norman didn't drink. He was just weak. It just looked like his equilibrium was off.

Not a week after we got back to California, Edward passed. We could see that he was losing strength from old age, so we knew it would be a matter of time. Edward was pastor of his church in Akron, and they had a big funeral for him, but I didn't fly back since I'd just been to see him.

Satchel would be in the Los Angeles area pretty regularly and, just like when I lived in Cleveland, he'd come stay with us. One time in the seventies, long after he had finished playing, we happened to be looking at a game on TV, and this boy John Mayberry was up for the Kansas City Royals. He was on a hot streak and pitchers were having trouble getting him out. Satchel watches him, watches everything he does up there. Finally he says, "Now Slow, lookit here. You could go to school on him. He never would hit nothing I'd throw at him but one time. If he hit me one time, he never would hit me no more." And he was talking about Mayberry. That was Satchel. He'd been retired for years but he couldn't stop sizing up batters. He believed that if you studied a hitter long enough, you'd spot his weakness. The problem, Satchel said, was that most pitchers don't pay any attention to how a guy was hitting. Satchel could have made somebody a great pitching coach if he'd have put his mind to it.

Later on we decided to do some singing. I was singing lead and Satchel was playing ukulele and singing background with my brother Norman. After we'd done a few songs he jumped up and said: "I'll take this group and make a million dollars." He'd say something like that, and I'd laugh at him. He was still the life of the party.

Another time he and the comedian Stepin Fetchit were visiting me in Los Angeles. Stepin Fetchit's real name was Lincoln Theodore Perry, and he'd made a show business career out of playing lazy, shiftless characters. He'd been part of Louis Armstrong's show at the Cotton Club back in the '30s and made a bunch of movies in Hollywood—some of them with Will Rogers. He was very popular with black and white audiences, and Step laughed all the way to the bank. The problem was that not enough of his money made it to the bank and what money that did, didn't stay there long. He had houses, cars, clothes—whatever he wanted he got. I don't know how he worked through as much money as he made. It took some doing because he made something like $2 million in his prime but was broke and starting over by 1947.

Anyway, a fellow that I knew by the name of Kelly heard that Satchel and Step were at my place. This Kelly ran a nightclub and asked me if I could get Satchel and Step to come down to his nightclub. This was on a Friday night. I told him I'd get them to come down. He thought it would be a drawing card and would bring quite a few people in, which it did. Word got out that they were there, and people flocked in to see them. A lot of people wanted an autograph or to talk to them, so we stayed for a while. Kelly was very grateful and had his wife fix dinner for us. He took us to a private dining room, and his wife brought out all this food. She said, "If anybody wants anything later, just ask for it and I'll fix it for you." It was a wonderful dinner and after we'd finished, we stayed there another two or three hours when somebody wanted some more chicken. Before Mrs. Kelly could leave for the kichen, Step decided it was time to turn in. He said, "Goodnight" and went back to his hotel. When Kelly's wife went in the kitchen, there wasn't any more chicken. She'd had a big platter of fried chicken in there. She didn't know where it went, and I didn't either so I asked Satchel, "I wonder where that chicken went?"

He said, "Didn't you see Step standing in that doorway?"

"Yeah, he was standing over there quite a while."

Satchel smiled. "I betcha his pocket is slicker than a rat hole."

I said, "Why? Would he steal chicken?"

Satchel laughed. "He'd steal anything."

His pockets must have been full of chicken when he left because the lady had fixed a whole lot of chicken. I don't know how Step got all that chicken out, but he didn't fool Satchel. Satchel figured it out right away. He was that way. He picked up little things like that. And so we laughed about Step going back to the hotel with a little snack.

Satchel was one of those guys who was funny even when he didn't mean to be funny. I remember in 1974 or 1975 they were going to have an Old-Timer's game in San Diego, and Satchel wanted to ride down from Los Angeles with me. For some reason Satchel wanted me to go his way, which was the old way down by the ocean. That's the way he'd gone twenty years earlier—before they'd built a freeway that goes straight into San Diego from L.A. We made it to the game without any problem, and you'd think that once he'd seen it could be done, he'd believe I knew the way. Not Satchel. On the way back to Los Angeles, can you believe he tried to make me go his way?

I told him. "I don't know but one way to go back. That's the way we come down."

"You don't know where you're going."

"Yeah, I know where I'm going. I got us there, didn't I?"

The whole time I'm driving, he keeps on arguing that I don't know where I'm going. After a while, a ladyfriend of his who's riding in the backseat says to Satchel, "He knows where he's going. He's on the right track."

That makes Satchel even madder. "Don't you say nothing. He *doesn't* know where he's going."

"Yes, he does."

Now they're starting. Finally, he told her, "Don't you say nothing else. Just be quiet and ride."

After that nobody talked. Satchel was mad at me and the girl. The girl was mad at Satchel. And I wasn't mad at anybody. I knew I was right, and I knew how Satchel could be. Finally, we got to my freeway exit. As I headed toward my house on 16th Street, I said, "Satchel, I live right up here, 'bout three blocks."

He wouldn't say anything so I looked at the girl in the rear view mirror and said, "I'm about two blocks from home. Since he's not speakin' to me, would you please tell Satchel that I'm almost home?"

"Well he *told* me not to say anything," she said, "and I'm not going to get into it. I'm not going to say a thing."

Despite what he might say, Satchel wasn't born in 1876, he was just celebrating the Bicentennial. Courtesy of the author.

Too Old to Play, Too Young to Retire

That's when I cracked up. I started laughing and couldn't stop. He wouldn't say anything. He just sat there with his jaw set, stonefaced. Then I pulled up, got out, told them goodnight, and said I'd see them tomorrow, and he drove from my place to where he was staying.

He come back over to the house the next day and said, "I was wrong. You did know where you were going."

Satchel never would get really angry with you. There might be a little bad feeling now and then but nothing serious. And it was tough to stay mad at Satchel.

He was always stubborn like that. He would want you to do what he wanted you to do—right or wrong—but I wouldn't go for it. Satchel was the type that, whatever it was, especially stuff around the house like plumbing and carpentry, Satchel would tell you he was the best at it. If he was good at home repair, I sure didn't see it. But that's the way he was; anything Satchel did, he thought he was great at it whether he was or not.

Just like Satchel liked to play pool, and he thought he was good but he couldn't play like Cool Papa, no. Cool liked to play pool if he played all day long. Cool Papa played for twenty-five and fifty cents, like that. He practiced shots constantly. That's all he would do is shoot pool and run you to death. Satchel never could beat Cool with a cue stick in his hand, but he still thought he was the best.

We'd get Satchel all the time. Winnie'd get him more than anybody because he'd always come up with way out ideas, and Winnie would laugh at him. He would eventually admit when he was wrong though. He was pretty nice about that.

After Satchel finished playing baseball, about the only time I saw him was when he'd come visit us. We just didn't get to Satchel's home in Kansas City much. After he began to get a little ill, he wanted me and Winnie to come and spend some time with him and his family. We never did get around to doing it because we were living in Los Angeles where we had a cleaning business and I just couldn't get away.

In 1981 they made a movie of Satchel's life story. It was called *Don't Look Back* and had Lou Gossett, Jr., as Satchel. After they finished shooting in Mississippi, Satchel stayed with us while he was in town for some meetings with the movie studio. He'd been having trouble with his lungs, and

Cool Papa Bell. That man was something to watch. And what a sweet man.
He liked to play pool and steal bases. Courtesy of NoirTech Research Inc.

he looked tired. He went to bed before I left for my late shift. He had breathing attacks that night, so Winnie turned on the air conditioner and that seemed to help. When he had an attack the next night, he decided he'd better see his own doctor, so our son put him on a plane to Kansas City. It was the last time I saw him.

I was in my car with the radio on one morning in early June of 1982 when I heard he passed. He had just called me the month before. We talked for maybe an hour and after I hung up, the phone rang. It was Satchel again. He said, "Slow, is that you? I just quit talking to you. I was trying to call Dick Bradley." He'd just gotten through talking with me and turned right around and dialed the number right back. He had done this once before when he was trying to call Jess Hubbard, an old time pitcher, and got me by mistake. So I figured then his mind was going a little bit, and it wasn't too long after that he passed.

What happened was that a big storm hit Kansas City and blew a big tree down in his yard. He asked to be pushed out there—he was in a wheelchair—so he could see how bad the damage was. Lahoma pushed him out on the porch and after a minute he said, "Take me back inside." She took him back inside, and he had an attack. She called 911 and he died on the way to the hospital. We'd been good friends for over forty years—right from the time I first caught him. He was a true friend until he passed.

Me and my stepson Ben and Archie Ware who'd played for the Buckeyes flew in from California. A lot of ballplayers from Kansas City were there. Monte Irvin was there, a lot of guys I hadn't seen in years were there. The funeral was in a big church, and afterwards they had so many people coming by the house that they had to have security. It was a big house, about twenty-three rooms, and Satchel collected antiques and they were worried that strangers would sneak off with some of that stuff. They had six detectives—three standing on each side—guarding that stuff from the first floor up to the top of his house.

Satchel's been gone now more than ten years, and there's not a day goes by that his name doesn't come up or that I don't smile about something he said or did.

Catching Dreams

Norman's health had been getting bad for several years, and he died on March 26, 1984, at home with his wife, Sarah, and son, Norman Jr., by his side. It was a shock to me, and it wasn't a shock. It was one of those things where I knew he was doing pretty bad, but I just wasn't ready when the time came. I don't believe I could have ever been prepared. It was pretty rough. No brothers were ever closer than me and Norman.

The last of my brothers and sisters passed about four years ago. This was Estelle, my youngest sister. Me and Winnie went to Tulsa for the funeral. Sarah, Norman's widow who still lives back in the San Fernando Valley, was there. It was good to see her, but it seemed strange to see her there without Norman. That made Estelle's funeral especially sad.

That Old-Timer's game in San Diego was the last time I caught Satchel, but it wasn't my last ballgame. Buck O'Neil still lives in Kansas City and wound up being pretty popular there and with good reason—he's a real gentleman. He called me not long ago and sent me literature on the Negro Leagues Baseball Museum in Kansas City, which is something he's been involved with for some time. He's also pretty active in getting old Negro League players together for reunions and banquets. In the mid 1980s several of us old ballplayers made it back to Kansas City to play in the Bruce Watson Foundation Golf Tournament. Before the golf tournament, Buck and some other folks had several of us old Negro and major leaguers play a game at a stadium named after Satchel. Satchel Paige Stadium. We had to play three innings. It was the players before Jackie Robinson against the ones after Jackie. They had Solly Drake, Bob Thurman, and a bunch of former major league ballplayers. They were old-timers but we were *real* old-timers. I was in my seventies. We played them three innings, and I was so sore. I had to catch all those three innings. I kept telling Buck to get somebody ready because I didn't want to catch and get so stiff I couldn't play golf. I didn't know we were gonna play no three innings. They beat us and that was the last time I tried to play any baseball.

Even though I'm done with Old-Timer's games, I still enjoy getting to as many of the reunions as I can. The last time I saw Cool Papa Bell was at a reunion at the Negro Leagues Baseball Museum in Kansas City. Don Newcombe was the master of ceremonies. That was the last time. Cool Papa died in 1991. What a sweet man. He had a nice disposition. He was quiet. You'd never hear him curse or nothing like that. He was just a good guy. He was somebody you'd never see get angry or be out of control. That's the reason you'd tag him as being a deacon or something like that. He was a nice guy. He liked to play pool and steal bases.

Winnie's people were from Kings Mountain, North Carolina. When we'd go there to visit we were impressed with how quiet and peaceful it was. Since Norman had passed, there was no reason to stay in California, and we decided Kings Mountain would be a great place for retirement. We built a home there and moved in 1988. Winnie and I never had children together, but I loved her two youngsters like my own. Carolyn grew up into a lovely woman and married the Reverend James Robinson who is no relation to me but by marriage. They moved close to us in Kings Mountain, and together they run a hobby shop in nearby Shelby. James is also the pastor of our church, the Antioch Missionary Baptist Church. I can't think of better people. Winnie's son, Benjamin, went to college, worked hard, married a fine woman named Dianne, and worked as an engineer in Cleveland. One day in the late winter of 1994 he came down with a very bad cold. It wouldn't go away so he went to the doctor. He thought it might be pneumonia. It was cancer and he died a few weeks later. It broke our hearts. Nobody should have to see one of their children die, but I guess the good Lord had other plans. You just have to put your faith in the Lord and pray for strength to carry on. Benjamin was quite a man and we were very proud of him.

All together, Winnie and I have nine grandchildren and ten great-grandchildren, and when they come for a visit you can believe they keep us jumping. I'm also very active with our church. I sing and Winnie writes the church bulletin. As for hobbies, I don't really have any. I believe that I could enjoy fishing if they were biting and I was catching something, but

Winnie and I outside our home in North Carolina. Courtesy of the author.

I never did really get into fishing or hunting. When I was a kid in Oklahoma I would hunt a little bit with my brother, but I just lost interest in it. I do like golf and went as often as possible until the doctors took one of my legs because of bad circulation.

I still enjoy getting out to card shows for signings when I feel up to it. People think autograph collecting is a new thing. Well, the business part of it is recent, but people have always been after us for autographs. You couldn't turn people down. Anyone that asked us for an autograph, we would just go ahead and sign. We autographed more for kids than we did for grownups. Winnie usually goes with me to these card shows. It gives us a chance to see a lot of the guys and their wives. There's a pretty good grapevine, so I get to keep up with everybody that way too.

I also like to follow baseball, football, and basketball on television, but I follow baseball more than I do anything else. I like Ken Griffey, Jr. I look for him to be a *great* hitter—one of the best ever. Barry Bonds is a good ballplayer too, but he's too flashy in the outfield. He'll catch the ball like he's mad at it or angry at it. He's kind of a showboat. One of these days he's gonna miss one of those fly balls, and it's gonna cause them to lose a ballgame and then maybe he'll stop. I think when Bonds got that big contract and went to Frisco, that Will Clark kind of resented it because Clark had been the big man at Frisco for a long time. I don't think Clark liked Bonds's big contract. No player likes to see a man get so much more than he gets when you're both on the same team.

As an old catcher, I love to watch Benito Santiago work behind the plate. He's pretty flashy at times, but I like the way he handles himself and the way he handles his pitchers. I especially like the way he'll try to throw a man out from his knees. He'll snap that ball to any base at any time and keep those runners on their toes. They'll cut down their lead, but if they don't, sometimes Santiago will pick 'em off. I love to see a catcher pick a runner off. It's one of my favorite things.

Would I do it all over again? I just love the game and even under the same conditions, I believe I'd do it over again. But I'd rather make a little more money. I'll tell you, you have to get a decent salary. You have to get a salary big enough to live off of. When I was playing I would play that summer, but I'd have to get a job that winter to survive. You'd have to get a job for about four months to keep things going or else you couldn't eat or pay the rent. I don't know what I would have done if I hadn't been a ballplayer. To tell you the truth, I just don't know.

I hear a lot of our players talk about being born too soon. I feel this way. I believe that, had I come along after Jackie Robinson, I could have made it too. These are things you think about quite often, but then again you don't let that stop you. You can't let it make you bitter. It's just something that had to happen. I'm glad to see that some guys made it. Some guys

Frazier Robinson, 1994. Courtesy of the author.

made it all right, but then there were quite a few that didn't make it. I just believe I would have made it and that would have made a big difference when I retired. If you play any length of time in the major leagues, you don't have to worry about nothing because they have a beautiful pension. I remember when Satchel wasn't eligible for his pension. He didn't have enough time in the majors so in 1968 Bill Veeck convinced Billy Bartholomay, the owner of the Braves, to hire Satchel on as a coach and keep him until he was eligible for his pension. And that's the way he got his pension.

I didn't make a lot of money playing baseball, but I left the game with a lot of good memories. I was lucky enough to catch two of Satchel's no-hitters and several of his one-hitters. I also got to catch one-hitters by Jack

Matchett, another by Bill Byrd, and, later in my career, one by Leon Day. I remember my best games with the bat especially that one stretch of three of four games in a row in 1939 where I broke things up in the late innings. Things like that. I enjoyed playing the game. Lot of times I wouldn't think about how the salaries was running. I was just happy to be able to play. We had a lot of thrills of winning games and playing in front of huge crowds of people. Reporters coming up to talk to you. That sort of thing. It was just something that I liked to do, went on doing it, and hoped it wouldn't end too soon.

It wasn't just the game though. It was the people in the game. I got to do something I loved, play baseball, and play it with my own brother, Norman. And I made a lot of good friends too. Leon Day, Pee Wee Butts, Al Wilmore, Junior Gilliam, Joe Black, Connie Johnson, Jesse Williams, Herb Souell, Willard Brown, Buck O'Neil, guys like that. I still stay in touch with Andy Porter, Ed Finney, and Jim Zapp—my old Baltimore teammates. I don't call Henry Kimbro anymore because when I saw him last at the 1993 All-Star Game in Baltimore, he'd just had a stroke and wasn't at himself. I'm not sure he remembers me anymore. We used to talk quite a bit.

And then there was Satchel. Satchel turned out to be what I would say is a true friend. Should I need something, all I had to do was let him know.

Satchel liked people, liked being around them and they liked to be around him. He'd kid people, tell them a story. He'd tell people most anything, especially about his age. After he'd retired, people would come up to him and ask, "Hey Satchel, how old are you?"

"Well, how old do you think I am?"

"You're about 65."

Then he'd look 'em right in the eye and lie, "You missed it by five years. I'm 70."

10

The Hall of Fame

Satchel and I talked about Cooperstown several times, and he had mixed feelings about going into the Hall of Fame. He was slightly bitter about the time it had taken for him to get into the Hall of Fame. And at first he felt that they were trying to bring him in the back door because they weren't going to put him in the regular Hall of Fame. He didn't think that was right. He told me, "I don't know no back door Hall of Fame." He said it reminded him of how little things had changed since he first started playing baseball in Chattanooga back in the twenties. That was his first try at organized ball. He pitched a couple of games; then they told him he couldn't stay with the club. He said the manager told him he'd hate to seem him go because he felt he could pitch and win for the team. The manager said, "You did everything I thought you could do, but your color's got you. We can't keep you."

"You mean to tell me," Satchel asked him, "I can't stay and pitch, something I want to do, because my skin is black?"

"I hate to see you go as bad as you hate to see you go," the manager said.

Satchel said he was so upset that he talked to his mother about it. He ended up playing for the Chattanooga Black Lookouts.

Anyway the Hall of Fame people changed their minds and decided that Satchel belonged right there with the other ballplayers. He called me in 1971 when he finally did go in and brought me his Hall of Fame card and signed it. I hear that card's worth some money now, but I'd never get rid of it.

I think they did great by putting some of our guys in the Hall of Fame because so many other major league players are sitting there waiting to go in too. It's great that the Hall of Fame finally let Satchel, Cool Papa Bell, Josh, Monte Irvin, Buck Leonard and some of our guys in. Even Willie Wells. I didn't care for Willie Wells's personality, but I don't hold grudges. I hope when I'm gone nobody holds anything against me. Wells was a great shortstop and belongs in Cooperstown. That's all that matters. And I'm so glad the Hall of Fame people finally chose Leon Day. I was so happy for him. Maybe now people will know about Leon Day. But look at the guys who are still waiting to be inducted. These guys have been waiting a long time to get into the Hall of Fame. How long do they have to wait? None of us are getting any younger. Leon was in a hospital bed with a bad heart, gout, and sugar diabetes when he got the good news in March of 1995. He was dead within two weeks. You can't get away from it. Death's going to happen to us all. I just wish Leon could have enjoyed being a Hall of Famer longer. I sure miss talking to him and seeing him at reunions and card shows. I feel sorry for people that never got to see him play. I feel sorrier for people that never got to know him.

Just off the top of my head I think Bonnie Serrell, Hilton Smith, and Bill Wright were all Hall of Fame players too. I think Bonnie will probably make it but it's too late now for him to see it. He was living in California when he passed in 1996. Last time I saw him was at a card show at the Meadowlands. Day was up there with us too and now they're both gone. Bonnie, Hilton, Bill—these are just the guys that I played with. What about old Smokey Joe Williams? They weren't just good players, they were great players—day in and day out. It's time.

It's just like black managers and general managers in baseball today. There aren't too many in the front office but it's coming. I was surprised that Al Campanis said what he did about blacks not being qualified for those front office jobs. He must know better. I figure he just slipped up and said the wrong thing. It's getting so black managers aren't so unusual and I think the day will come when black GMs get hired and fired like the white ones. I just hope it comes sooner than later.

Catching Dreams

Who were the best players in the Negro Leagues? I caught a lot of great pitchers but the greatest were Satchel Paige, Hilton Smith, Connie Johnson, Booker McDaniels, Jack Matchett, Lefty LaMarque, Dick Bradley, Joe Black, and Leon Day. Any one of these guys could have pitched in the major leagues and, of course, Satchel, Connie, and Joe did. The one thing these guys had in common was that all of 'em had a lot on the ball and they had control. When you had a pitcher out there with control, it made it easier on you. You didn't have to be jumping here and jumping there. It made your game easy too. But if you had one out there that didn't have control, well, it's pretty rough on you. I think out of all the pitchers that I caught, Satchel had the best control.

I get asked a lot who would be on my Negro Leagues All-Star team. Of the guys I played against, saw play, and played with, I'd put my team together like this. I'd have Cool Papa Bell in center field, Willard Brown in left, and Bill Wright in right. Cool would give you speed, and Willard would give you power—maybe 56 or 57 home runs a season. Bill Wright wasn't the best hitter but he could switch hit, would bat around .275, hit a few home runs, and his base stealing would make up for his bat. In the outfield he had speed, a good arm, and didn't make mistakes. Not much is written about Bill because he was pretty quiet and played many seasons in Mexico. He had one season down there when he even beat out Ray Dandridge for the Triple Crown. Bill was a good all-around ballplayer.

In the infield I'd have Buck Leonard at first. They compared him to Lou Gehrig. I'll go along with that. And I'd have Ray Dandridge over at third. Those two are easy. At second I'd have to go with Bonnie Serrell. You couldn't get nobody to beat him playing second base. And he was a good hitter too. I'm not forgetting Larry Doby, but I have to put Bonnie Serrell ahead of Doby because Bonnie Serrell could play second base like nobody else. There were a bunch of good shortstops. I saw Willie Wells and played for Wells. They say he was a good shortstop, but he was way ahead of me. I've seen Ernie Banks too, but he was after my time. Judy Johnson could play shortstop. Dick Lundy played shortstop. These were great players, but I'm just calling the guys that I played with for a time. So my pick at short is Monte Irvin. That was his position at Newark when I saw him, and he was the best at the time that I was coming along.

Catcher's another easy one. Nobody but Josh.

There were a lot of good pitchers to choose from. Of course you'd go with Satchel. That's an easy one. Same with Leon Day. You also had Dick Bradley. He was faster than Satchel, but he didn't have the control that Satchel had. When I played with Dick in 1939 and 1940 he was faster than Satchel, and I caught both of them. Hilton Smith was about your best curveball pitcher. He played for the Monarchs a long time. Connie Johnson pitched for Kansas City a long time too. He was a good pitcher. If he would have ever gotten really serious about the game, he could have been a better pitcher. After the Monarchs, he pitched for the White Sox and Orioles.

I'd feel pretty good with any of those guys on the mound, but if I had to win one game, I think I'd want to put my chips on the old man. Satchel. When he wanted to beat you, he could beat you. Flat-out beat you. I only knew Satchel to have one superstition. Satchel just believed when he put that ball in his hand, he was gonna get you out.

My line-up would be:
Cool Papa Bell, cf
Bonnie Serrell, 2b
Ray Dandridge, 3b
Buck Leonard, 1b
Josh Gibson, c
Willard Brown, lf
Bill Wright, rf
Monte Irvin, ss
Satchel Paige, p

and the rest of the pitching rotation would be:
Dick Bradley, p
Hilton Smith, p
Connie Johnson, p
Leon Day, p

Catching Dreams

I believe you'd win a few games with that team. They were the best in our league, and they would have been the best in any league.

As for me, I'd just be happy for people to remember me as a baseball player and a nice fellow. That's all I ever tried to be.

A Postscript

While this manuscript was in preparation, and unbeknownst to Mr. Robinson, his church, the Antioch Missionary Baptist Church of Kings Mountain, North Carolina, chose to honor Mr. Robinson by building a recreation center. Money was raised and ground broken. Construction dragged and, during the summer of 1997, Mr. Robinson's health declined. Contractors were pushed and the building completed. The Frazier "Slow" Robinson Gymnasium was dedicated on October 12, 1997. Frazier Robinson died on October 13, 1997. [PB]

Index

Parker, Bonnie, 5

Parker, Charlie, xxii, 65, *66*, 67, 131

Parker, Tom, 140

Partlow, Roy, 92, 93, 94

Pearson, Lennie, 157; hitting ability of, 94; plays for Baltimore Elite Giants, *150–51*; plays for Newark Eagles, 119, 125; singing and, 155; slumps and, 156

Perkins, Bill, 108

Perry, Alonzo, 137, *138*, 180

Perry, Gaylord, 44

Peterson, Oscar, 78

Pettiford, Alfonso, 68

Pettiford, Harry, 68

Pettiford, Ira, 68

Pettiford, Leontine, 68

Pettiford, Oscar, 68, 171

Philadelphia Phillies, 15

Philadelphia Stars, 79, 81, 85, 86, 90, 108, 118, 130, 142, 143, 179

Philpott, Joe, 186

Pittsburgh Courier, 73

Pittsburgh Crawfords, xxi, 43, 149; formation of, 12. *See also* Toledo Crawfords

Pittsburgh Pirates, 14, 56

Pollock, Syd, 172–73, 175

Polo Grounds, 118, 120

Pompez, Alex, 142

Porter, Andy "Andre," *107*, 111–12, 114–15, 169, 192, 208

Portland (ship), 99

Posen, Brad, 170

Posey, Cum, 10, 13, 94–95, 104, 139

Powell, Dick, 150, 162–63

Preston, Robert, 162, 170

Provincial League, 176

Prysock, Arthur, 134

Radcliffe, Alex, 47, 114

Radcliffe, Double Duty, xxii; character of, 163; hitting ability of, 154; and illegal pitches, 43, 114; as manager, 162–63, 164, 167, 170

Reese, Pee Wee, 183

Renfroe, Othello "Chico," 108, 148

Richardson, Gene, 129, 157, 158

Rickey, Branch, xx, xxii, 103–4, 108, 124, 127, 145–46

Ricks, Bill, 129, 144

Rizzuto, Phil, 54

Roberts, O. B., 181

Robinson, Bill, 98

Robinson, Brooks, 175

Robinson, Carolyn Griggs (stepdaughter), 188, 204

Robinson, Catherine (first wife), 105, 165, 183

Robinson, Corrine (mother), 1, 2, 103

Robinson, Edward G. (brother), 2, 9, 117, 183, 186, 195–96

Robinson, Estelle (sister), 2, 203

Robinson, Frank, 181

Robinson, Frazier, *205, 207*; on aggressive pitchers, 158–61; on alcohol, 63; All-Star team and, 122–23; on all-time all-star team, 211–12; on ballparks, 117–20; on batters with quick wrists, 90, 116; on best defensive catchers, 108; on best curveballs, 56; on best fastballs, 34; on best fielding pitchers, 154–55; on best hitting pitchers, 154; on best knuckleballs, 39; on best outfielders, 142–44; on best screwballs, 128; birth of, xix, 1; birth of son and, 84; calling of pitches and, 31, 113–14, 120–21; Canada and,

167, 184; on candidates to integrate major league baseball, 104, 126–27; and catching, xix, 7, 68, 70, 206; catching instruction from Biz Mackey and, 106–7; catching no-hitter and, 41, 84, 207; childhood of, xvii, 1–8; Christmas and, 3; on clowning, 105–6; contracts and, 78–79, 83, 164; and courtship of Wynolia Griggs, 188, *189*, 190; dancing and, 63, 132, 190; on difficult managers, 167; divorce of, 183; early baseball experience of, 6–8; education of, 7; ejection of, 45; on fastest base runners, 68, 70; on fights, 160–61; fights with House of David players, 36–37, 59; first sees Satchel Paige pitch, 19–20; and forfeit of 1948 playoff game, 141; foul tips and, 68; on gambling, 17, 36–37; game against Hobbs, New Mexico, team and, 16–17; in game against Jackie Robinson's All-Star team, 182; in games against Marshall, Texas team, 176–78; on gamesmanship, 45, 80–82; on guns and ballplayers, 148; on Hall of Fame, 210; and harassment by Newt Allen, 14, 57–58; health of, 19; on Hiroshima and use of atomic bomb, 102; hitting philosophy of, 129, 173–74; on illegal pitches, 43–45, 55, 113–14, 163, 173–74; injuries to 14, 25, 157, 162, 173; on inside-the-park home runs, 69–70; on integration of major league baseball, 103–4, 123–24; invasion of Emirau and, 99; invasion of Peleliu and, 99–101; invited to play for Oakland Oaks, 172–73; invited to play for Satchel Paige's All-Stars, 21; on

Japanese baseball, 171; jazz and, 63–68, 131–36; longest home run witnessed by, 120; marriage of, 105, 190; military service of, 97–103; as player-manager, 180–82; Native-Americans and, xix, 5; nicknames of, 58–59, 155, 188; and Old-Timer's games, 198, 203; plays for Abilene Eagles, xxi, 13, 15, 16; plays for Baltimore Elite Giants, 80–82, 108–9, 112–15, 116–19, 121–22, 125–26, 128, 129–31, 137–41, *150–51*, 155–57, 161, 162; plays for Brandon (Man-Dak) team, 183–84; plays for Chicago American Giants, 163–64; plays for Goodyear Wingfoot Tigers, 9–10; plays for Jacksonville, Florida, winter team, 105; plays for Kansas City Monarchs, 53–63, 83–85; plays for Nashville Black Vols, 115–16; plays for Odessa team, xxi, 16; plays for San Angelo Sheepherders; plays for Satchel Paige's All-Stars, 22–25, 27–28, 38–39, 41–43, 45–48; plays for Sparrows Point Giants, 78–80; plays for Tulsa Blackballers, 8–9; plays for Winnipeg Buffaloes, 165, *166*, 167–71, 176–81; punishment by father of, 6; on racial "passing," 61–62; racism and, xxi, 8–9, 16–17, 123–24, 62; relations with father of, xix, 1–2, 19; relations with mother of, 1–2; relations with Norman Robinson of, 6, 41, 130, 192–93; relations with Satchel Paige of, 37, 40–41; 74–75, 191–92, 196, 198, 200; on relief pitchers, 154; religious upbringing of, 1, 3–4; retirement from baseball of, 185; revival attendance of, 3–4; rigors of catching